# LITERATURE
# & PHILOSOPHY

*The Century Philosophy Series*
Justus Buchler, *editor*

*Stephen D. Ross*
State University of New York
at Binghamton

# *LITERATURE*
# & *PHILOSOPHY*

## an analysis of the
## philosophical novel

New York

*Appleton-Century-Crofts*

Division of Meredith Corporation

PRINTED IN THE UNITED STATES OF AMERICA
E 76320

# *Preface*

There are two major parts to this book. The first takes up the difficulties that arise in trying to explain how a work of literature can at once be of artistic value and yet also and in the same respect contain philosophic ideas of importance. The nonphilosophical reader will perhaps wonder at the absurdity of the view that works of literature are devoid of philosophical content, and marvel even more that certain philosophers have maintained that literature *cannot* be at once philosophical and successful in literary terms. For this reason I have played devil's advocate to an extreme, to develop and sustain the view that is well known to philosophers, that literary and philosophical forms of expression are very different and cannot be combined without detriment to both of them. What is of greater importance, however, is the analysis given in Part I in which I attempt to set forth the methods employed by writers to express philosophical convictions, how they preserve and even enhance the literary value of their work, and also set forth philosophical theses of great significance, though often in a rather implicit and indirect fashion. Most important is the way in which the devices of literature permit the building of a case for a philosophic position without the characteristic forms of argument.

The second part may be read independently of the first, though it is intended to provide exemplification of the various arguments and positions presented in Part I. The novels selected for analysis are among those most susceptible to the combined modes of literary and philosophic analysis required, as well as being novels of particular interest to students today. Again, it is of major importance that the reader understand that the philosophic positions

262620

found in these novels are not there accidentally, nor are they dis-
connected from their literary values, but that within the forms of
literature the authors of these novels have built rather strong cases
for definite positions. In short, such novels may be read with profit
as works of philosophy, and their positions accepted or rejected on
the basis of the support given them.

S. D. R.

# Contents

# I

*Philosophy and Literature*

# 1

## The Role of Philosophy
## in Literature

There are two rather different ways in which philosophic views are thought to enter into works of literature (and art in general). These may be summarized as the view that art only *displays* philosophical positions, and the view that it in addition can legitimately *adopt* philosophic positions and *make claims* about them. These rather different treatments of the role of philosophical material in works of art reflect very different conceptions of art in general and literature in particular. And although almost everyone would admit the legitimacy of a work of literature using the thoughts and writings of a great philosopher within a novel, by no means everyone would agree that a work of literature can make claims about the philosophic positions it displays.

It can easily be seen that authors have often dipped more or less deeply into quite reputable philosophic material and embody the views they find there in their own work; or else they may show in their work the influence of attitudes and ideas which may be considered philosophic in spirit if not in form. The various intellectual and artistic disciplines usually interact with each other, if only accidentally and asymmetrically, and it may be very interesting and illuminating to study the ways in which a work of art exemplifies the philosophic spirit and the temper of an age as well as the ways in which philosophers are influenced by the very-compelling modes of literary persuasion.[1] Much of great interest can be discovered by treating Greek drama as a manifestation of a historic, cultural, and intellectual world-view. The artistic and philosophic are both products of a given time and can be treated to advantage from this point of view.

To many, this is the only way philosophy enters works of literature, and it is an extremely important one. I have called it *philosophy "displayed" in literature:* a novel, poem, or play in its imaginative contrivances simply presents or adopts certain philosophic attitudes and general points of view. Sophocles' extant plays all reveal a sense of the tragic hero apart from society, enriched by a consciousness of purpose that sets him apart at the same time as it renders him heroic. This teleological vision of human moral power is quite absent from plays like Beckett's *Waiting for Godot* or Miller's *Death of a Salesman.* The moral quality of *Oedipus Rex* is a display of a conception of human capacities and powers that may well be both general enough and rich enough to be considered philosophical, as well as of a metaphysical vision of the polarity of the rational and the irrational. The paragon of rational excellence is ruined by the ineffable working of Fate. The vision is of a double teleology that treats human purposes as only a part of the teleological nature of things. Yet the nobility and glory of Oedipus shine through nevertheless.

Such philosophic views found in works of literature are not interpretable so much as explicit philosophic claims but as the embodiment of a philosophic position without argument—often a mirroring (distorted or clear) of views found elsewhere. Here it is usually appropriate to note the philosopher whose views are presented, the cultural world-view which is portrayed, the temper of an age which is revealed through the work of art. Even when the views are the artist's own, they are not so much asserted as revealed, for us to behold, not appraise. The assertions of a scientific or philosophic treatise are regarded as claims to truth, and are expected to be treated as such. The world-view of a people, embodied and articulated in their art, is not *therein* to be regarded as true or false, but as just what it is—of interest to historians and anthropologists. We read Homer to find the Greek (or even his) conception of the gods. Whether or not there really are gods is quite irrelevant. The existence of attitudes or positions in art in this sense I call "display" because it is fundamentally derivative. Here art is not interpreted as making claims, but as portraying or displaying positions that properly belong elsewhere. A work of art reveals a philosophic position normally to be found somewhere else, as it may also display the character of a man, the look of a scene. The man, the scene, and the philosophic position have natural locations: men inhabit the social world, scenes belong to nature, philosophic views can be found in philosophic treatises. Art borrows and uses these, to a very different purpose from that normal to each of them.

Even reading a poem to discover the poet's own views is derivative in this sense, for we are not concerned with their truth, but simply with what they are. An act of interpretation from the medium of art to that of declarative language is undertaken, but without appraisal or cognizance of the merits of the claims as interpreted. It may even be argued that all art displays some stance or point of view that when put in words (by the critic) is indeed philosophic; but surely not all art can be interpreted as making definite claims, or supporting some position by its devices and structure.

The act of interpretation is a fundamental one, and can be misleading. Philosophy in painting and poetry is present in a second-derivative sense—it is expressed in a medium that is not properly its own. The proper medium of philosophy is discursive language. Until philosophic views within a work of art are stated in their own terms, they are not genuinely philosophic. The role of the philosophical literary critic is often to express as philosophical—in language suitable to philosophy—views and attitudes which are found in works of art in a totally different form, and which are therefore not quite philosophical. The interpretation makes them so. It is a fact that the medium of art is not the medium of philosophy, and this is one of its consequences. Thus one may extract from Dante's *Commedia* a conception of an orderly universe within which justice and piety reach their fulfillment. One may find as well his attitude toward the purity of women and their innocence, which is far closer to the requirements of faith than rational understanding, or his incredible sense of the attractiveness of souls doomed forever to Hell. But the poem itself does not *say* these things. It is the task of the interpretive critic to reveal them. They are there, but not in assertive form.

What is misleading here is that philosophic views in art can be doubly derivative—derivative in that they are in the wrong medium for their expression, and derivative in that they are not, *even in the interpretation,* to be regarded as genuine claims. Having brought the views of a work of art into the light by interpretation, a critic may well imagine that no further task exists, and ignore the entire question of the truth or falsity of the positions set forth. The critic who sensitively and profoundly represents the philosophic temper of a great work of literature does not thereby render it genuinely philosophic. It may well be that although now in a form proper to philosophic expression, the views themselves are still not claims or assertions. Even if we agree that Dante "believed" in an orderly and just universe, we need not interpret the *Commedia* to be taking and supporting the position that the universe is that. Rather, it may be viewed simply as showing us a vision of what that order might be like—a possible, not an actual, conception of the world we live in. On the other hand, it seems possible to interpret *some* works of literature to be making and supporting definite theses—at least, that is the possibility I wish to explore.

The question might be raised here whether the interpretation of works of literature in order to find philosophic attitudes and convictions below the surface is a legitimate enterprise; whether it properly finds what is "in" the work, or imposes its own methods and techniques upon it. Does not the interpretation of the content of a painting into words violate its spirit? And is not this much the worse when the positions reached are highly intellectual and abstract? I shall quite arbitrarily refuse to face such questions, and assume the legitimacy of finding at least displayed philosophic positions in works of art—perhaps (to a very sensitive critic) in all works of art. Interpretive criticism is not only a proved method of responding to works of art, but has its own methods of defense and justification. Some interpretations of a work of art are indeed more defensible than others. Given this, I wish to show that some works of literature permit justifiable interpretations which view such works not only as displaying theoretical positions, but as supporting them as well, in a manner much like an argument for them.

On the one hand, we have works of literature that lend themselves most congenially to interpretations which, however philosophic they may be, assert nothing, and provide no support within the work itself. In such cases, we do not ask "is the author correct?" but rather "what is the view he is setting forth?" On the other hand, it is worth considering those *few* works of literature which not only display such philosophic positions, but are constructed in such a way as virtually to make a case for the view presented. The question is whether a work of art can simultaneously be a work of philosophy. (The converse question, set aside here, is whether some works of philosophy—like Kierkegaard's *Fear and Trembling*—are not also works of literature.) Cannot some works of literature be masterpieces of philosophy and literature at the same time and even in indistinguishable respects? Is there not a literary form of philosophical writing, which makes its case in an indirect and nondeclarative fashion?

To a much greater extent than composers and sculptors, authors have felt the burden of an inner vision of Truth which they are called upon to reveal through art. We ignore Wordsworth's intentions if we consider his views merely displayed and derivative. Surely it does injustice to treat in all cases alike the claims of writers as mere revelations of views that are no more than accidents of historic circumstance. Artists themselves have certainly been convinced that they possessed special insights that only literary expression could convey. If only their convictions could be taken at face value!

For there is a virtually unanswerable reply to the aspirations of artists who claim to possess definite knowledge of important truths —that they are presumptuous in their claims and foolish in their aspirations. Art is art; and it cannot be expected to serve philosophic purposes. In the argument of Plato's *Republic,* "The dramatic poet sets up a vicious form of government in the individual soul: he is an image-maker whose images are phantoms far removed from reality." [2] On the one hand, if the artist makes a claim to wisdom, just because art is but an imitation of things far removed from their true essences, "the artist knows nothing worth mentioning about the subjects he represents, and . . . art is a form of play, not to be taken seriously." [3] But as a source of pleasure, poetry "waters the growth of passions which should be allowed to wither away and sets them up in control, although the goodness and happiness of our lives depend on their being held in subjection." [4]

Plato has made two points here, the first of which we can either reject or set aside without difficulty: if we regard art (including literature) as nothing but a source of pleasure and entertainment, without great intellectual pretensions or serious content, then it destroys the moral fibre of our souls and corrupts our very being. It appeals to sentiments that overpower reason and rule without knowledge or understanding, leading to moral degeneration. The poet produces in us fear, sorrow, terror, and pity, all of which weaken the character and degrade the mind rather than strengthening the noble part of us and inspiring us with conviction and self-discipline. To this Aristotle offered two replies: that men learn by imitation, which is natural to them—this is why Tragedy should portray men nobler than ordinary; and that properly done, Tragedy produces a *catharsis* of pity and fear which transforms the nature of such feelings, even into morally desirable attitudes and orientations. The portrayal of terrible events in the theatre is not necessarily corrupting; it may well serve to develop revulsion and repudiation in the audience, and end by strengthening rather than weakening moral conviction. Indeed, Aristotle's reply goes far beyond the mere affirmation that art *can* serve a moral purpose, and suggests even more that it may do so in ways far from obvious. To those who, like Plato, are willing to permit art a place in society only if its moral function is assured, Aristotle's reply is that such a view requires careful judgment and exceedingly fine perception, for art works in ways less direct than propagandists would have us believe. Catharsis of pity and fear (as well as other strong and undesired emotions) may demand the arousal of precisely those feelings in order to appease them, contrary to the opinions of those who seek to stifle all unwanted feeling. Turning to Freud it may be pointed out that suppression of aggressive desires never eliminates them but only diverts them into unforeseeable and perhaps worse manifestations, such as war or sexual aberration. What is needed instead is what Freud calls "sublimation"—the diversion of psychic, usually sexual energy into desirable and productive areas such as science, art, or politics. Such diversion is not very different from Aristotle's catharsis in releasing the force of undesired feeling in worthy and valuable ways. Art can serve in both arousing and controlling such energies, for it manipulates both material and surroundings in ways that *indirectly* (and thus harmlessly) release such forces. The fear aroused by a horror movie is not the fear one feels for himself in a house alone in the dark, or in the Great Blackout in New York City in 1965. Controlled and organized, such arousal of feelings may strengthen rather than weaken one's abilities to withstand panic and self-pity.

Plato's second point, however, is both far more significant and far more relevant to our subject matter here. The question is not whether art *properly directed* can serve important moral purposes—for Plato himself utilizes myths, legends, and tales to inspire the populace of his Ideal State with worthy attitudes and ambitions —but whether an artist *qua* artist can make legitimate claims to particular insights or specific knowledge of things. Rather, should not the artist be directed by the philosopher (for Plato), or the scientist, and represent known truths given him by others? What legitimate right has an artist to claim that he possesses any kind of knowledge? What could this be? What could be its source? Most telling of all, what possible reason is there to think that art is a medium congenial to the expression of knowledge? Does it not indeed distort whatever truths it may possess through the use of emotionally loaded words, the reliance on metaphor, and the use of legendary and fantastic tales? If an artist had something to say, would he not do better to say it in any other way than he actually does? The bizarre, emotional, and fantastic means used by authors arouse our feelings, but have no right to touch our reason or enlist our intellectual capacities.

The metaphors, ambiguities, and indirect means of expression used in literature (and other forms of art) are often blamed for its unliteral and imprecise qualities. But lest we conclude from this that such lapses could be corrected if only artists so desired, a further point is often made. That is, it would not be appropriate to treat a work of art,—for example, a poem—with or without its uniquely expressive elements, as argumentative or literally significant. A philosopher may utilize metaphor and expressive language, but his claims to truth reside in the justification he provides for being taken seriously. Both philosopher and scientist seek to make their views authoritative and to justify their acceptance by others. If they are wrong they are responded to as such. The artist, however, need not be considered knowledgeable at all; a poem's truth or falsity is irrelevant to its value as a poem. If there are truths to be found in art, they are obscure and vague. It is thought far more accurate to recognize that truths (and falsehoods) play a role in art only in passing, by chance, and that literature is valuable in its expressive and evocative function without regard to the wisdom of its author. As I. A. Richards puts it: poetry consists of statements "which only the very foolish would think of attempting to verify. . . . All that matters in either case is acceptance, that is to say, the institution and development of the further response." [5]

Lurking throughout this point of view is a distinction that should be made explicit—between referential or literal uses of language as in science and philosophy, and emotive or expressive uses of language as in poetry. It is proper to speak of knowledge and truth with reference to the former; for the latter, only the kind and strength of response aroused are of importance. According to this view, in discussing a Shakespearian sonnet we may speak of the forcefulness of imagery, the faithfulness of alliteration, the effectiveness of representation, but not of the truth or falsity of what is said nor of the arguments given to defend claims made. As for direct assertions that cannot be evaded—such as Shakespeare's claim: "Not marble, nor the gilded monuments/of princes, shall outlive this powerful rime"; (Sonnet LV)—defenders of this distinction suggest that at best we consider the import of the author's lines, the nature of *his* belief, and react to *his* point of view. Regardless of whether poetry confers lasting fame, that is what *he* is claiming. But we can appreciate his sentiments without taking seriously his claims for ourselves. The last thing in the world we are supposed to do in response to the lines above is to start writing poetry to immortalize ourselves and our loved ones.

The conversion of every statement uttered in a work of literature into at best an autobiographical claim, either of the author or of the character in whose mouth it is placed, and otherwise an emotive utterance working only upon the sentiments of the reader is artificial, without any basis than that of saving a distinction that is without great plausibility. Is it really possible to read the above poet's presumptive declaration without reacting to its overwhelming arrogance and self-conceit? And does this not include a distinct judgment as to whether poetry does or does not usually convey immortality? It is true that the reader cannot *learn* about the durability of poetry from a sonnet; but knowledge of the truth or falsity of what is said is essential to the aesthetic value of the poem. If the sonnet is primarily expressive it is so through the medium of its referential content. This suggests that the distinction requires reworking, that perhaps no utterances are ever exclusively literal or expressive, that scientific reports convey some expressive elements and that many poems and novels are loaded with literal content. And this last cannot be rejected as irrelevant to the main aesthetic values themselves.

The point of the distinction is to resolve the difficulty mentioned above—to explain the value of literature independent of the legitimacy of the author's claims to wisdom. The "art for art's sake" school simply sets aside the assertive claims of the artist as irrelevant, letting art be purely entertaining or pleasurable. (Although there are frightening and ugly aspects of some works of art, I presume all art is intended to produce some pleasure, amidst terror and pain.) Its members completely accept Plato's repudiation of wisdom in art and relegate the artist to a purely borderline function in the intellectual community, however effectively and successfully he fills it. The artist who claims special vision is laughed at for his presumption and naiveté, and judged solely for his expressiveness and forcefulness. The fact that so many authors and poets do make claims to special truths that men not only lack but urgently need becomes a peculiarity of psychology; for such claims are wholly without merit.

Yet something is missing from the doctrine of art for art's sake so far as literature in particular is concerned. Looking for the truth of music or the wisdom in Michelangelo's *David* or Raphael's *Madonna* (La Belle Jardiniere) is a vain and hopeless enterprise, and we do well to heed warnings not to look everywhere for edification and wisdom. Some art does best taken solely in terms of values properly called "aesthetic." But other novels and plays cannot without severe injustice be treated in this way. How can *Faust* be read without constant appraisal of what Goethe has shown about man and the goals of life? Does not the strength of Dante's *Inferno* depend on its portrayal of a moral world-view taken toward the events of human experience as lived, not merely imagined? Fascinating as the vision would be if we thought of it as nothing but a fantasy revealing the power of human imagination, its truly transcendent quality is embodied in our awareness of its relation to our lives and world. Novelists have always been social critics; can it seriously be maintained that Dickens, George Eliot, and Tolstoi are to be read without concern for the truth or falsity of their often violent criticisms of the social environment in which they found themselves?

Theoretical difficulties can be raised for the distinction between expressive and literal language: in particular, can it be maintained that linguistic utterances ever serve solely one or another function; or is it not more correct to say that now one, now another function is emphasized or subordinated? If the point of the distinction is to tell us how we *should* read a novel, then its supporting argument is lacking: the distinction carries no argument by itself. Even if some art is best viewed in terms of criteria independent of content, it does not follow that *all* literature should so be viewed. There is something particularly sublime about novels that not only succeed in purely literary terms, but contain and develop ideas of great philosophic worth without destruction of the literary values. Is not *Faust* greater than it would otherwise be precisely because of its fusion of philosophic and artistic elements? We can grant that art is not science or philosophy without demanding that it be wholly exclusive of considerations relevant to them.

But the attack against the art for art's sake point of view can be made most effectively by simply spelling out the ways in which the intellectual content—philosophic and otherwise—of literature plays a fundamental role when it appears. A few examples are considered in Chapter 2, for this purpose as well as to show the wide range of philosophic ideas to be found in literature.

# 2

# *Some Important Themes*
# *in Works of Literature*

## 1.

In *The Magic Mountain,* Thomas Mann spends almost an unbearable amount of time and the reader's patience on long speeches given aloud to his hero Hans Castorp, and on internal monologues in which Castorp addresses himself. If such speeches are not taken seriously—indeed, if they are not of fundamental importance to the novel—then our time is being wasted unmercifully, and the novel must fail abysmally. The reader who seeks characterization (in which the novel is rich) or plot (which it is not) rather than thought and intellectual conflict cannot but find this novel an utter failure. Thus without regard for ideas as such, for intellectual confrontation in its important as well as exciting elements, such a novel cannot be appreciated for what it is.

Mann sets the scene in a tuberculosis sanatorium high on a mountain, far removed from worldly considerations and immediate concerns, where life and death are critical issues indeed—for many patients die or are in terminal stages, and all wonder at and fear possible death. In a setting which thus reflects man in confrontation with life and death in a most urgent sense, Mann reenacts the intellectual history of man in which the great themes of human understanding arose in response to the human condition and its desperate needs. He thus sets as a background the intellectual and cultural elements that surround Castorp, the good and worthy German youth. Quite explicitly Mann retraces the great controversy between the Church and Science—which is at once that between man of despair and man of hope, man caught in primeval sin and man of optimistic potentiality, between man irrational, superstitious and man rational and noble. Here are the options facing Hans, to choose one or another path, to recognize the greater truth of one or another way. How can the reader forego, with Hans, evaluating the arguments, the styles of life, the attitudes, and the characters of the men who are so much at odds? Hans Castorp is, if not Everyman, then every German; unless his acts represent *our* acts and his thoughts in some way are our thoughts, he becomes only one particular man, faced with one particular decision. And however important that decision is to him, can it be of much value to us unless we can take those issues seriously and weigh those alternatives in our own minds?

Of course, as a novelist Mann makes use of means that are unavailable to the historian of ideas or the philosopher, who might present to their audience the same great conflicts and ask for us to make some great decision. Important characters work their influence on Hans. His cousin, a man very close and important to him, dies. He is torn both by the unworldliness of his surroundings and his utter passivity and willingness to remain without decision. Finally Mann spills out this composite of rich characterization, timelessness, intellectual conflict, and human history into the First World War, and we suddenly realize that *if* that war was the great pivotal point it was then thought to be—and that Mann took it to be—then Hans Castorp now has come to recognize where Man stands and stands there himself as emissary or representative. The speeches made by the various characters in the novel are not always either literal portrayals of a true or false thesis, nor are they speeches to which we must bring definite and detailed analysis. But the overriding considerations of the novel are revealed by such intellectual developments and depend unavoidably on them. Mann is not satisfied with portraying *some* people found on *some* mountain, with *their* problems and needs. Their problems are ours, their decisions mirror ours; Hans Castorp's intellectual passivity and confrontation are at once the reader's. What actually can be made of man in the twentieth century, a culmination of a history of more than one thousand years? Can we reach any conclusion without both a confrontation of each man with the immediacy of his surroundings—which Mann's skill as a novelist provides—and an awareness of what other, wiser men have made of the human condition?

## 2.

Sweeping historical visions of the poles of human thought are not alone to be found in philosophic literature. Nor is the only way to examine or expose intellectual considerations to the reader through speechmaking, either by the author or by some of his characters. It is also possible—and *perhaps* even more successful—to portray ideals implicitly in the structure, events, and characters of the work of literature. No doubt the very implicitness of such a portrayal calls for some modesty in our analysis, but unless we recognize this way of representing a point of view in literature—often forcefully and persuasively—we cannot succeed in our analysis of the relationship of literature to intellectual issues and problems.

Consider here two novels of social criticism—and two ways of expressing distaste for certain elements or practices in society. In *Middlemarch,* George Eliot introduces us in the very beginning to Dorothea, a young girl of great longing, who yearned to make some great man a worthy wife.

Her mind was theoretic and yearned by its nature after some lofty conception of the world which might frankly include the parish of Tipton and her own rule of conduct there; she was enamoured of intensity and greatness and rash in embracing whatever seemed to her to have those aspects; likely to seek martyrdom, to make retractions, and then to incur martyrdom after all in a quarter where she had not sought it.

The novel may be Dorothea's, but it may even more be Lydgate's, who appears later in the novel marked as a capable and perhaps brilliant doctor, an apostle of *science* and the new enlightenment. Eliot even offers us insight into the nature of science and its relationship to man through her portrayal of Lydgate, who has a

conviction that the medical profession as it might be was the finest in the world, presenting the most perfect interchange between science and art, offering the most direct alliance between intellectual conquest and the social good. Lydgate's nature demanded this combination: he was an emotional creature, with a flesh-and-blood sense of fellowship which withstood all the abstractions of special duty.

Characters such as Dorothea and Lydgate are not and cannot stand alone in themselves. This is the fundamental point in literature—that characters always either "imitate," "represent," or *are* Man to us, humanity crystallized in print, in the author's imagination. Perhaps some characters are too odd or distasteful to us to accept as our representatives—like Quasimodo in *The Hunchback of Notre Dame* or Smerdyakov in *The Brothers Karamazov*. But even the latter is used by Dostoievski explicitly to show the unavoidability in art, perhaps in life, of *our* confrontation with the question of whether we are our brothers' keepers. The question Ivan must face is whether his own deeds, innocent as they may be in intent, are not the very cause and source of Smerdyakov's crime. The question of whether we are indeed like the characters we read of, or know people like them, whether we would or would not act as they do, succeed or fail as they do, is unavoidable in literature. Because of it no *particular* thought in a work of literature is ever only that; its reverberations compel us to take larger, perhaps occasionally intellectual perspectives. So to return to *Middlemarch,* the utter destruction of Dorothea's hopes and Lydgate's ambitions—"Lydgate's hair never became white. He died when he was only fifty. . . . His skill was relied on by many paying patients, but he always regarded himself as a failure: he had not done what he once meant to do"; and "Dorothea herself had no dreams of being praised above other women, feeling that there was always something better which she might have done if she had only been better and known better"—is a *portrayal* of Eliot's conviction that society can be deadly, and often destroys just the exciting individuals that arise within it. Parochialness and narrowness of vision permeate our world and threaten all of us. But they threaten the most important and hopeful far more than the timid and conforming.

Eliot's thesis is not wholly original. The effects of social pressures on individual quests have been testified to by many other novelists, philosophers, and dramatists. The pressures of social conformity can be found in Sophocles' chorus, repeated over and over. Eliot only portrays it somewhat differently, in a context in which the scientist rather than the hero or statesman is of prime concern. The range of her generalization, the extent to which society *always* effects destructive conservation, is of course unclear. Yet what *is* quite clear is that we are being warned of danger, shown a possible mechanism of social control, and told, moreover, that no degree of ambition or desire can alone permit success. A man of great and noble ambition might well learn some of the enemies against whom he must prevail. Of course, Eliot does not argue her case; but is not the very portrayal an argument? Can we not (*should* we not) respond by rejecting her portrayal as unfaithful, inaccurate, or idiosyncratic if that is what it is? If we decide "that could not happen here," are we not repudiating a *thesis*? And is not the novel, however moving and effective somewhat the less when we do so?

Consider here Emile Zola's *L'Assommoir* (or any other "realistic" novel by Zola, Balzac, or Dreiser). Zola does not harangue the reader; he does not even succumb to the temptation to sentimentalize and represent Gervaise as a paragon of virtue ruined by the economic conditions in which she finds herself. Gervaise's own lack of discipline and softness are the conditions of her decline. Yet the novel is unquestionably a portrayal of a way in which many men live, one developing from a sparseness of intrinsic values and opportunity in the environment, from the utter lack of concern for others in Gervaise's fellow Parisians, and from a limitation of Gervaise's own vision and ambition. Here is utter emptiness of beauty, hopelessness, and perhaps a virtual absence of humanity. What would elsewhere be virtues—Gervaise's softness, her desires, her enjoyment of what she possesses—become the source of her ruination. The beauty of life, the heights of human aspiration, are alien to Gervaise's world. The novel is not read as a pure and vicious social critique, against capitalist and exploiter. But its revelation of human misery—and the lack of awareness of pain and of greater human possibilities—portrays a thesis concerning what men can become if they are not prevented from doing so. Zola reveals here what poverty really is—and it is something different from starvation, perhaps worse. We may again ask if Zola has *proved* his case: but he has looked and seen. Does a sociologist really do so much more? The degree of precision the sociologist seeks may be far greater, but is this not a function of his unique statistical methods rather than greater truth or accuracy? Does not Zola "know" what people are and how they act as well as any psychologist?

3.

In 1651, in apology for the right of the monarch to prevail in the face of new demands of the English middle class, Thomas Hobbes wrote his *Leviathan*. The great burden of this work was to justify the power of the king in order to avoid what Hobbes called "the state of nature," in which there is "continuall feare, and danger of violent death; And the life of man, solitary, poore, nasty, brutish, and short." Some 250 years later, Freud warned of the dangers inherent in the irrational impulses of the id, and testified to the need for some internal psychic mechanism to prevent them from being destructive. It is interesting to note that Hobbes' main argument rests neither on special psychological insight nor on ethical considerations. Its basis is the fact that, in as orderly, calm a society as we live in today, men *do* lock their doors and fear harm from each other. How then face the prospect of life without a force to compel order? Anything is better than anarchy.

William Golding, in *Lord of the Flies*, takes a more Freudian than Hobbesian view of the matter, revealed in his use throughout of such sexual symbols as the conch, sticks pointed at both ends, and the "younguns'" fear of *snakes* or other creatures that creep in the night. Out of this material he fashions a tale of British boys, whose society is the pinnacle of civilization, cast adrift on an uninhabited island. In the absence of adult authority and sanctions they descend into a vicious state of depravity and cruelty, motivated by fear of the night creatures, but even more by their innate fascination with death and pain. The return of the adult world in an abrupt fashion at the end marks as well a return to order, but for the remarkable fact that the adults are sailors of Her Majesty's Navy, en route to a secret testing ground to engage in war maneuvers of some unspecified type.

Considering Hobbes and Freud, Golding has nothing *new* to tell. But the question is not whether Golding learned or invented his intellectual position; rather, it is whether the value of the novel depends on the definite awareness of a message we should not overlook, both from our own moral and political point of view and from the point of view of the aesthetic values of the novel. Once again, if these are just *some* boys, cast adrift on *some* particular island, we can read with interest their hunt of wild pigs and decline into savagery a bit like we read the *Swiss Family Robinson* or *Robinson Crusoe* (though not *Gulliver's Travels*). Life on a desert island has its intrinsic fascination, and reading about it has direct rewards. But Golding has written a novel about *man,* and shouts it aloud over and over in his symbols and almost caricatured treatment of very important characters—like Piggy and his glasses, or Simon the mystic. Great human possibilities are portrayed here, and their importance revealed in the face of human bestiality. Beware, Golding warns, of man's natural condition and what lurks beneath the surface. Hobbes and Freud too have the same warning, and in addition provide argument to defend it. But surely Golding's *portrayal* of decline is no less persuasive or legitimate than is Hobbes' appeal to human distrust. Unless we feel quite sure that Golding is right about any or most boys in a like situation, generalization fails. The novel functions on only a literal level. In order to make something more of it—and Golding surely asks us to—we must grant the possibility of its central thesis and admit its being proved to us by illustration or example. This means of proof is not as adequate as scientific experimentation or philosophic argument. But it is by no means without justification or support. It can be attacked, even by saying that man is not like that!

## 4.

Literature has always had a fundamental moral purpose, however discredited authors have been as bearers of moral vision. From Aeschylus' attempt to allegorize the coming of civilization and the relinquishing of a vengeful morality in the name of social justice in the *Oresteia,* through Sophocles' portrayal of man the hero apart from and set against ordinary needs and moral demands in *Philoctetes* and *Ajax,* to Gide's utter repudiation of social norms in *The Immoralist,* the artist has struggled to represent man confronting ethical values and commitments. Perhaps moral "criticism" has arisen only in recent times—Sophocles and Aeschylus seemed content to work with moral attitudes to be found amongst their contemporaries—but the peculiarly moral issues of evaluation, decision, and responsibility are the byways of literature. Here of course the artist runs afoul of Plato's attack, since he presumes to offer advice on matters he may well be thought less than expert on. And when writers stray so far as to offer just advice and little more, they slowly descend into the abyss of unsuccessful literature. But that does not imply that moral objectivity is desirable, nor that moral values are out of place in great literature.

Consider a twentieth-century novel steeped in a moral tradition, though with a stance of rejection and repudiation. In *The Stranger,* Camus presents a young man who from the first violates ordinary codes of behavior, and in the worst ways. He does not weep at his mother's funeral, and indeed cares little if at all whether he should marry or not. It's all the same. He is an empty shell of a man, one we would find easy to accuse of *alienation:* a man divided from himself, from a place in the world, from any sense of belonging to or of meaning in existence. The alienated man is the man out of touch —with others, even with himself, perhaps with ultimate purposes of things. He endures, but he fails to live. Meursault is a man to whom nothing has value, for whom nothing lasts, nothing is worth time or effort. He cannot but arouse our pity and our condemnation. His utter lack of sensibility eventually leads him to a senseless murder for which he is condemned to die. Yet if our reactions could remain on this level alone, little of either literary or moral value would have been gained. Camus shows us the emptiness of the lives of all the other men who pretend commitment or social purpose. They are horrified at Meursault's strangeness, yet it is no less genuine than theirs. The so-called involvements and feelings of men are but absurd shadows of possible humanity. And Meursault concludes by affirming that his utter repudiation of humanity in that garb was completely justified, and that he would do it again. His impending death only strengthens his resolve.

If Camus' moral message were completely clear perhaps he would be less a novelist than he is. Sartre, for example, is all too often in his literature marking aesthetic time to tell us something very specific. Overt and specific messages can destroy literary forcefulness and indeed result in utter lack of persuasiveness. Sometimes we find a novel the greater when we can say that the author's intentions were diverted in execution. Tolstoi sought in *Anna Karenina* to portray Kitty and Levin as moral solutions to a corrupt and degradingly worldly Russian society. The moral message is that we should return to the soil, even to the life of the peasant, to be cleansed and restored. But Kitty and Levin are the most boring of people; and Anna and Vronsky, doomed by the world in which they find themselves and which Tolstoi wants to criticize, are both appealing and exciting. Tolstoi succeeds in developing a powerful criticism of a destructive society. But that very society also produced our two attractive characters. That is far more than can be said of the society Levin seeks to join.

If Camus' message is obscure, perhaps even intentionally murky and unintelligible, if Tolstoi's message is fortunately subordinated to pressures which develop within the novel itself, still we may not conclude that moral issues are irrelevant in either case. Camus is groping with a moral problem of critical importance: the source of value in human life, and the extent to which rationality and propriety become confused by social pressures and propriety comes to represent the only form of value. We may indeed reject Meursault's caprice, his conclusion that death marks all life as absurd, and that the only values that matter are immediate and personal. Perhaps we demand that humanity stand forth in the face of emptiness and absurdity and *create value,* rather than destroying it in the name of nihilism. Things *do* matter. But the thesis of the novel is not as important as the themes with which it deals. And so with *Anna Karenina:* Tolstoi's explicit *intent* is subordinated to the exploration of the relationship between Vronsky and Anna. But the novel's meaning rests heavily on a generalization from the two characters to the nature of their relationship and their ostracism from a definite kind of society. Anna is a wonderful creation; and her despair is all the more real because of it. Her despair, though, is part and parcel of the circumstances in which she finds herself, a married woman in adultery. The moral repercussions of such a portrayal are immense and virtually unending.

Perhaps the point is that if we are not going to hold moral prejudices so fixed as to be utterly without possibility of rejection or reconsideration, then the events of our lives will serve as testing grounds for our generalizations and moral conventions. What Tolstoi and Camus do is to forcefully render events which contain possibilities we might be unlikely to encounter directly for our moral appraisal and evaluation. These too can serve as testing grounds, perhaps even more clearly than the events in our own lives in which we are so directly involved. Therefore, if we fail to bring moral analysis to bear on such novels, we miss their point altogether.

### 5.

Artists have often in the twentieth century focussed on themselves as objects of scrutiny. Self-consciousness is a theme of our age, a vestige of romantic loss and quest after self. The artist, however, seeks himself in the forms and nature of his art. He views art as the harbor of self; in the play or novel we find our very being. Occasionally the artist professes unique acquaintance with his art; but often he claims far more—that, as artist, he represents the highest achievements of man.

Thus Joyce, in *Portrait of the Artist as a Young Man,* reveals Stephen Dedalus as the young and tormented artist seeking his own nature and individuality. He finds himself in direct antagonism with the Church, which stands firmly in his path as man. The tortures of hell are revealed to him, but neither assuage nor enlighten him. The pervading quality of Irish Catholicism is the hurdle he must win over; and in doing so Dedalus the artist steps forth, not only as man against cruel and demanding Church, but as artist with a higher truth. It is not enough that Stephen become a man, aware of his feelings and the oppressive nature of the Church, but that he be revealed a higher truth, embodied now in Art, not in endowed religion. "Welcome, O life! I go to encounter for the millionth time the reality of experience and to forge in the smithy of my soul the uncreated conscience of my race." Joyce's image is thus that man the artist is man crystallized, closer to true humanity than ordinary man, and also that art becomes the vehicle for the fulfillment of life and takes on a special role in human experience. Of course, we who read may wonder if Joyce is speaking literally in Dedalus's mouth; and so we should. Great intensity of expression is here developed precisely through the question of the *truth* or *falsity* of Dedalus's discoveries, which are wrapped up in the nature of the novel itself, in its revelation of the artist as person and believer, and in how his own art exemplifies his dicta. When the artist speaks we turn automatically to his work to find exemplification. Thus Joyce's novel must itself *be* the art Stephen Dedalus speaks of; it must mark a higher vision and a greater self. "The dramatic form is reached when the vitality which has flowed and eddied round each person fills every person with such vital force that he or she assumes a proper and intelligible esthetic life." Otherwise the words dissolve into mere polemic. If Joyce succeeds in unifying aesthetic vision with its execution, then the synthesis of content: that art can reveal special truth, with its form: the execution of the truth, marks that very truth itself.

While I think that Joyce fails here (as he does not in *Ulysses*), Hesse in *Magister Ludi* offers a different vision. This is, spelled out in great detail, the primarily intellectual function of the artist-scholar to bear the weight of tradition and the foundation of aesthetic and moral values through the history of man, set against a separate and remote background of the political and worldly life of the active man. Here the artist seeks and finds a new medium of expression, in which the discoveries of science and mathematics, music and the other arts, are unified in a glorious exercise which is only a *game*. The artist withdraws, to increasingly sterile achievements. In an utter repudiation of the Rationalistic, NeoPlatonic, and Eastern mystical abdication from active engagement, Hesse portrays in his hero Knecht an awareness of responsibility that is the very core of his being Master Artist. The artist as such has a moral and pedagogical function to serve. Tragically, however, he cannot both serve it and remain a functioning artist. In the most pessimistic conclusion I know of, Hesse reveals both the obligation and the impotence of the artist as man, repudiating the beauty and grace (with only a touch of human frailty) which are found in the realm of pure art.

What is most remarkable is Hesse's unification of form and content. By utilizing a third-person narrator who, as a member of the artistic-intellectual community knows no more—and often less—than we do, Hesse portrays Knecht's wandering through the realms of man and art to his final fruition, neither lecturing on his need to serve nor explaining events to us, but simply letting us see that life demands in its own terms something more than Castalia can offer. We are less told than shown, less lectured to than given revelation. And thus we too are enlightened by a fusion of art and intellectual awareness.

## 6.

There remains one further example to consider in a far from exhaustive set of examples to show the kinds of philosophic positions and attitudes which are to be found in works of literature. The work of Franz Kafka is perhaps the most general treatment of the *human condition,* on so abstract a level as to merit the term "metaphysical." Kafka's awareness of the "plight" (if that is the correct term) of man is expressed through parable-like exhibitions of men in strange, dream-like, yet altogether familiar situations and circumstances. Guilt permeates Kafka's world, and men move in strange ways through an unreal setting that somehow mirrors the actual world in which we find ourselves. Amidst the chaos and absurdity of events are revealed—so we think while reading—great truths about the characteristics of human experience, but on so allegorical a level, in so indirect a fashion, as to call for *translation* into languages we understand. Sometimes Kafka offers such a translation within the framework of the novel itself; sometimes he does not.

The literary form here is essential to Kafka's purpose, which could not be met by any other. Partly this is due to the literal terror that the circumstances of his main character, K., would arouse if we were to take such circumstances literally or even as very possible. Art properly performed and appreciated stands at a distance from the beholder. Conventions of response exist which make it impossible to take too literally the events of a play, the circumstances of a novel—at least, while remaining appreciative of the work of art as such. As E. Bullough puts it:

> The working of Distance is . . . the cutting out of the practical sides of things and of our practical attitude to them. . . . As a rule, experiences constantly turn the same side toward us, namely, that which has the strongest practical force of appeal. . . . The sudden view of things from their reverse, usually unnoticed, side, comes upon us as a revelation, and such revelations are precisely those of Art. In this most general sense, Distance is a factor in all art.[1]

As works of art, provided we treat them as such, Kafka's novels do stand at a sufficient distance—aided by obscurity, ambiguity, and allegory—to permit us to read them without finding ourselves too involved, faced with too horrible a prospect to behold. The ability of art to perform its cathartic function depends on our awareness that it is art we are beholding, not reality; fictional, not real people. A jealous man who identifies wholly with Othello will become so involved in his own feelings as to miss the value of the play. We learn conventions which enable us to set ourselves aside from a work of art in order to appreciate it. These permit us to tolerate murder in *Titus Andronicus* and *Macbeth,* the atrocities of the Marquis de Sade, even to enjoy musicals based on violence and deprivation such as *West Side Story.* If children learn early to read fiction as fiction they may well be aided and purified by distilled violence, rather than corrupted by it.

If we grasped immediately and directly what Kafka is only suggesting by innuendo and various literary devices—that the world of man is oppressed, irrational, absurd, and permeated by guilt, that order only apparently prevails yet we are ultimately responsible for our acts even when we have chosen on the basis of the little we really know we would find the world unbearable to face. Moreover, since Kafka, along with Beckett, Ionesco, and Genet, is concerned primarily with the absurdity, irrationality, and disorderly nature of the world we live in, it may be held that rational analysis is out of place, virtually self-contradictory. Lurking behind the rational and intelligible is the dark and unforeseeable, the blind and incommensurable. Sophocles knew it and revealed it in the remarks of his Chorus at the ruination of the paragon of rational existence, Oedipus. Artists are in touch with the irrational aspect of things. As Freud would have it, they are more in contact with the unconscious and primitive elements in the psyche, which by its very nature can only be pointed to and revealed. It cannot be analyzed; analyzability is a characteristic only of the rational. Plato and Nietzsche, two philosophers who recognized this dimension of existence, both turned to myth, to poetic expression, to indicate it. I must confess my sympathy with Plato's view, however, that rational understanding of the object of myth and poetry is possible. He does not claim that there is an aspect of things that is opaque to philosophy, but that under some circumstances, an appropriate myth is more appropriate than is technical analysis. If there is an irrational dimension to existence, its presence if not its nature can be rationally comprehended. But a work of literature may enable us to feel qualities far more deeply, simply by exposing us to it.

If, then, *The Castle* is man in quest of authority, whether political, intellectual, religious, or parental—and the latter two seem most likely to have been intended explicitly—Kafka portrays this authority as hidden, opaque, mysterious, meaningless, even perhaps nonexistent but for the myths that the townspeople tell and believe. Man's condition is one of desperate need for authority, one so great as to permit no turning aside. Like Lancelot, K. is in search of the Holy Grail, but his search is aborted and twisted by everyone and everything; his faith that the castle is truly inhabited is never really tested or rendered significant; and if he were to reach his goal he does not nor can we know what he will find. If man is doomed to eternal restlessness and seeking, then only a Romantic could find value and achievement in that quest alone as Goethe has Faust do.

Literature can capture, as no rational analysis quite can, the feelings that are part of our systems of value. Reason examines, but we may wish to taste and experience. And art can provide so controlled an experience for us as to make us tolerate what we couldn't bear in any other form. To Kafka, the world of man is so unbearable in its emptiness, its cruelty, its meaninglessness, that no virtue can be found therein except that placed there by man; and this he also finds but a mockery of genuine and literal value. *The Castle* literally shows us that the world is . . . . But here we must stop, since spelling it out only makes it so intolerable as to compel our rejection of its thesis. Hope and reason rule hand in hand. No rational arguments can really be given to support the utter futility of reason. It is the poet who must then carry the necessary message in his own manner and style.

# 3

## The Unique Wisdom of Art

The problem which has been posed, and which most philosophers accept in some form or other, is that on the one hand art utilizes its own techniques that render it quite different from philosophy and science, and rule out treating literature as if it contained definite truth claims. The judgments to be found in scientific journals and philosophic treatises are to be judged as true or false by weighing the evidence offered, evaluating the arguments set forth. Both philosophy and science seek warrant and justification. This art cannot provide. Of course, the conclusions of both science and philosophy can be taken out of context and, independent of justification, presented in almost any form. But this is precisely the derivative presentation of truth claims I have called "display," and is not to be confused with the presentation in works of literature of philosophic views to be judged in the work of art as true or false. For on the other hand, it would seem that many works of literature not only display positions, but adopt and support them. Not only do people look for truth in literature, but it would seem that in the works mentioned above, it is legitimate to do so. In short, the problem is that literature cannot be philosophical except in a derivative sense. It cannot make claims. But it nevertheless does so—or at least, many people including artists have thought so.

As is to be expected, the history of philosophy reveals a wealth of approaches to the problem. I shall argue later that literature can be (though it is not often) literally philosophical, can take positions and can support them by using its own special techniques. And I shall show and explain how philosophical literature can be first-rate literature. On the other hand, many philosophers have tried to solve the problem I have posed by arguing that men who look for philosophy in art are wrong to do so. I hope the examples I have given speak to this point for themselves.

There is, however, another alternative. If art seems to provide wisdom, but does not do so in a manner appropriate to philosophy or science, then it is only necessary to claim that art offers unique wisdom and special insight, that the wisdom it conveys is of a different kind altogether from that of science. We seek to learn from art what art alone has to offer. Put another way, truth in science and philosophy is a cold, logical, and rational truth, reached through nonhuman and emotionless methods. Truth in art is alive, vital, and rich in human significance. Art reaches wisdom through the imagination, science through logical rigor and understanding.[1]

Knowledge has two forms: it is either *intuitive* knowledge or *logical* knowledge; knowledge obtained through the *imagination* or knowledge obtained through the *intellect;* knowledge of the *individual* or knowledge of the *universal;* of *individual things* or of the *relations between them;* it is, in fact, productive either of *images* or of *concepts.*[2]

It is clear, however, that if one counterposes the logical and the intuitive, even the intellect and the imagination, he is implicitly denying that the imagination and the intuition can offer the kinds of justification afforded by the intellect, which rely on logical rigor and meticulous analysis and experimentation. Surely the *prima facie* case is that it is precisely the logical rigor of science and mathematics, the movement from premises to conclusions, that provides them with their arguments, proofs, and justifications. The intuition, however profound or particular its insights, cannot test and evaluate them.

If, then, we take argument and experimentation—proof—as essential to knowledge, art fails to provide knowledge, in that sense. On the other hand, if we maintain with Croce in the above quotation that the intuitive is as legitimate and valuable a form of knowledge as the logical and analytic, even though it cannot provide logical and analytic proof, we must cope with the relationship between these two forms of knowledge. It is interesting that even if one grants the existence of two forms of knowledge, the place of philosophy in such an epistemological picture is far from clear.

Philosophical arguments are of vital importance, it would seem, for no great philosophers simply offer pictures of the world without argument. Yet the importance of strict rigor in philosophic argument is a matter of violent controversy. Spinoza offered his *Ethics* in almost a purely mathematical form; but it is not clear that his lapses in proof are liabilities, nor his valid proofs strengths. Hegel argues tightly for his dialectical movement of spirit in history, yet in a manner rather different and greatly out-of-style from contemporary philosophers. To most contemporary philosophers, philosophy seeks truth as does science, seeks to prove where science seeks to confirm, and it weighs evidence wherever that is relevant. Art does not. And when all is said and done, we have not broken the fundamental dualism with which we began, which leaves no room for literature seeking to provide scientific or philosophical understanding.

Other views can be found which hold, for example, that philosophy lies closer to art than science, that it employs imagination rather than understanding, and seeks order rather than proof. Thus Abraham Levi has attempted to show, in *Literature, Philosophy and the Imagination,* that the categories of art parallel the categories of philosophy.

Metaphysics, and particularly the metaphysics of the imagination, is not just a system which one constructs like a physical theory or a mathematical demonstration. It is the expression of self in its confrontation with the world. And therefore it can be expressed equally in the Platonic dialogue, the Schopenhauer treatise, the Cervantian novel, and the Pirandello play. The imagination can attempt to uncover the mystery of existence in a philosophic treatise or evoke it concretely in the theater, and each will be an adventure in metaphysical vision.[3]

Note, however, at how far a remove is metaphysical "vision" from discursive and rational philosophy. Kant does not merely envisage— he analyzes and demonstrates. Even Hegel, though through a very different sort of logic, attempts a logical derivation of the development of Spirit. We may turn Hegel into an artist in our minds, but we deny, when we do so, that he is a great philosopher.

Without going into the details of a view such as Levi's, it may be pointed out that the dualism between the imagination and the understanding cannot be used to solve the problem under consideration. Ultimately, only two alternatives seem to remain within the dualism: Literature can display philosophic and scientific positions, but these are not claims, and are not to be treated as scientific or philosophic judgments themselves. Or art offers its own unique content and attitudes, through the imagination and not the understanding. But whether or not this is then to be called "cognitive" and art is to be thought to provide its own unique kind of knowledge is no more than a terminological question. Call whatever you wish "knowledge"; art and science are radically different in the kind of task they perform and what they accomplish. Those who assert the province of art to be imagination and intuition, while that of science to be logic and understanding, defend and support the dualism. If both are kinds of knowledge, they are nevertheless worlds apart.

The alternatives that remain within the dualistic view for understanding philosophy all seem unsatisfactory. Philosophy must be thought of as one of the following: (1) A science—which would seem to make it dependent upon empirical evidence and experimentation, unsatisfactory to everyone. (2) An art—which seems equally to confuse the issue and neglects the role of justification and proof in philosophic works. (3) A mixture of each of them—which requires an explanation of how they are to be merged in any but a nonessential and arbitrary manner that would permit a simple separation of the two kinds of elements, while this is just what cannot be done, for we would then be able to divide philosophic works into artistic and scientific components without destroying them. This last view fails to explain how philosophy can enter art without giving up its ability to make claims and support its judgments, or how art can be philosophical without finding a way to justify assertions—which the dualist claims is just what cannot be done. Or philosophy might be thought of as (4) some very different kind of enterprise which resembles both science and art somewhat, but which is radically different from each of them nevertheless—which turns the dualism into a triad and opens the door to a pluralism. And are all of them to be considered knowledge?

But a very different approach to the role of philosophy in literature has been neglected throughout these different approaches. They all presuppose a radical gulf between science and art, as well as the legitimacy of each of them, and argue only about whether philosophy is closer to one or the other, and which provides the greatest wisdom. From this point of view, either all art provides wisdom (more or less), or none does.

May I suggest that not all works of literature are equally philosophic? The examples I have given above are far more philosophic in a very literal and judgmental sense than the plays of Shakespeare. In short, are there not particular works of literature that provide not only whatever wisdom art uniquely offers, but make claims and even justify and support definite conclusions? Are not some novels particularly philosophic, not only in display, but in that they also do indeed adopt philosophic positions and defend them? How can they do so? This is the question I propose to answer.

# 4

## *Moral Values in Literature*

Two strains, although virtually incompatible, find common ground in denying ethical significance to literature. On the one hand, the rationalistic in temperament seek truth through analysis and investigation, through the collection of evidence and the mustering of argument. The paradigm chosen is that of the painstaking laboratory scientist, or the meticulous compiler of arguments, to substantiate a given position or claim. From this point of view art fails to contain wisdom precisely because it offers no arguments, provides no evidence, and appeals to no justification. It is at best an expression of a point of view, and at most an attempt to persuade rather than to enlighten, to exhort rather than to teach, to propagandize rather than to demonstrate. A scientist who makes a claim to discovery may properly be asked for proof or justification; presumably he has checked his hypotheses through carefully designed and executed experiments. The philosopher must justify his claims by carefully devised arguments. The author of a novel, however, usually does not provide such evidence or argument; and if he did, that would be irrelevant to his function as artist. Thus if there are ethical truths, authors are not in a position to claim to know them except through special artistic inspiration or on a superficial and uncritical level. Here the poet who seeks to teach us something new about moral conduct or our values and obligations is a propagandist or moralizer, not a philosopher or teacher.

The antipodal view is that there are no ethical truths, no messages to be learned, only attitudes which vary from person to person. One cannot learn what is good and right, for there is nothing that is truly so. There are only feelings or attitudes different men have toward things around them. Thus when two people dispute on an ethical matter, they cannot properly settle their dispute as they might if the issue were a factual one, by collecting evidence. They can only try to persuade each other. According to this view, any "moralist . . . is one who endeavors to influence attitudes," [1] and

the most important of the non-rational methods will be called "persuasive" in a somewhat broad sense. It depends on the sheer, direct emotional impact of words—on emotive meaning, rhetorical cadence, apt metaphor, stentorian, stimulating, or pleading tones of voice, dramatic gestures, care in establishing rapport with the hearer or audience, and so on. [2]

This is, of course, art.

Thus two widely divergent views of valuation and man's ethical life are able to take a common attitude toward the role of the artist on ethical matters. This is that literature and other forms of art are at best propagandistic, persuasive, rhetorical, and emotive; that they play no cognitively significant role in man's choice of the good life or in his evaluation of the goods and evils that surround him, in his judgments about his achievements and failures. They differ, of course, in one fundamental respect: the view that holds that ethical judgments can be made rationally and methodically, critically and analytically, differs from the view that ethical judgments are but expressions of attitude in holding that at least *some* legitimate methods do exist for appraising moral choices, and that these may properly be called "rational" or "cognitive." The view that all moral judgments are persuasive cannot distinguish artistic from non-artistic means of expression except by their degree of forcefulness and persuasiveness. Here the role of the artist is to compel assent to his doctrines through persuasive and rhetorical devices. But if all ethical claims are but persuasive rhetorical devices, why then are we so struck by art which is too propagandistic, whose authors are too obviously hammering their views upon us? Is this but irritation at the obviousness of the methods employed, at the doctrinaire opposition to our own views? Not always, since a novelist with whom we agree in fact may be rejected as a poor novelist if his attempts at persuasion are too overwhelming. Art seems different from mere persuasion in some important respects.

Furthermore, if all ethical judgments are but persuasive devices, the literary author is granted no *special* right to make his. Our concern is whether some *special* connection exists between art and moral evaluation, whether a writer makes use of moral considerations only as he makes use of time and place, character and plot; whether art is indeed harmed by too definite an ethical bias, or whether there exist particular ways in which literature can reveal great moral wisdom. We must assume, then, for purposes of analysis, that some particularly appropriate domain does exist in which ethical, metaphysical, and other intellectual values properly belong. The question is whether art—particularly literature—is part of this domain.

Perhaps it is worth considering again the suggestion that intellectual matters, even science and philosophy, play a role in literature only in the same way that character and place do. Henry James set many of his novels abroad—in Venice or London—and utilized his setting as one of the many devices with which he could develop a strictly aesthetic appeal. The fact that Dostoievski has Ivan make speeches in *The Brothers Karamazov* need not imply either Dostoievski's own attitude toward the content of the remarks, nor the truth or falsity of Ivan's position. Rather, it permits Dostoievski to develop tensions of great dramatic value—in Ivan's self-loathing and cynicism against Alyosha's simplicity—to portray character, and to set off against each other lyrical passages of sentiment and intellectual analysis. Properly speaking, James does not offer a travelogue in his descriptions of Venice; C. P. Snow does not psychologically or sociologically study what it is to be a scientist: Dostoievski does not explain to us what holiness is in his portrayal of the monk Father Zossima.

We are appraising the position set forth in the last chapter—that scientific and artistic methods both may be brought to bear on the same subject matters, but in different ways. The scientist collects evidence to solve cognitive problems; he forms hypotheses and checks them by performing appropriate experiments. This properly permits him to make claims to knowledge of the subject matters which he studies. An artist may choose exactly the same material—for example, the life of a butterfly—and by carefully-selected images excite his readers' passions and fancies. But nothing in the latter seems to mark anything known—except the trivial or irrelevant knowledge of the craft employed. Or whatever knowledge exists in art does so only in a radically different sense from that of science or philosophy. What must now be analyzed is the relationship of intellectual content to the particularly aesthetic values of literary works, as well as the particular elements the artist may be best fit to consider because of his unique methods and forms.

So far as the former is concerned, it may be suggested that blatant intellectualism and polemic in a novel or play actually harms it, that the artist may toy with issues and express positions, but never in such a manner as to harangue the reader, either implicitly or explicitly; for then the work becomes a piece of propaganda devoid of aesthetic content. Consider again Tolstoi's *Anna Karenina*. When Levin is carried away by a feeling of belonging to the earth and oneness with the peasants, our reaction can be historical: "how interesting that that should have been Tolstoi's own view." Or we may, as I am inclined to do, reject Levin as a decidedly insensitive and dense young man. But if we take the novel to be *arguing* this point, does it not lose its grace and charm—most of which is embodied in the creation of the character of Anna herself—becoming a naive and inept presentation of a foolish and unworldly panacea for social ills? Yes, but that is uniquely Tolstoi's quality. He cannot enter his work as a thinking author without lamely twisting our arms and making us grit our teeth in despair, yet he can also let his internal compulsions lead him far from polemic to the qualities of character and description that make him a great novelist. Tolstoi is an author split in two. Not every great author shares his dualism.

The main example to prove this point is *Magister Ludi* (and Chapter 8 may be read to that end). Another example, however, might also be useful, and I shall discuss another work that might be labelled "propagandistic" to its discredit—Ugo Betti's *The Queen and the Rebels*. In this work Argia, a woman of pleasure, is found at a border outpost preparing to leave the country—an unknown land which has just been taken over by an unknown group in the name of man and his salvation. "The queen," who had fled from the revolution and led a band of followers some years ago, is supposed to be in the neighborhood. She turns out to be an empty shell of a woman, destroyed by fear, eaten away by despair, devoid of courage and will. To help the queen escape and as an act of self-ridicule (for she knows full well that she is anything but a queen), Argia pretends to be the woman sought. But she discovers that she cannot cease pretending. First the others will not let her; slowly she discovers that she wants to be the kind of woman who should be queen. She comes to realize that in this one night she has become Man at his height. She began as a party-girl, bereft of all dignity and self-respect, and has through tragic self-affirmation become a queen. And she has learned that it is worth it, though she must die at morning. Betti shows us that man finds who and what he is in his capacity for self-assertion; that self-denial and abrogation are the antitheses of human greatness. Most of all he shows that heroism is not a virtue solely for others, for society. It is a "good in itself" as well as a good in what it will bring (indeed, in this case perhaps it will bring nothing).[3]

The play involves much talk and little action, though it does include a couple of deaths and an execution. It is almost wholly a play in which an ordinary woman discovers how to be more than ordinary, though it mean her death. It is tragic not because she dies, but in its triumphant affirmation of man. There is no flaw to Argia —we have here the antithesis of Aristotle's conception of the tragic. Yet the play indeed reveals man at his noblest, and shows us—at the proper distance—the strengths of being noble. Like anyone else, Argia could easily succumb to the temptation to be ordinary; and the play shows us both these temptations and the internal and external pressures that enable her to withstand them. If the play has any effect at all, it is in its portrayal of the noblest possibilities of man—made even more compelling through the use of a particularly base example of womankind. In revealing that such possibilities are the pinnacle of human potentiality, the play cannot but be moral to the fullest extent.

Is it then merely persuasive? If it is, then it is difficult to understand what would constitute a stronger case. Aristotle argues in the *Nicomachean Ethics* that the highest life for man is a union of virtues—human, intellectual, and moral. But amidst the arguments is the question of just what the various priorities are, how they are to be apportioned in particular circumstances. Specifically, what grounds exist for demanding of an individual that he place moral demands higher than self-interest? Betti simply demonstrates, through the medium of art, that moral heroism can be true self-interest, far more than mere self-preservation. It cannot be shown that everyone will feel that way; only that this is a definite and genuine possibility. Thus the panicked act of Bad Faith[4] that men indulge in when faced with great moral demands—that they are too weak or unheroic to accept their responsibilities—may be discounted by telling them that they fail to see the worth *to them* if they act nobly. Like the advice given if the water is too cold—jump in, you won't mind it a bit; in the case of moral hesitation—act and you will discover that it is both easy and wonderful. The evidence for the former can only be that in other times and places other people did jump and didn't mind it. It is difficult to imagine what kind of evidence would be relevant if this is not. So Betti shows that Argia, human as she is, gains from her realization of who and what she is. Presented in such a compelling form, it constitutes justification for the claim that the reader too, or other men, should act in like manner and that they will have similar experiences. If we have evidence that Betti is wrong in his sense of the rewards of Argia's decision, then the experience Argia undergoes is unreal, incredible, beyond human capacity. And the play degenerates into an egoistic fantasy. If at any point we feel Argia is unreal, the play loses its force. And as we affirm the realistic qualities of the play, we *generalize* its claims, until they constitute definite support for Betti's thesis. If the point of the play were only to show us *one* woman undergoing *her* special experiences, the level of identification, the rapport between audience and actress, and the power of the play would be lost. It is only as moral, both with a thesis and with a defense of that thesis in its very form and arrangement, that *The Queen and the Rebels* is a wonderful play.

Let us consider this notion of the arrangement of the material of the play as constituting justification (see also the chapters on *Magister Ludi, The Brothers Karamazov,* and *The Trial*). Argia has pretended she is queen, has been believed, and now wishes to admit her pretense. But she cannot find anyone who will testify in her behalf—neither the queen herself who tries to escape and dies; nor the young man she knew very well, who denies her out of fear and dies also. Powerfully, Betti uses the countermotif to heroism—self-abrogation out of fear—to force Argia into a heroic position. On the one hand we see the others panic and deny what they know to be true, and must ask ourselves what such cowardly self-denial is worth. "What is a man profited if he gain the whole world, and lose his own self?" On the other hand, just because others are not to be trusted, we cannot rely on them. Heroism arises in the most absurd places, in the most unjustifiable ways. Argia cannot win a cause, reach a goal, nor justify what she is doing. Nor can Antigone in Anouilh's play of that name. She is explicitly forced into a position where all consideration of goals and consequences is rendered irrelevant. Should she not then capitulate, to live and perhaps fight again another day? Antigone cannot because she is a born heroine, Oedipus's daughter: to live is to deny herself. But we don't really understand what Anouilh means here in speaking of affirming oneself. It is Betti's strength that he shows precisely what this does mean. Death is a lesser evil than living poorly—the lesson all moral cowards must learn, yet find so difficult. After having been denied, Argia finds that she must continue. And once having chosen (because she must) to be queen, she discovers the intrinsic rewards of self-affirmation. Thus when asked to repudiate all her actions in rebellion, which after all are not really hers but for her having chosen to accept them, she finds strength in the very deed itself.

Consider the student who has joined a protest march. The march itself may well be dreary and interminable; that is what most nonparticipants would expect. Yet it may indeed become an experience with great significance and vitality. How can the student argue to his friends who share his point of view but not his willingness to act, who never participate in such activities out of fear that they would feel demeaned and prostituted, that they should do so? His claim, based on his experiences, can only be that acting forcefully and openly for one's political and ethical beliefs is an exciting and rewarding thing to do *in itself* as well as in its fruits. Indeed, so rewarding are the immediate satisfactions that they render ethical activity worthy, assuming that one's motives and values are noble, even when definite consequences cannot be envisaged. They render the participant more of a man than he would otherwise have been.

The claim that any given individual has been changed by a particular act need not have any implications at all for any other person. Yet evidence to support any claim that A should act in a certain way can only be derived from information about B, C, and D, or at best A at another time. If an argument exists to support Betti's thesis, it is that other men have found it immediately and directly rewarding to act nobly rather than to humble themselves out of fear. But such an argument must also include evidence to show that those other men are not unique, that they are not superior beings different from other men. Betti, precisely by presenting Argia in such humble form at the beginning and showing how events could render her both heroic and pleased to be so, presents precisely this argument in both its forms. However, since it is not given explicitly in discursive language, with premises and conclusion, it may not be useful to call it an "argument." Furthermore, the presentation is made in the realm of possibilities, which renders it rather different from a typical argument. Argia is not a person to be found down the street or around the corner. But after all, what significance can a sociological study based on individuals from a carefully selected sample have for me unless I grant that I and they are men and thus have much in common? So too, if Betti can render Argia credible as a human being, then her possibilities are also mine.

Predictions and moral arguments to show that a person should do something in the future, compared to claims about the past and what should have been done, always take place in a context of possibilities grounded in past and present actualities. The future has not yet happened. We can only point to what is most likely to occur on the basis of what has already taken place. Implicit in every such argument is the claim that the analogies drawn, the situations offered in evidence, are indeed relevant. A scientific proof that an eclipse will take place in the future at such and such a time depends both on evidence offered as to past eclipses and our having good grounds for believing that past eclipses are indeed relevant to predictions of future ones. The problem of induction arises if one denies wholly and completely that any relevance ever exists between past and future events. That problem with its fruitlessness and self-stultification can be ignored. The point is that arguments can be given to support claims of evidential relevance.

In literature, situations are presented to us, often in fantastic and imaginary garb, which we must accept to a greater or lesser extent. Sometimes we relish strangeness and absurdity, as in *Alice in Wonderland*. Or we may be charmed by Dante's vision of the world yet feel the incredibility of his image of Hell. There are many ways in which one can enjoy a work of art without direct acceptance of its realism or of the similarities of its situations and characters to the world around us. Of course, if there were no resemblance or relationship at all (since radical contrast also may be envisaged), a work of art would stand only in itself, and indeed some do just that. However, it is just as clear that when resemblances exist by intentional design that we as audience are being called upon to react to and judge them accordingly.

Thus, if Argia's feelings and actions are unreal, according to what we know of men, then the play is one thing. Perhaps we may feel fascinated by the imagination Betti shows in inventing such unlikely possibilities. But if Argia is credible and realistically drawn, if she could be one of the people we know, then we may well at least consider the possibility of generalization. A work of literature calls upon us to identify with its characters both as individuals and as something more. They are never so richly drawn as to be quite real—so they suggest possibilities that lurk behind and beyond their apparent being. At the very least, Argia represents a possible vision of man. This is what man might become, if he or the world were different. On this level Betti is offering at least a moral vision, though only a possible one.

But if we grant the credibility of Argia's portrayal, her resemblance to people that we know, to ourselves if we need not strain too far to understand and appreciate her, then we are in effect granting Betti's *premise:* that her fortunes and experiences are indeed relevant to our own. Therefore his conclusion follows, virtually as if argued for; though it follows from the manner of presentation, not from the logical arguments set forth in propositional form. In *Crime and Punishment,* Raskolnikov's conversion is irritating just because Raskolnikov, as human and understandable as a literary character can be, suddenly becomes inhuman, converting as no man we know could possibly be expected to. Perhaps Dostoievski is correct that redemption may be achieved through suffering and the acceptance of guilt, but the argument fails to convince us when Raskolnikov suddenly acts out of character. What, though, is meant by this phrase, "out of character"? Is not Raskolnikov Dostoievski's toy, to manipulate as he chooses? Perhaps, if art is mere arrangement of material for no purpose or end. But if we are to be convinced or simply thrilled by Dostoievski, then Raskolnikov must be true to our conception of humanity. Otherwise he is an exceptional case and his experiences are not relevant to ours. If only in the realm of possibility, a work of literature can offer itself as an example of humanity at work. And if it is relevant to our experiences and knowledge, then it can indeed compel assent as can an argument, though by its own special methods and designs.

# 5

## The Merging of Aesthetic Value and Philosophic Themes

Even if it is decided that intellectual content may belong properly to literature and other forms of art in that the artist does have something he can say particularly effectively because of the nature of artistic expression, it does not follow that in choosing to do so he is improving his work as art. Perhaps intellectual and philosophic notions do destroy the aesthetic value of literature even though they add to the forcefulness and conviction with which we hold such notions. We have not fully considered the ways in which philosophic material can enhance the value of poetry or drama.

It is a fact, after all, that some beautiful and surpassingly great poems and even plays are utterly devoid of philosophic content. Keats' sonnet, *When I have fears that I may cease to be,* has some meaning that no doubt can be formulated in unpoetic terms; but it is an expression of Keats' own feelings, given to us to share and respond to. Need the lack of intellectual content render the poem less beautiful, less perfect a work of art? No one would dream of considering music for its edifying or enlightening properties. And *Anna Karenina* is wonderful as a novel precisely where Tolstoi simply offers his characters and events for our consideration, without proselytizing or preaching. How then claim that art needs or requires philosophic content to fulfill its purpose? Why need a poet, such as Goethe, claim special insight into truth?

But is not *Faust* the greater just because it rises above imagery, juxtaposition of feelings and response and expression, to provide yet more than these—a vision exemplified rather than

43

stated, placing the various parts which internally cohere into a more significant and vivid organization? Are there not times we seek to understand the thesis of a novel or play precisely because such understanding enhances our appreciation? The desire to find a thesis in some novels—such as Joyce's *Ulysses*—can take us away from the purely aesthetic or sensuous pleasure to be found there. In such instances it is appropriate to reply that conveying a thesis was not this particular author's intent. Doing so, however, suggests that intellectual and philosophic enlightenment may be another author's intent in another place.

It is often said that science musters argument, develops evidence to confirm or disconfirm hypotheses, and thus is the paradigm of objectivity and reason. As a language, science is literal, referential, and cognitive; as an enterprise it is the seat of methods devoted to cognitive analysis and investigation. Compared to it, art is but expression or evocation, the arousal of feelings and passions, but without the right to make claims as to truth or falsity. Now it is true that science on an immediate or factual level—of direct experiment and report—is very far from the poetic and metaphorical, the fanciful and aesthetic. But science may also be considered with regard to its theoretical level, cosmological speculations, comprehensive visions, portrayal of universes at birth and death, conception of the harmonious balance of things, and its no less wondrous fancies and delights.

What science rests on is the ostensible objectivity and dispassionateness of individual scientists whose experiments are accepted and whose reports become evidence. A scientist egoistically involved in his work, either out of concern for his reputation or simply by dint of prior conviction and judgment, is dangerous to the scientific community. Social scientists whose social, ethnic, or political prejudices are of such force that they cannot be withheld from experimentation and judgment often fail to achieve the objectivity necessary to scientific discovery. Thus an overriding concern with the goals of science independent of immediate and personal concerns is necessary for a practicing scientist. Science demands distance in order to persevere.

This distance in science, called "objectivity," rests on methods developed through its history, methods which can be employed independent of passions and fears of its users. In this sense, a scientist gains distance from his subject matter by holding it apart from him and *generalizing* or *abstracting* from it. Practically speaking, only the particular is of concern to one—the people he knows or meets, the house he owns, the character of his immediate environment. A psychiatrist can withhold personal involvement from his work by treating his experimental subjects as members of humanity, as symbols or forms rather than friends, by letting his methods lead him to general, abstract, and therefore impersonal conclusions. By separating his immediate feelings about the particular people he knows from the methods he employs in experimenting on other men, who represent Mankind, a particular psychologist may be enabled to make a discovery that would otherwise be repugnant to him. It is often said that scientific research not free of the experimenter's values and prejudices is worthless; that personal values have no place in science except as objects for study in themselves. Such objectivity is achieved by a kind of generalization, independent of the actual tests being run on actual people. Science is concerned with laws, not particulars; with fundamental principles, not individual events. Objectivity and distance depend on the ability to withdraw sufficiently from the concrete and particular—perhaps to the point of seemingly malicious and cruel experiments. This is not necessarily intentional cruelty, though that has been known to exist, but too-great distance, to the point where experimenters lose sight of the moral being and concrete capacity for pain of their human or animal subjects. In more Kantian language, science demands that things be *used* to discover their fundamental properties. In the name of science, then, generalization can proceed to the point where men cease to be ends in themselves and become instead only means—to the advance of science. Surely scientists who have helped to perfect nuclear and biological weapons have often done so in the name of scientific discovery and truth. We may feel, however, that they have done so unwisely and without sufficient moral forethought—a consequence of their too-great objectivity or scientific distance.

Aesthetic distance works quite differently from that of science. Where the scientist can withdraw personal involvement in the consequences of his work by *generalizing* them so that they are treated quite apart from him and his special circumstances (as we feel accidents always strike others, not anyone close to us), the beholder of a powerful and emotional tragedy remains distant from the play only by recognizing that the characters are in particular different from him and involved in circumstances apart from him. That is, he gains distance by virtue of the particularity of the drama, with its characters and situations which do not permit him to generalize from them to all mankind—at least, not immediately. My jealousy is not Othello's; I can appreciate the play only insofar as I recognize that Othello is but a character in a play, that above all he is himself, and I am not he. Overidentification with a character in a work of literature destroys its value as art. It becomes a part of life itself, arousing wholly immediate and practical responses. Art succeeds only when distance is maintained.

Aesthetic distance arises from response to characters and events as *Other*—though in contrast to science, Other as particular and concrete rather than general and abstract. Recognition of this side of aesthetic value suggests that characters are particular, events are concrete, and that generalization is wholly out of place in art. If this view is adopted completely there is no room for intellectual content as such in art. It too would remain Other, without concern for the reader, therefore without import or value. If the characters in literature are but themselves, implying nothing about mankind, representing nothing, then literature cannot offer insights or truths about man or the world in general.

However, too-great distance is also unaesthetic and valueless; it produces no response at all. This fact suggests that somehow the events, characters, and situations in works of literature must be made part of the reader's life and feelings or he will be unable to respond at all. Art cannot achieve the general and objective Otherness that is found in science precisely because of the intensity and kind of feelings that are aroused. In science, the only permissible feelings and values are properly in the name of Science and its progress. Consequences of action are set aside if they arouse personal feelings of a different sort. The very substance of literature, however, is found in the personal feelings of the characters, and the experiences they undergo and choices they make. If these are wholly concrete and particular, they mean nothing. They become vital only as the characters either arouse our sympathies or our personal identification, however restricted or minimal. But sympathy depends on identification—men are undergoing these experiences, their choices are ours. Therefore, the proper balance of distance can only be achieved when the individuality of particular characters is bridged with their portrayal as men and women, like you and me, with whom we can identify—though not too much. On this level, events portrayed, choices shown, characters revealed, situations set forth, are human events and situations, human choices and characters. It is impossible to avoid the kind of generalization that is intellectual and philosophical when confronted with these issues. The kind of situations and choices that arouse our pity and fear are usually either deeply emotional or excruciatingly moral. Insofar as we are capable of responding to the point where the work is successful, it demands that we entertain the events portrayed for ourselves. This is how men act, how they choose. Perhaps they should choose otherwise. The very portrayal itself is a setting forth of characters as men, events as real or probable. As such they reveal important truths about what they represent.

The proper balance of distance necessary to the successful use of philosophic and intellectual ideas as art can be achieved in different arts in different ways. In painting and sculpture the very medium holds us off from overidentification and involvement. These can achieve great beauty and feeling without additional means to provide distance. Music too, abstract as it is, withholds overly immediate or practical feelings. When it capitalizes on them, as in highly programmatic music, the uniquely musical values may be destroyed. But literature—particularly the drama and the novel—if it deals with men and women, their feelings and decisions (which it may not, as in lyric poetry), must struggle to achieve the proper distance. The greater the force of presentation, the more vital the events with which it deals, the greater the struggle must be to avoid overwhelming the audience with personal and unaesthetic responses.

Where the writing is vivid and compelling, and the situations portrayed fearful and devastating, one way of holding proper perspective is to place the consciousness of the work on such a high level of intellectual awareness as to produce some degree of objectivity. The author utilizes obscure symbols, double meanings, and absurd connections to separate his reader from the action and characters to a proper distance. Symbolic and intellectually self-conscious literature may well be the stronger for utilizing such explicitly intellectual means, compelling the reader to seek out meanings, forcing him to confront the most horrible events as part of a wider meaning, demanding the consideration of the most terrible decisions as revealing something greater than themselves. Philosophy is the lifeblood of such literature, for it becomes both an aspect of its means—to greater literary effect—and its end as well, insofar as the artist has something to say.

A fundamental element of literature is its *multivocation*—the multiple meanings of words and phrases, situations and events. In poetry it is the suggestive multiple meanings in language that enrich words with significance. Even poetic alliteration is a form of suggestion. The enhancement of meaning with sounds appropriate to it, or inappropriate to convey another meaning, provides a further suggestiveness to the literal meaning of the words. So too, multivocal symbolism on a philosophic level can stimulate and enhance aesthetic values. In literature we are constantly called upon to go beyond one or two levels of response to something more, which may well suffuse the other modes of response with wider and deeper meaning. Some types of multivocation point to philosophic vision and comprehension; and not only does this provide richness and multiplication of value, but it may provide distance, simply by always meaning something more than an immediate response can do justice to. Thus the greater significance of philosophic literature can actually enhance its aesthetic values.

# 6

## The Sublime

Here we may introduce the same distinction made in the first century by Longinus, in his work *On the Sublime*, between the careful, harmonious, and beautiful on the one hand; and transcendent works of passion and vision on the other. Some art is balanced and ordered, graceful and immaculate in its finish and working. The paintings of Raphael and the early statues of Michelangelo probably belong here. Displayed is a wonder of craft and arrangement that marks beauty in art. Creative inspiration is put to the task of harmony and order. Here are found the particular and idiosyncratic in works of art which we may say stand for nothing but themselves most purely, crystallizing in themselves order and arrangement to its summit heights. Among the greatest works of art that we have are those that go no further than themselves. The facade of Chartres in Monet's painting is just there, resplendent in its glory of light, but complete in itself. Chartres itself might have existed only in a vision like Kubla Khan to Coleridge—without affecting the beauty of the painting. Here is an example of Keats' words "beauty is truth, truth beauty." Just because that is all that is offered, that is all that has to be known.

Yet art is capable of something else. It can widen its range to include visions of Man and fantasies about the world, of torment and passion. It can strive in the glow of inspiration toward a fusion of balanced structure with greatness of capacity and breadth of insight. The content of a work of art can include far more than the formal and often sterile elements harmonious beauty permits. When the pity and fear of man are brought into drama to render it tragic, it transcends order and balance to become a sublime fusion of aesthetic

49

distance with the vital in the world of man. Vision, insight, and passion become endowed with beauty of expression; the formal aesthetic elements are imbued with a significance that only nobility of import and glory of intent can provide. This is the sublime. In Kant's words, it can "be as it were, an outrage on the imagination, and yet it is judged all the more sublime on that account."

As has been suggested, philosophic attitudes can endow works of literature with sublimity by at once providing them with the intensity offered by great insights into the nature of the human condition, yet restricting the degree of identification to the point where these can be considered apart from their immediate consequences. Sophocles' *Oedipus Rex* is sublime because of something beyond its purely formal assets—its beauty of language, unparalleled dramatic necessity, economy of presentation, and development of dramatic tensions. It also touches the pinnacle of human aspirations and needs, the greatest and most compelling of human problems. Oedipus is man of Reason, the savior of Thebes through rationality and knowledge; he has answered the Sphinx's question. He is man of dedication to truth, unwilling in the face of dire warnings and omens to turn aside from the pursuit of knowledge, whatever it cost him personally. He is also man of pride and self-respect, refusing to take seriously the possibility that there is more in the world than he knows of or dreams of in his philosophy. In an absurd and irrational world, his very strength is a liability. He is therefore man trapped in that world, caught in the paradox of Reason that blinds itself explicitly to the possibility of Unreason. His tragedy is not only the working of Fate upon one man, but the tragedy of men who dare to strive beyond the ordinary and secure. Oedipus' *hubris* is our own, if we have any self-respect at all. It is in the context of such awareness that the play reaches a transcendent height of vision that is sublime.

On the other hand, sublimity can be achieved in literature without the aid of philosophic theses, though not without a stance that is transcendent in some other sense—either through passion, psychological insight, or some other vision of great breadth and importance. *King Lear* transcends its formal elements in many ways, by the convention that as king, Lear must be respected *ipso facto,* making his lapse one larger than life, beyond the bounds of ordinary error. The very richness of language Shakespeare provides in Lear's despair enriches the play about a king with an opulence that is truly royal. Sublimity here stems from the portrayal of a royalty in grievous lapse through a language properly suited to the expression of royalty. Shakespeare here transcends the ordinary and formal art by a felicitous matching of language, development of plot, and theme that could not be achieved by one less gifted in poetry. It is the passionate fusion of elements that is sublime.

*Hamlet* is sublime in a very different way, for Hamlet is not king—though he would be if he could—nor is his bearing noble and royal. His hesitation and brooding, his inner despair and torment, make him the truly human hero, the prince with whom we are most in touch, because he exhibits just those weaknesses we suspect most in ourselves. Procrastination, rationalization, self-doubt, great ambition, a touch of neurotic self-destruction, and an ability to hurt others in his own despair mark the everyday life of man. Prince Hamlet, of greatness of aspect, brilliance of wit, and deviousness of planning (witness the play within a play), whose language too matches the hero larger than life, is Man himself caught in situations of great demand. His failure is ours; his passions reveal us to ourselves—though at the remove proper to our willingness to behold them. Sublimity can arise from transcendence of passion and revelation as well as from philosophic import and significance. It would be difficult to state the meaning of *Hamlet* as if there were some philosophic message contained therein. And yet it is profound in its import, and sublime to the fullest. It is so, however, only insofar as Hamlet represents to us Man himself. It is a very small step indeed from such representation on a passionate level to a theoretical confrontation of some aspect of the human condition.

In *Magister Ludi*, Hesse sets forth the notion of the Bead Game as a totally encompassing form of art, to the point where it virtually becomes a way of life. Distilled within it are the essences of science, music, various languages, and all the different schools of philosophy. These are the tools it employs and the material with which it works. Yet the Bead Game is completely sterile, a perfect example of art for art's sake, capable of being appreciated only by men who have totally withdrawn to a monastic existence. What Hesse shows is that mastery of this form of art, despite its apparent internal completeness, leads inevitably to the awareness that a master is in reality the perfect teacher, and that the compulsions built into art in its pure form demand the acceptance by the artist of his role as teacher. Great art depends on a mastery both of technique and the essence of the great products of man. Otherwise it will become sterile and trivial. Sublime art is vital and transcendent because of the in- sights and wisdom possessed by its authors. Such insights render art itself the great teacher and compel the artist to recognize his worldly role or accept his impotence. In his own way, then, Hesse portrays the substance of my argument.

The recognition of the sublime in art as against the merely beautiful, suggests that although beautiful things can exist in a purely formal manner, something even greater can be brought about if form and content worthy of it are unified in an achievement that is greater than either alone: a sublime and transcendent work of art. Formalists who claim that only the order and arrangement matter in beauty may be correct—but then there is an art-form that goes be- yond beauty to the sublime, confronts the vital and necessary, the wondrous and possible, and unifies them in a work of art which is both beautiful and something more.[1]

In fact, most novels and plays have a definite didactic pur- pose. Not only do they contain intellectual issues as part of their material, but they may express a particular point of view toward them. Sometimes too explicit a polemic may ruin a play by dis- rupting the distance necessary to great aesthetic value. Sheer argu- ment in literature may draw the audience in as antagonist, making aesthetic responses difficult to maintain. Propaganda suffers even when elegantly and gracefully designed. Argument set forth explic- itly, either by the narrator or various characters themselves, is often dangerous for this reason. On the other hand, a work of art may set forth a particular point of view without a word of polemic, simply by virtue of its arrangement and organization. Consider Shaw's de- lightful comedies whose characters argue continually. Shaw plays with disputation and rhetoric, and we enjoy his plays to the extent that we are entertained by ideas in conflict. Yet so much disputation can sometimes weary us, and can stand between aesthetic and intel- lectual appreciation. Contrast with this Kafka's *The Castle,* which contains not a polemic word, yet which has at least as much theo- retical significance as any or all of Shaw's plays put together.

# 7

## *Philosophic Themes*
## *Appropriate to Literature*

One point remains for consideration before particular works are analyzed to exemplify the points made above. That is whether any particular philosophic theses are most suitable for incorporation into art, or whether anything at all may have aesthetic significance. What possible grounds could exist for claiming that artists should deal only with certain theses or points of view?

A parallel can be drawn with philosophy that may be enlightening. Would it not be presumptuous of a philosopher to offer technical claims which are dependent on particular experiments for their justification? The material with which philosophy works is the material of experience available to everyone. Its claims can be tested without specialized knowledge which is dependent on special instruments and experiments. It is true that philosophy does study special fields of knowledge, such as science and art, and must depend on knowledge of the intimate details of such areas. The point is that its claims are external, not competitive with science itself. For example, contrast the sociology of science with the philosophy of science: the former is a specific discipline which possesses experimental techniques for validating its claims; the latter seeks to generalize about the methods and techniques of the sciences without depending on information available only through experimentation. Technical distinctions are made for clarity in philosophy; but they too are independent of special experimental tests. They are technical only in that they enter systematic frameworks that call for arduous reinterpretation and modification of older concepts. The grounds for such transformations are not special or hidden as are the evidence for modern scientific theories. In short, philosophy offers new and highly controversial claims about systematic and organized views of the world we live in, but justifies these on the basis of uncontroversial and easily obtained information. Science is thus both more controversial—in its reliance on difficult tests; and less controversial—in its claims, which follow clearly from the evidence presented.

The technique of much art, and especially literature, is more controversial than either science or philosophy, in that different interpretations are possible and desirable. Aesthetic value is inextricably tied up with the multivocal aspect of art which provides enhancement and enriched possibilities for response. This multiplicity of meaning also renders the actual claims and justifications provided by such works of art open to ever-new analysis, confrontation, and reinterpretation. Perhaps this is what suggests that art cannot be cognitive; its very multiplicity renders its positions opaque.

However, this conclusion would follow only if an author were playing the role of scientist in making very technical claims. Where precision is necessary, as in science, the nature of the claim made depends on the accuracy and clarity of the assertion. A constant determined to only the fourth decimal may be insufficient for scientific purposes. A work of literature which offered positions to be interpreted precisely could not both do so and remain art. Yet an alternative remains: that the positions appropriate to literature are not so precisely formulated as to call for scientific investigation, nor are they so systematically organized as to call for philosophical analysis. They remain on a relatively uncontroversial level of justification —which is by no means to say that they are unimportant or prosaic. They may be definite and valuable, but also somewhat vague with unclear boundaries. The positions of a work of literature are not really difficult to collect evidence for—which would make them scientific—nor so carefully formulated as to call for critical analysis. They are sophisticated methodically in their presentation and exhibition. This does not make them less definite as positions.

It may be asked, what of variant interpretations of a given novel? If a number of readers come to and can defend a variety of interpretations, how can we know which philosophic position the novel is written to defend? And how can there be any genuine defense of a variety of different, if not conflicting positions? In short, the multivocal nature of great works of literature is often essential to their aesthetic value; yet it would seem to create terribly difficult problems for philosophic analysis.

Note, however, that many great philosophic works suffer from similar difficulties. The writings of Plato, Aristotle, Spinoza, Hegel, and Whitehead, to name just a few, all suffer from a welter of interpretative analysis. Hegel's *Phenomenology* must be interpreted to be understood and appreciated, and variant interpretations of it can be and have been given. Of course, each interpreter offers his as the one and only true analysis of the work in question, but so too do literary critics maintain the unique wisdom of their own analyses. Critical analysis and interpretation are essential to the understanding of many great works, in literature or philosophy, and even if many great philosophical works are somewhat less open to multiplicity and difficulty of interpretation, the latter are without doubt essential elements of some of the greatest of them.

The task of the critic or interpreter, then, is to bring into the open—often by the intentional sacrifice of the aesthetic qualities, the architectonic structure, the force of the work he is dealing with— the intellectual theses, positions, and justifications that are rather obscured within the work. Obviously, he can defend his position only by an appeal to the text itself or by the use of other indications such as other writings of the author, biographical information, and the like. The art of interpretation is one of pulling together all the various threads of life and art relevant to the analysis, even to the point of creating another work of literature; one which reveals or articulates, elaborates and exposes, what can be found in the original. Equally obviously, two sensitive and intelligent critics can defend rather different interpretations without violating the original work—that much multiplicity of meaning is essential to works of art like those we are considering.

The force of the positions presented and their substantiation and defense will clearly depend on the interpretation offered. One critic may find rich and profound insights displayed in a work of literature, without substantiation. Another may find significant ways in which such insights are defended, or he may have to weaken the richness of the positions taken in order that they can be defended. A critic who reads too subtly may find that no possible defense could exist within a work of literature for the positions he finds therein. This is another reason for not interpreting the position of a work of literature too precisely or technically: no work of art which preserves a multiplicity of meaning can defend extremely subtle positions—those which require technical philosophical analysis or scientific precision.

It is the interpretive critic's task to reveal the work of literature in its various aspects. Perhaps no critic can reveal the totality of a work of art, for works of art are virtually inexhaustible. The critic chooses and selects what he will emphasize. In Part II, I shall try to interpret various novels from the point of view expressed in Part I. I shall seek those philosophic positions and theses that are presented, defended, and grounded. The question I shall be most concerned with is whether the novel makes and *defends* its point. Another critic may find it possible to defend a rather different interpretation, but one that is not defended or substantiated by the novel itself. See the chapter on *The Stranger* for a particular example of that.

Art has a fundamental contribution to make that is difficult for science and philosophy to offer consistently—that of revealing the irrational, the horrible, or the obvious (simply by showing it). The former two are most important here, for they are precisely what the medium of art can instill with distance and control to reach sublimity, and what science and analytic philosophy can only face literally and unbearably. On the one hand, the basic commitments of both science and philosophy to a world intelligible in important respects and to methods fundamentally rational and consistent prevents either of them from attacking these commitments themselves, except in a partly artistic fashion. Science can only pursue its investigations by adopting criteria for such investigation; it cannot then take the position that no such criteria have any foundation or worth, nor that every scientific discovery is really without value to man. Philosophy too cannot represent sincerely to itself the poverty, lack of value, or utter failure of *every* method of rational inquiry. It would have no way of continuing in its own ways if its basic devices were destroyed. Nietzsche claimed inarticulateness precisely because he wished to philosophize about the irrational, the strong but unprincipled, the hidden, and was forced into complete silence or obscurity. If the rational tradition is on the wrong track, only a basically artistic medium can represent that fact. (Or this can be done through philosophic works that are as literary as they are philosophical. Kierkegaard's *Fear and Trembling* is a highly literary work which calls for literary as much as philosophic analysis. It may well be that some works of literature are works of philosophy, in the same way that some works of philosophy are also works of literature. I am arguing that a mixture of the two modes is possible.)

On the other hand, some events or facts of life are too horrible to be faced in anything like a literal or standard fashion—concerning human depravity, worthlessness, weakness, despair, or hopelessness. The excremental in human life, the absurd or nauseating (in the words of Freud or Sartre, respectively), are not accessible to direct confrontation. Men choose various ways to avoid face to face confrontation with the worst side of life. Art can provide it with sufficient distance by methods so well-controlled as to permit some consideration of its aspects. It is thus the irrational, harsh, and violent elements of experience that are most suitable to literary exploitation, which can be uniquely presented by artistic means.

Here then we may see the difference between propagandistic or exhortative works of literature that are weakened by the author's intent to enlighten and educate his audience, and works of literature that reveal truths and convey understanding by the very means that render them art. This difference is twofold:

1. In content, the author must remain out of the proper domains of science and philosophy. Instead of seeking precision, he must deal with the side of things that science cannot and remain rational, or with uncontroversial positions that do not demand either special means of proof or technical analysis. Such positions are obvious in the sense that they can be supported by fairly well-known facts of experience; all the author has to do is show us events which reveal them. In short, art reveals great insights that can be supported by nothing more than the events portrayed within the work, though they are often missed until pointed out. Goethe's *Faust* shows us the wonder of man in his incessant and tormented seeking, reveals to us the beauty and value in such a life without the existence of anything greater toward which it can strive. Henry James reveals to us the nature of moral decision in *The Princess Casamassima* by simply letting us see a moral situation. Hyacinth Robinson must make a decision or refrain from one, which is the same thing. How and on what

basis? That, James lets us see without comment or justification. Nor does he try to convince us of a detailed polemical position. Art cannot do so without overstepping its bounds. Art supports its theses, where it does so, by the presentation of events that are related to such theses in a nontechnical, nonspecialized fashion. The appeal to our experience is fairly direct and uncomplicated, once we grasp the essential position of the work by interpreting it. Where careful and detailed analysis is offered, however literarily, which leads to very specific conclusions, we tend to consider the work primarily philosophical, rather than artistic—as in the Platonic dialogues.

2. The second difference is the technical correlate of the first: the means used to convey wisdom must be proper to it. When events are structured so that we feel manipulated to the author's particular end, art oversteps its bounds again and enters the domain of explicit argumentation. If we are argued with in literature, either obviously or even in the outright incredibility of events designed by the author, then we desire definite argument, to be found outside art. The particular developments within a play or novel must move of themselves, out of the momentum of character and situation created by the author. Only then are we being *shown,* from which we can directly gather wisdom for ourselves. This does not imply less self-consciousness or reflection on the part of the author. Polemic is far easier to indulge in than the fusion of art with significance that great literature requires. The point is that art can only be successful in its own terms as an exhibitive medium, not in assertive or declarative terms appropriate to philosophy and science. When it fails as art, it fails too as philosophy. In order to succeed as literature, it must utilize means that preserve its internal compulsions and values. These are never purely polemic, dependent on the same kinds of proof as are philosophy and science.

Two areas are particularly amenable to artistic analysis—areas in which technical analysis is not necessarily called for, and which contain elements of the irrational and mysterious—ethics and religion. The former has already been considered in some detail. Those elements of the moral which depart from the rational and trespass upon the mystical, the intuitive, and the absurd, may be faced by art which has not made any logical commitments. These elements cannot be faced by philosophy and science, however, which have made such commitments. The latter two always seek explanation and justification, though in the domain of ethics we may be satisfied with nothing more than being shown. If we are not sure what the qualities of a moral problem are, a work of literature can show us without the careful analysis philosophy is expected to provide. Perhaps we wonder what would be the right thing to do in a complex moral tangle. A work of art can show us, exhibiting a decision made by a character; once so shown, we recognize the decision to be valid. Moral choices involve the balancing of various principles and fundamental needs, to the point where elaborate analysis may be impossible. But we can still be shown a balance, perhaps grossly, that genuinely resolves the problem at hand. Such an exhibition is, of course, not as precise as we might desire in other circumstances. But often a general answer is enough.

In the domain of the religious, however, we find that although preempted by theology, the truly religious has aspects that cannot really be examined theologically. In general, these may be pointed to by emphasizing that theology is a rational discipline, while all religions have mysterious elements in them. In short, reason must be supplanted by faith. But faith is something very difficult to capture, and if we cannot reach an understanding of faith, we cannot genuinely grasp what it is to be a religious man. Above all, the saints are men of faith—as well as love, humility, and charity. What literature can do is to reveal to us, by choosing various models of different kinds of men, what faith actually is, in practice. We cannot be *told,* for the very reason that faith is not subject to analysis. But we can be shown.

I consider it absurd to hold that faith is a real quality of human life, but cannot be studied rationally. What may be said, however, is that the analysis of the man of faith, the holy man, is always only partial, while it is the *integrity* of faith—its unification of all aspects of life into a whole—that is fundamental. Here art can offer us a vision of faith, and can present it in such a way as to show us why alternative versions are inadequate. In a very profound way, then, art can reveal, by its own techniques, the nature of faith, of mystery, of holiness, by letting us see them in action. The holy man compels others to follow him by example, not only by analysis. The artist can capture that holiness, as science and philosophy cannot, retaining the integrity of the saint, if at the sacrifice of some details of understanding.

In response, then, to the Platonic claim that artists can make no legitimate claim to special wisdom, the answer may be that they do not have to, for they are not specialized or technical in their claims. The knowledge that the artist has to offer is not precise. It needs—in the framework of art—neither philosophic analysis nor scientific proof. It represents possibilities of such general character as to require only appreciation and recognition. Such possibilities may often be shown to exist only by exemplification. Truths about man and what he is capable of need only be revealed. The world is what it is and we all know it: Kafka need only expose us to it to prove to us that it is indeed as he sees it; for we too see it that way. But we may not have been aware of it before.

# II

*Five Philosophical Novels*

There are many ways to approach the critical interpretation of literary works. Yet if justice is to be done to the fusion of form and content in the works considered here, the structure and organization will have to be treated as primary. The most useful procedure, though not necessarily the most sophisticated or analytic, will be to present a commentary—of necessity quite curtailed and schematic—in which the form and sequence of the events presented to the reader are analyzed as they appear. This procedure will be employed more or less throughout—though somewhat less explicitly in *The Princess Casamassima,* and in effect four times in *The Trial*—in order to show how the very organization of literary works marks definite theoretical attitudes and claims,

These chapters are not intended to exhaust the novels with which they deal. Many considerations of style, symbolism, and other literary matters will be omitted in order to focus more carefully on the philosophic content. Moreover, considerations of space prevent even a very detailed philosophical treatment of the novels. I trust that enough detail will be provided, however, to ground the analyses given.

Even more important than the foregoing remarks is, I believe, the indication that the following chapters are somewhat uncommon in their approach to the literature with which they deal in that they are not intended to summarize the views of the *authors* of these works, but to analyze the philosophic aspects of the five novels considered. This is not a minor difference. When considering a man's total body of writing, it is possible to collate the various individual pieces so that a total world-view emerges, though it cannot be found directly in any of the works taken singly. Although this mode of criticism is of inestimable value, it does often succeed in giving to the reader only the author's views *displayed* throughout his work. The individual writings are to be read, from the point of view of such criticism, as exemplifications or indications of the author's total position. They represent instances of such views. They reveal part of the total picture. But they do not stand alone as novelistic embodiments of a particular theoretical position to be judged for its truth or falsity.

I shall, then, stay within the boundaries of the particular novels under consideration to study what views *they* take, and shall even discuss whether or not they succeed in substantiating those views. References to other works will be made only to clarify particular points where they require clarification, or where such reference provides enrichment of the thesis being considered, The main point of concern here is that particular novels do take positions, defend philosophic theses, and render compelling points of view. This will be demonstrated in considerable detail.

# 8

## *Magister Ludi*
## *by Hermann Hesse*

"Magister Ludi"—the Master of the Game: thus Hesse sets the atmosphere of his novel. These words forebode both the significance of the man who is master and the frivolity or sterility of a game—all in the sonorous sounds of Latin, lending both irony and force to the juxtaposition. To the narrator, the title is quite literal and serious, the mark of nobility and rank. The Magister fits Aristotle's specifications that epic and tragedy deal with men of great stature, to lend significance and value to the events portrayed. To the reader, games do not mark events of such stature. Indeed, is not the very idea *ludicrous?* We discover moreover that the Magister Ludi of the novel—a particularly worthy example of Magister—is named Joseph Knecht, which quite appropriately means "servant" in German and "increaser" in Hebrew. It is no coincidence that the master is at once a servant and a provider. In the very names themselves we are warned of important meanings, and to watch for further connections that will be set forth. Also, we are told even more of the important themes of the novel by the opening quotation (of Knecht's): "There is nothing more necessary than to place before the eyes of men certain things the existence of which is neither provable nor probable, but which, for this very reason, pious and scholarly men treat to a certain extent as existent in order that they may be led a step further towards their being and their becoming." (ML13) [1] Is any description more succinctly an account of the role of art in forming the understanding of men? Distance as well as import are thus suggested even before the novel opens, to be revealed through the events in a single character's life.

Further distance is achieved through a device that Dostoievski also uses, one of great value in philosophic novels—the presence of a narrator who is no better informed (and occasionally considerably less) than the reader. By this device the author keeps his own opinions from intruding too obviously. Most of all, it permits the consideration of the narrator's views independent of the thesis of the novel, both creating dramatic tension and forcing the reader to take thoughts seriously insofar as the narrator presents them as such. Particularly since the narrator is a member of Castalia, with all its prejudices and narrowness of vision, we are called upon directly to reply to his views with our own. Of course, we are not aware of this at the very first, taking the narrator's views quite unquestioningly. But when the problems arise, he himself tells us that he is not in possession of all the facts. He knows no more of Knecht's end than a legend, has no definite information to go on, and remarks: "we must be content with this." (ML310) And so he must; but can the reader?

In presenting Knecht to us for the first time, the narrator irrelevantly makes reference to Knecht's death, to its legendary quality, calls Knecht's end a coincidence. The irrelevance of these remarks and the striking nature of the word "coincidence" cannot but arouse us to doubt the narrator's view of things. (ML45) Can a reader not feel challenged by such a word to examine the nature of such a coincidence? Particularly since this is not life itself but art—in which even coincidences have definite significance.

The tale the narrator will tell us is that of a particular individual's life. Yet we must be cautioned that "the extinction of the individual . . . [is] one of the cardinal principles of our spiritual life," that "the spiritual life of our province . . . has taken anonymity as its ideal." (ML14) Contrast with this the words of Schopenhauer: "it is true we see the individual come into being and pass away; but the individual is only phenomenal. . . . The individual . . . neither has nor can have any value for Nature. . . . Only the Ideas, not the individuals, have, properly speaking, reality." [2] and "Hatred and wickedness are conditioned by egoism, and egoism rests on the entanglement of knowledge in the *principium individuationis*. . . . The penetration of that *principium individuationis* is the source and the nature of justice, and . . . by abolishing the distinction between our own individuality and that of others, renders possible and explains perfect goodness of disposition, extending to disinterested love and the most generous self-sacrifice for others." [3] Or the words of Nietzsche (who is referred to by the narrator): "egoism belongs to the essence of a noble soul, I mean the unalterable belief that to a being such as 'we,' other beings must naturally be in subjection, and have to sacrifice themselves. The noble soul accepts the fact of his egoism without question." [4] We are being treated from the very beginning to an analysis of individuality, its importance and responsibility. The life of Knecht is being set off against a social life in which individuality is submerged, in which the individual finds its achievement. "We of today [Castalia] only speak of personalities when we meet with men who are beyond all originalities and peculiarities and who have succeeded in achieving the most perfect possible self-identification with the general, and in rendering the most perfect possible service to the supra-personal." (ML14–15) It is true that the narrator makes some reference to a hero's "strong fresh urge," but remarks that a man is such a hero only when he finds a place and remains within the hierarchical structure. Like Schopenhauer, the narrator turns to the East for the saintly or self-denying hero, finding little admirable in neurotic rebellion and empty self-assertion. The ideal reached is indeed *Greek* in its fusion of urge and order in a balance that is most proper. But the flavor is a denial of individuality as such, and a placing of the uniqueness of men in a relationship to something larger than the person. To the modern reader, as in Plato's *Republic,* elements of totalitarianism are suggested where it is claimed that men reach their satisfactions by participation in the destiny of a state larger than any of them. Yet also suggested here is the aesthetic ideal that the greatness of man is to be found in his participation in ideals of beauty or contemplation. The goal of life is the achievement of a fusion of individual man with overarching principles of Reason or Beauty (depending on whether one chooses scientific or aesthetic values).

The issues raised here are transcendent in scope and overwhelming in generality. The history of philosophy from Plato to Schopenhauer, expecially in the extolling of science in our time, has found the highest life in the quest for Truth and Beauty, residing in the rational principles of things which are independent of and greater than individual men. The ideal for man is suprapersonal, whether natural or supernatural. Against this is the strain of Protestantism, Romanticism, and Existentialism in which individuality itself is a paramount value. Idiosyncracy and uniqueness have their intrinsic values; creativity itself is a virtue. Faust is a hero just by being man the individual, ever seeking for something greater, but finding only a world foil to himself. The rational and beautiful in Castalia and in Knecht's life are thus set off against the idiosyncratic, irrational, and incommensurable elements of his nature, insofar as he ultimately comes to believe in ways that the narrator finds inexplicable. The narrator himself tells us that individuality cannot be ignored in a functioning hierarchy. But what is the place of the idiosyncratic man in a structured order? That, the novel tries to show, and in fact concludes by suggesting that he must transcend that order, though such a step is one of dire peril. What can be concluded about the relationship of the individual to the suprapersonal is found in the events, situations, and actions portrayed. Knecht is offered as the height of Castalian achievement, the transcendent member of the hierarchy. He is no rebel or iconoclast, but a genuine master of the Castalian world. If he must leave this world behind, it can only be because of demands implicit within it.

The introduction is designed for the lay reader, and in it we are told something about the Bead Game—though of necessity obscurely and vaguely. A secret language is devised in which all the sciences and arts are unified. If comprehensiveness of vision is an ideal for man—which it would surely seem to be—then the Bead Game achieves the ideal, though remarkably in a *game,* played by aficionados. Here is art in its highest form, as pure art, isolated from practical matters; a way of life rather than a part of life. The extremity of the Castalian way of life cannot be overlooked, but neither can its beauty and comprehensiveness. In a world filled with gaps and distinct perspectives, where the total vision of the Christian world-view has been replaced by discrete and separate domains—art *and* science *and* philosophy *and* politics *and* religion—Castalia offers a reunification through the medium of art. By sundering art from the practical, a fusion of all the spiritual elements in human life is achieved. If art can offer anything but subjective or personal visions, it will do so in some comprehensive and total Art in which all the life of man will find a place. But Hesse calls it only a Game.

The Bead Game is not only a vision of the possibilities of art, but also of science. In fact, it is a portrayal of the ideal possibilities in the spiritual life of man. Everything the philosophic, aesthetic, and scientific deem ideal is synthesized in a comprehensive glorification of man's achievements. Perhaps such a synthesis is indeed impossible. Perhaps it can only be achieved by the creation of a sterile and empty Game—though Hesse's later description of the game in action should not be overlooked:

> The basic feeling of the celebration like a fundamental chord, like the deep quavering note of a base bell, which for the less sophisticated members of the community is the best and nearly the sole experience of the festival, but which is also felt with a shudder of awe by the inspired Game virtuoso and critic of the elite, from the lowest ministrant and official up to the leader and Magister. (ML237–238)

Such a description sounds enormously aesthetic; but the experience of solidarity and import, beauty and reverence, can be found as well in Kepler:

> [A] very few days ago the pure Sun itself of the most marvelous contemplation has shown forth—nothing holds me; I will indulge my sacred fury; . . . The die is cast, the book is written, whether to be read now or by posterity I care not; it may wait a hundred years for its reader, if God himself has waited six thousand years for a man to contemplate His work.[5]

If there is anything sublime in science it can be distilled in its wonder and beauty and rendered as art. Science, then, in its pure form—the quest for knowledge and truth—is as beautiful and wondrous as the arts, seeking in its own ways the comprehension and explanation of all things in a total vision.

Posed for us, then, is a new way of life, arising from the splintering of the intellectual and artistic world in our time. The poverty and meaninglessness of modern life, its empty forms and rituals, its complicated machinery which in no fundamental way instill life with purpose and depth, are described by the narrator in great detail. (ML23) Castalia and the Bead Game offer an imaginative and aesthetic alternative to today's painful and mediocre life— a spiritual or artistic solution to man's emptiness of vision. To today's stoical acceptance of everything as it comes and lack of concern about anything of importance, the alternative is to find and develop beauty in a world devoid of larger meanings. Once music and art served the Church, even the greater values of human purpose. In our desperate time, neither religion nor human reason offer legitimate alternatives. A resigned spiritualism thus has great appeal. The quality of modern life seems to offer as ideals only nihilism or resignation. The former can be found stated perfectly by Camus' Meursault:

> What difference could they make to me, the deaths of others, or a mother's love, or his God; or the way a man decides to live, the fate he thinks he chooses, since one and the same fate [death] was bound to "choose" not only me but thousands of millions of privileged people.[6]

The latter resignation and acceptance of loss, accompanied by an attempt to find beauty in what does exist is found in Castalia—"that secure, resigned and courageous attitude towards the problem of the age of culture." (ML27) The spiritual life of man is separated from ordinary life, and offered as an escape from its torments.

The resignation Hesse describes, the decline in creativity, and the separation of art from surrounding life are of a piece. The spiritual achievements of man are rooted in the events of his life and the needs that give rise to them. What would happen if the two were separated and treated in isolation? Surely the result would be a decline in vision and significance, a loss of creativity, a resignation before the absurdity and meaninglessness of experience. "Art for art's sake" is a repudiation of possibility, a renunciation of order and intelligibility, a withdrawal into aestheticism and sheer adoration of tradition. All this is embodied in the Bead Game. Yet Hesse, wisely recognizing the appeal of traditional and venerated art in a world of declining values, takes the alternative very seriously, trying to show just what rewards it is capable of providing. Out of hand rejection would be neither convincing nor just. The Game "represented a select, symbolic form of the quest for perfection, a sublime alchemy, a self-approach to the inherent spirit beyond all images and pluralities—and thus to God." (ML40) In a world without larger meaning, the fusion of aesthetic, scientific, and philosophic visions offers virtually the only remaining alternative. The question is whether the purely beautiful can suffice for a full and complete life. For it would seem that art can be achieved only at the expense of the repudiation of active engagement in everyday life.

The fundamental schism between Castalia and the outside world mirrors the fundamental split between the political and economic, and the contemplative and spiritual. The alienation of the artist from immediate concerns is mirrored in the withdrawal of painting and music from the outside world. Where Rembrandt and Michelangelo reveal man's place in nature, and reveal significant meaning in life, contemporary forms of art withdraw from the human and the natural into a private domain of the purely aesthetic, requiring special degrees of devotion and reverence. The artist feels maligned by society and scorned for his efforts; the man of business repudiates involvement in learning for its own sake. The gulf between the practical and spiritual widens unbearably. Perhaps at no time in human history has the spiritual truly had a place, but when life was fundamentally religious, painting and poetry could play a definite and useful role therein. The view that art has no special purpose or moral function, however, leads it to its own private domain, however beautiful and worthwhile that may be. Art has no external values but only its own; therefore the ordinary man cannot learn from art, and the artist need not concern himself with the mundane. If science is for scientists, and art for artists, untrammeled in their domains by external considerations, then let us look at them and what they wish to become. This is exactly what Hesse does.

In the introduction, then, by describing to us the Bead Game and its origins in the desperation and alienation of men in our time, their preoccupation with an idiosyncratic and neurotic self, Hesse sets for us the problem of the novel. And a problem it truly is: whether the monastic, isolated, aesthetic, and spiritual side of man, isolated from exterior considerations but unified in a communal organization and hierarchy, truly offers man a solution to his desperation. By rendering Castalia sympathetically and appealingly, rather than disparagingly, Hesse makes its strengths even greater, yet finds in the end that its strengths are not enough. Analytic argument could not present so strong and compelling a case. On the one hand are all the views that counsel the achievement of peace and fulfillment through escape from the immediacy and pain of everyday existence—from Epicurus to Schopenhauer in the West and including the Greek conception of the security of contemplation, the religious escape into monastic retreat, the purely scientific or aesthetic life in our time, and the Eastern goal of Nirvana. One reply is Freud's: that the quest for peace is doomed to failure, for the pressures of immediate needs are too strong. Another is John Dewey's when he claims that "nothing but the richest and fullest life is appropriate for man." [7] Hesse's is a third: that the very nature of the spiritual calls for a return to the responsibilities inherent in the human condition. Ultimately this is truly a Platonic conception of responsibility. So too must the philosopher-king leave his contemplation to administer to the needs of the community. It is Nietzschean as well.

The story of the life of Joseph Knecht is begun in his childhood. He is without parents, implying the detachment from worldly ties and responsibilities necessary to becoming a member of Castalia. A man bound by economic or emotional obligations cannot simply set them aside—simply consider the constraints upon Plinio Designori. We must then ask if external fortune is necessary to satisfaction in Castalia and the life of Spirit. Knecht himself seems to have been "predestined" for Castalia. (ML44) To others, with parents or strong outside ties, Castalia was more a burden than a reward. They couldn't endure Castalia, mainly because of the requirement that they sever every tie with family and country, that they enter Castalia's service quite completely. (ML57) If so, then the solution Castalia offers to the problems of life is neither available to everyone nor even admirable when attained. It becomes the kind of solution expressed by the sigh—"if only all men were more noble." But they aren't, and unless some means exists for making them so we are only railing at Fate, not proposing a way to satisfaction. Compare with this the tale of the Grand Inquisitor in *The Brothers Karamazov*. Ivan is also condemning the human condition, and it is precisely his inability to do anything but repudiate the world he lives in and condemn human frailty (though he claims that he understands and sympathizes with it) that labels him the hopeless and tortured soul he is. If even in Castalia external fortune and arbitrary chance are necessary to peace, then Castalia offers only another way of life for some men, not a path to peace for all. To the old Music Master, it is quite clear that the Game is dangerous: the weak ones are sent away. (ML75) Moreover, Waldzell, the home of the Bead Game, is the smallest of the Castalian schools, implying at once the aristocratic and elite nature of the aesthetic and intellectual life therein, and its insufficiency for other men. In what sense, then, can Castalia be thought of as a solution to the problems of life, except a narrow, sectarian one? To whom is this proposed way of life addressed—those who like Knecht are "called" to the life of mind, or those who cannot experience its appeal?

A second theme arises here in the narrator's telling us that Knecht's life seem to him an organic whole, even to its unknown beginnings and legendary end. (ML45–46) Knecht is thus offered simultaneously as a legend, whose life is indeed a structured whole, and as a person of exceptional stature. The sense here is of a life lived itself as a work of art, set against a background in which individuality is minimized and fulfillment is found in communal satisfactions. If Castalia represents the communal and spiritual side of man both idealized and realized, then Knecht represents the same theme of the life of the spirit, found in the same tradition in fact, of the holy man whose life is itself art and philosophy. Quite apart from the sense of philosophy as a mode of knowledge independent of particular men and their actions is the conception, found even in Plato and Aristotle, of philosophy as the saintly *portrayal* of the Good in the philosopher's very being (Socrates is an example). Against the background of the isolated community of artists and scholars—which is not without rather specific point in the Germany Hesse knew very well, whose scholars had for fifty years withdrawn from active political engagement—is the mark of the exceptional man who carries the life of Spirit simply by being it. Which then is the most truly beautiful—the worship of beauty, or living and being it?

It is interesting that Knecht comes to Castalia through music, not science, mathematics, or painting. Music is to many the perfect art, but how? It would seem in its utter purity, its relevation of values independent of any but its own. Is not program music a lesser form, dependent on extramusical and therefore inferior values? The sense of art withdrawn into wholly internal and intrinsic values— albeit quite wonderful ones—is found most clearly in music. Hesse often chooses music to reveal the soul of man. In *Steppenwolf* he portrays the complete romantic soul torn asunder, seeking after beauty but alienated from a world essentially sterile and bourgeois.

To the man Hesse calls the Steppenwolf, Mozart stands for the pinnacle of human achievement in the complete purity of his music, the revelation of a whole and complete soul. As he discovers, however, Mozart too is a man, with the feelings and torments proper to man whatever his art. From the standpoint of his music, however, this is irrelevant. Art transcends its maker in time and place, rendering ordinary human cares out of place. Its deception, of course, is that its very timelessness suggests to men at other times a freedom from torment that no composer himself has ever really known. The utter perfection of music draws us away from the immediate as no other art—particularly literature—can. If music is taken as the paradigm, then Castalia is again portrayed in its isolation from human concerns other than the purely aesthetic. To quote Schopenhauer again, music

restores to us all the emotions of our inmost nature, but entirely without reality and far removed from their pain.[8]

The will, existence itself, is . . . a constant sorrow, partly miserable, partly terrible; while, on the contrary, as idea alone, purely contemplated, or copied by art, free from pain, it presents to us a drama full of significance.[9]

Music and the values of Castalia are introduced to the reader through the person of the Music Master, just as the values which Hesse wishes to show us are revealed through the person of Joseph Knecht. Simultaneously, the boy Knecht is introduced to reverence and love for the essentially saintly and holy person of the Music Master, and the beauty of spirit coupled with law and order found in music. And, quite naturally, Knecht's whole life is transformed. Great possibilities in human life are always art insofar as they transform and remake human experience. What the narrator refers to as "the first call" is precisely that—the obligation beauty imposes on those who are capable of receiving it, to add to it and preserve it. One theme Hesse repeats over and over is the importance of the call or obligation to Knecht. One may escape life to peace in pure egoistic self-gratification. But if one is *called* to any particular way of life, he accepts the ethical requirements that go with it. "Whoever receives the call not only receives a reward and a command but takes upon himself something in the nature of an obligation." (ML56)

Knecht is given a definite vision here—of the ideal, the orderly, the beautiful, the sublime. "Joseph had experienced his first call, which one may rightly term a sacrament—a vision, an inviting revelation of the ideal world." (ML52) Such visions are precisely the possibilities of human inspiration, in art, science, philosophy, even religion. They bring with them a new way of seeing the world, at least for the individual involved. They often create a sense of mission. The remarkable word "call" cannot but suggest in the Western world the notion of *grace*, bestowed rather than achieved. The unreality of inspiration, its rarity and its wonder, are captured for us here. The ordinary is far away; something special and very strange has happened. The life Castalia provides must be compared with this vision to determine if they are compatible. The ideal of art is discovered by Knecht in his first encounter with the Music Master. Is this ideal preserved in Castalia, which is ostensibly so dedicated to the service of the spiritual life of man?

Knecht is selected, and Hesse draws for us, in passing, a picture of his complete and immediate isolation from his fellow students who had not been selected. On the one hand is the average students' disdain for what is so demanding that they cannot meet its qualifications. They ostensibly despise what they have failed to reach. On the other hand, and mirroring their rejection, is the internal change in Knecht: he no longer lives amidst ordinary things. One of the failures of excellence in modern society is that it receives little of the reverence and appreciation it would seem to merit, but rather disregard, hostility, even contempt. The hostility might be a form of jealousy; but the contempt marks again the gulf between the patient and the visionary, the inspired and far-seeing and the immediate and practical. The man of action, though guided by no ideals and goals of greater value than immediate pleasure, scorns those who find in life the marks of something wider and more wonderful, because he cannot understand it. In Plato's words:

On every occasion, private as well as public . . . when he [the philosopher] appears in a law-court, or in any place in which he has to speak of things which are at his feet and before his eyes, he is the jest, not only of Thracian handmaids but of the general herd, tumbling into wells and every sort of disaster through his inexperience. His awkwardness is fearful, and gives the impression of imbecility. . . . But, O my friend, when he draws the other [the lawyer] into upper air, and gets him out of his pleas and rejoinders into the contemplation of justice and injustice in their own nature and in their difference from one another and from all other things . . . when that narrow, keen, little legal mind is called to account about all this, he gives the philosophers his revenge; for dizzied by the height at which he is hanging, whence he looks down into space, which is a strange experience to him, he being dismayed, and lost, and stammering broken words, is laughed at, not by Thracian handmaidens or any other uneducated persons, for they have no eye for the situation, but by every man who has not been brought up a slave.[10]

The gulf revealed here between the clever man of action and the man of sensitivity and intellect has been repeated again and again throughout the history of man. What Hesse does that is remarkable is to take sentiments like those of Plato seriously and literally and to portray the ideal world in all its beauty and richness of possibility. But he also takes seriously the price paid for idealism—impracticality and isolation from the common man. To the common man, Hesse offers the beauties and values of the life of mind; to the intellectual he offers the compulsion to recognize human life as lived. The burning question is whether the two are necessarily and forever separate, or whether they can be conjoined. The jealousy and rejection come from both sides, and the prevention of reconciliation may be due to both. To most men, the values of education reside only in the success that is their consequence. The intrinsic worth of spiritual achievements is scorned and misunderstood. Even in the United States, where higher education for all has become a rallying cry, this is achieved only by the subordination of the intrinsic values of education to life-success, however it is measured. In the middle classes today, desire to learn for its own sake comes long after emulation, conformity, and desire for success. College is popular when it represents a norm, not when it marks the transcendent experience that Knecht discovers with the Music Master. Of course, there are exceptions: some students discover great visions and possibilities in the intellectual world opened to them. But that this is an exceptional and occasional event only supports the schism. It does not narrow or obliterate it. It is often said that the humanities play a crucial role in preserving and extending culture. But only for a very few, and by a very few. What then is this "culture" that belongs to so few, and transforms the lives of men so seldom? What meaning can it possibly have for men in general? Shall we claim that true and beautiful lives are achieved only by the arty and intellectual? Or that art and mind are only escapes for the weak from a life too cruel for them? Or is there not a third alternative?

Our first introduction to Castalia portrays the standards and value inherent in the life of mind, the beauty and order, the concern for genuine talent (compare here Plato's description of the education of the philosopher-king). The life is "contemplative, painstaking, and intellectual." Scholars are allowed freedom in their own pursuits; and the narrator clearly portrays to us the sterility and fragmentation which result for some who are allowed free rein in even the academic world. (ML60) There is much to laugh at in the realm of pure scholarship. But on the other hand it may be of immense value for future generations. The utter isolation of academic life from ordinary concerns—such as money or power—is portrayed in its sterility as well as its discipline. Celibacy is a matter of course, to exemplify the complete and final schism between the poles.

The poverty of some pure scholarship raises the separation of the active and contemplative lives in a somewhat different form. Presumably the scholar and artist contemplate the beautiful and fine —things intrinsically good in themselves. On the other hand, the politician or realist must be concerned with means to the ends he has chosen. The life of means alone, with no respect for the beautiful and good, is the outside world, the mad scurrying of men with no end in sight, no worthwhile aims. Castalia, however, represents a life of pure ends, isolated from the means necessary to achieve it. It has come about in a rather fanciful, almost incredible way. Even granting the beauty of the life of mind as an end, can life be lived without concern as well for means? Put another way, is it really possible for the philosopher to be so farsighted as to see nothing near him, and yet be a philosopher? Can an exclusive concern for the *goals* of life possibly be of any worth? As the narrator tells us, the privilege of wasting one's life is granted as a reward for the price Castalians pay in the renunciation of worldly pleasures.

In violent contrast the poles of worldliness and the ideal are set forth by Hesse. Throughout we wish to shout that this is all too extreme, though aware that its extremity is only being exaggerated, not invented, by Hesse. Surely a union of means and ends—as John Dewey desired—a merging of the spiritual and worldly, the immediate and ultimate, the beautiful and the urgent can be achieved, particularly in the life of the holy man, a life made art. By portraying a divided world representing divided world-views, Hesse forces us to seek a union, a greater synthesis. The question we are forced to pose, though never stated by anyone in the novel explicitly, is whether this third alternative is possible. Knecht, of course, is that alternative, carried by Hesse to a degree of perfection that we probably did not expect. His life, then, is the answer to the question posed.

The same question receives impetus from another side as well. Knecht is quite concerned about the boys who fail—which is remarkable enough, considering how egoistic most men are. Why not simply take the view that they are not worthy, that the disciplines of the contemplative life are too great for most men to bear? Knecht tells us that at first he pitied those who were expelled, and he also feared a bit for himself. (ML66) This is very natural. But he goes on to say that "perhaps it was not the weaker and inferior that the outside world attracted . . . perhaps it was we who remained steadfastly at Eschholz who were the weaklings and cowards." (ML66–67) Such sensitivity would be but self-abuse in a lesser man than Knecht. The fear of failure exists in even the most successful, even to the point of desperate anguish that one's success is itself a failure—in having chosen wrong. Graduate students, well on the way to professional success in every public aspect, torture themselves with the fear that their field or specialty is wholly without value. Yet in Knecht this means something more, as the novel goes on to show: it marks the fundamental question of whether Castalia is truly viable. Only three pages earlier Knecht speaks of the beauty of music, in a way that brooks no questions as to the value of Castalia. The other question that remains, though, is Nietzsche's: whether "the ascetic ideal springs from the prophylactic and self-preservative instincts which mark a decadent life." [11]

Tied in with the same issue is the problem of *freedom,* one which in the context of the Castalian ideal becomes crucial. The idealistic traditions—whether rationalistic, religious, or aesthetic—come to a common position concerning freedom. The free man obviously chooses the ideal whatever it is; if he *cannot,* then he is in bondage. Thus to St. Augustine, in *The City of God,* the "freedom of will shall be superior inasmuch as it shall not be able to sin," [12] and to Kant "a free will and a will subject to moral laws are one and the same." [13] If there is a truly ideal principle, part of its worth lies in freeing man from his worst side. As Plato puts it, the man who seeks only his own pleasure at the expense of the good and the beautiful "will hardly be able to call his soul his own because the best elements in him will be enslaved and completely controlled by a minority of lower and lunatic impulses." [14] The truly free man is the disciplined and controlled man, not dominated by his desires or impulses.

There is another side to freedom—the freedom from constraint and the influences of other men. To the ordinary man, freedom is the ability and right to choose, not to be at the beck and call of others. On the most ordinary level, where men speak of freedom they refer to the "liberty" of the Declaration of Independence, the right to pursue their own goals, to make their own choices. The value of such freedom, particularly in a time when dictatorial and totalitarian governments have shown their inhumanity so clearly, should not be overlooked. It has taken thousands of years for just a few men in the world to achieve democratic rights and privileges, rights which are constantly in danger of being subordinated to other considerations. The first sign of danger seems to call for a return to older, more organized, and thus constrained hierarchical organization. The values of individuality—found in creative urge, in novel insights, and private visions transformed into public advantages—are clear and definite.

But the other side of the coin is too often neglected in the name of freedom. As Erich Fromm points out, "we have been compelled to recognize that millions in Germany were as eager to surrender their freedom as their fathers were to fight for it." [15] Certainly freedom *from* constraint is not enough, and as Fromm claims, "there is only one possible, productive solution for the relationship of individualized man with his world: his active solidarity with all men and his spontaneous activity, love and work, which unite him again with the world, not by primary ties but as a free and independent individual." [16] The achievement of freedom from the constraints of others is no achievement if it is not accompanied by a gain in the principles and satisfactions which make life worthwhile. Mere freedom from bondage may result in "alienation"—the isolation of men from one another and from the purposes and needs surrounding them; a complete loss of a sense of belonging, of place and role in society; the feeling of utter futility, that nothing has meaning, that no particular person has any important function to serve.

All these theses are brought in by Hesse in the context of the separation of Castalia and the outside world. The narrator has already told us of the organic union of individual and hierarchy in Castalia—perhaps sometimes to the point where individuality is lost, but always in the context of definite principles and ideals. This is the antithesis of ordinary totalitarianism in the fact that the Castalian scholar, once he accepts the fundamental principles of the Order, is free to do anything within its bounds. There is no social control over his particular choices, provided they conform to the intellectual and aesthetic values upon which Castalia is based. On the other hand, only if the values remain ideal is this true. Just as in Plato's *Republic,* if the state is corrupted, the modes of organization and control are as constraining and confining as can be imagined. If Plato's state were best under a philosopher-king, it would nevertheless be horrible under any other rule. Castalia rests upon the repudiation of neurotic idiosyncracy, the obsession with self and personal egoism, and offers a social community within which individuals have a definite and fundamental place. Without doubt, Castalia offers a haven from self-loathing and alienation, the achievement of community and togetherness, perhaps even Fromm's "active solidarity." But it perhaps does so only by submerging individuality.

To this fear of Knecht's the Music Master replies that the only freedom for the average person lies in choosing his vocation, whereupon he is swept up into all the concomitants of that choice: ambition, success, desire for fame, and so on. The scholar, however, chooses no vocation, but accepts the disciplines of his scholarly world. Yet thereafter, he is free to pursue whatever is commensurate with the life of scholarship, which is truly a very great freedom. (ML68–69) This is a perfect expression of the ideal view of human freedom, achieved through order, discipline, and standards of excellence, which literally free men from their worst sides. To this point of view must be compared Nietzsche's powerful words (in a section entitled "The Free Spirit"):

The sentiment of surrender, of sacrifice for one's neighbor, and all self-renunciation-morality, must be mercilessly called to account.[17]

We believe that severity, violence, slavery, danger in the street and in the heart, secrecy, stoicism, tempter's art and devilry of every kind,—that everything wicked, terrible, tyrannical, predatory, and serpentine in man, serves as well for the elevation of the human species as its opposite.[18]

Is not such a view that of license rather than freedom? But is there not also strength to admire and envy in the ability to free oneself from the cavils and standards of others? Nietzsche is often taken as the spokesman for immoralists of all persuasions, for all forms of nihilism, even for the Aryan *Übermensch* of Nazism. What is continually overlooked is the element of discipline and obligation amidst individuality: "Signs of nobility: never to think of lowering our duties to the rank of duties for everybody; to be unwilling to renounce or to share our responsibilities; to count our prerogatives, and the exercise of them, among our duties." [19] Is it not incredible how closely Knecht's life fits these words, in his utter awareness of the responsibilities even his privileges bring, his acceptance of his obligations as solely his own, to be placed upon no one else? Can it truly be said that the communal and the ethical are identical, or is it not necessary for the exceptional individual to render moral insight simply by living well, by *being* the good—however incomprehensible his actions then become by ordinary standards? Simply note that Knecht's choice to leave Castalia at the end cannot be understood by men who have made Castalia their whole lives—except that Knecht too has made Castalia wholly his. Is it not perhaps true that he has *transcended* Castalia, risen to something higher, and therefore unintelligible? Knecht is, after all, at the pinnacle of achievement in Castalia when he decides to leave. Is not the making of oneself into something more noble, in the face of great personal deprivation and at great cost, truly one species of *freedom*—that which is at once accompanied by an increase in responsibility?

It is important to recognize the ambiguity in the themes we have been considering. Concerning boys who have failed, Knecht says: "those fallen ones have something imposing for me despite everything, just as the apostate angel Lucifer has a certain grandeur. . . . they have dared to take a leap forward, and that requires courage." (ML70) His friend replies, "Oh! I don't know. Some of them neither did nor dared anything at all, but simply went on the loose until they were expelled." (ML70–71) And he is perfectly correct: in the name of independence and courage, fearful atrocities as well as waste and vacuity can be maintained. The difficulty lies in grasping the significance and value of courage within the context of principles of order and beauty. What Knecht says makes no sense whatsoever if we think of how little it takes to fail. Yet his life itself retains all that is of value in his words without succumbing to the temptations of arbitrary willfulness. Clearly Castalia comes first, in the tools it offers to one who would transcend in Nietzsche's sense. We must recognize this essential fact through and beyond Knecht's own words.

It is revealed, for example, in the fact that by far the greatest amount of space in the novel is devoted to Knecht's preparation to become Magister. This preparation is thus fundamental in our understanding of him and what he represents. Only one chapter is directly concerned with what it is like to be a total success in the life of mind; immediately thereafter Knecht begins to make his plans to depart. The novel as a whole, then, if it is a revelation of the holy life as lived by an ideal man, is virtually all preparation. There is very little enjoyment or self-satisfaction. Most important is the final acceptance of responsibility above and beyond personal joy. (Though in fact Knecht's stature is so great as to let him enjoy the acceptance of his responsibilities. There is no sense at all that he is driven by moral compulsions. We might compare him with the existentialist heroes—Antigone in Anouilh's play, Argia in *The Queen and the Rebels,* and Orestes in Sartre's *The Flies.* Their humanity renders them vulnerable as we are, tortured by moral obligations as are most men. Yet Hesse offers us credibly an alternative to tortured and violent heroic demands, found in the preparation undergone to free Knecht from the torture of the Romantic soul.)

The main themes have now been stated and recognized, as early as the first chapter. What is left is the further development of Knecht's life, the hardening of the alternatives even further, and the denouement which in its necessity and legendary quality expresses very important views about the nature of the human condition. And although by far the greatest portion of the novel is devoted to Knecht's preparation to become Magister, it only leads to the recognition that this highest of all human roles in indeed not sufficient. Let us examine, if somewhat sketchily, the preparation undergone. The resolution of the novel follows quite directly from it.

## 1. *Meditation*

Knecht learns to find spiritual solace in this most private of activities, in which he becomes independent of all external needs, capable of sustenance within himself. The frantic and passionate life offers its escapes and satisfactions, but only by creating even greater dependence on external circumstances. The narcotics addict may indeed achieve escape into beauty and freedom from emotional pain, but only by his utter dependence on further supply. In meditation, Knecht becomes self-sufficient and free from emotional torments and cares. Implied here is the self-discipline and training necessary to a self-sufficiency which is not achieved at the price of coldness and inhumanity, for Knecht never loses his concern for others, his sensitivity to their feelings and needs. Meditation marks, in its development—for it does grow and change—spiritual peace which is the achievement of self-discipline and control. It marks strength—the strength of the saint, the mystic, the Eastern holy man. The Music Master teaches Knecht to meditate, and offers to him the image of the most human and transcendent achievement of all—the beautiful life—which he too marks in his own life by what he becomes.

The confrontation of the divided life of man in his later encounter with Plinio Designori is overcome by Knecht only through meditation. The world offers us no solution to its own problems. Strength can be found only in a third alternative—other than the active or contemplative life—individual harmony and contemplation, the development of inner capacity. Here Hesse offers on a fairly gross level a merging of the meditative strain in the East with the alienated and tormented West. Intellectually speaking, perhaps the West requires new blood, new views from which it can draw courage and sustenance. But what meditation offers is not new; it is one side of individual possibility, the achievement of order in a single soul. The purely aesthetic in Castalia is sterile and void—Plinio is profoundly correct about that. It is the peace of mind and freedom from torment that Knecht achieves in Castalia that is its greatness and ultimate virtue. It is the achievement Plinio wishes most to have, and falls most short of. The demands of external life can only be met through an internal strength: "the more we demand of ourselves . . . the more we are thrown back upon that source of strength which is meditation." (ML95) It is through the central role played by meditation in Knecht's life that Hesse portrays the Bead Game as the sterile and isolated aesthetic and intellectual exercise it actually is.

On the other hand, of course, the strength that Knecht gains does isolate him somewhat from personal warmth and feeling for others. Truly this has some of the elements of the stoic ideal: Knecht "had no such passionate and exclusive need for a friend, and he could, if necessary live without one and turn his sympathies freely toward new objects and new people." (ML138) Perhaps some of Knecht's inner harmony is itself achieved only through withdrawal from active concern for others. Yet it also provides him as well with the serene strength that enables him to meet Plinio and Tegularius when needed, without the pangs that overinvolvement in narrow self-gratification would have occasioned.

Knecht represents the spiritual life of man at its peak in an all-encompassing sense—taken from as many sources as possible and synthesized in a person, almost a reflection of the way the Bead Game synthesizes all the various spiritual aspects of human life in a single art. Yet such a synthetic achievement, however powerful, cannot but lose something of its comprehensiveness. Meditation plays a very important role in Knecht's life and in what he becomes. But it is never more than a part of his life—he is too busy and has too many definite obligations to be free to meditate when and as he wishes.

A wonderful comparison, then, is drawn by Hesse between Knecht's comprehensive spiritual being and the being of pure spirit, pure mind, even pure goodness (where goodness is taken in spiritual form) as exemplified in the old Music Master. In his first encounter with the Music Master, Knecht is aware of great spiritual beauty, and it is that awareness that makes up his first call. He is led to Castalia by the beauties of the mind, the deep and moving qualities of music. And the Music Master teaches Knecht the inner strengths of meditation, the peace of mind that is essential to all resolute and secure action. But that is not all: as he ages, the Music Master becomes an embodiment of purity—we suppose through continued meditation and internal peace of mind—that is the greatness of that aspect of the spiritual tradition divided from the external world of action. Thus at least one of the sacrifices Knecht must make for his worldliness and concern for the future of Castalia is revealed

here. And we are shown as well the quality of deep spiritual achievements isolated from external affairs, to realize the greatness and
beauty Castalia is capable of.

It would not seem that Castalia is to be judged by its having
created a Knecht—for he is truly a rare, even incredible individual—
but by the Bead Game on the one hand, and the Music Master on
the other. Knecht represents a man who, by exceptional capacities
and circumstances, may be able to reconcile the spiritual and active
elements in man—to save the spiritual beauties in the life of man
from vanishing. The Music Master represents those beauties at their
peak. In Knecht's words:

> I felt only that he had accepted me into his peace and illumination,
> . . . Without my having meditated voluntarily and consciously, it was
> comparable with the experience of a particularly successful and gratifying
> meditation, the theme of which was the life of the aged Magister. . . . he
> was now only a symbol, an apparition, a personification of music. At last I
> experienced all that radiated from him . . . as nothing but music—com-
> pletely unnatural, esoteric music. (ML235)

## 2. Tradition

"Knecht felt the powerful magic of this atmosphere, for everything
here seemed old, venerable, hallowed, and saturated with tradition:
he felt that he was a little nearer to the center of things." (ML80–
81) Perhaps with responsibility this is one of the recurrent and pervasive elements in Knecht's preparation. Castalia itself is the heart
of traditions preserved—to the point where nothing new or truly
novel is offered to promote new traditions. The Bead Game crystal-
lizes all the arts and sciences into a profoundly moving ritual which
both preserves its own traditions and that of the various elements so
crystallized. Its actual form, in a given festival, may be quite singu-
lar, just as different critics may find something different in *Hamlet*
or *Oedipus Rex*. Still it is virtually a parasitic bearer and maintainer
of tradition rather than a breaker of the old to achieve the new.

It will be recalled that the very purity and apparent unworldliness of music is both the narrator's and Knecht's path to the Bead
Game. Hesse presents to us, only two pages after the above quotation, another from Knecht's later writings: "He who knows music

only in the extracts which the Bead Game has distilled from it, may be a good bead-player but is far from being a good musician." (ML 82–83) Knecht's own rejection of the pure aesthetic spirit apart from its roots in the active and passionate life of man is thus made very clear. He at first has nothing to do with the Game, until he has mastered music. Beginning with art in its real, not distilled or virtual essence, Knecht takes the Bead Game as it properly should be taken—as but a part of man's spiritual heritage. Compare with this the fact that in Castalia "the composing of verses ranked as the most impossible, laughable and prohibited of all activities," (ML97) and that Knecht, at the time of his deepest crisis, turns to poetry. Hesse marks the sterility of Castalia in its rejection of perhaps the most passionate and personal art of all, yet marks Knecht's own richness of spirit and soul.

This is the negative side, which the reader cannot but be aware of. Yet for Knecht, tradition, with its beauties and values, is the heart of his preparation. In fact his education and life till he becomes Magister are virtually a tracing of the entire spiritual tradition of man, for he indeed represents everything holy and beautiful. Knecht's larger-than-life status surely is based on the fact that he becomes a living symbol of mankind's intellectual and artistic aspirations, in his willingness to learn everything and his fortune in finding it possible to do so. The maker of the new can destroy the old and valuable only at his peril, ere he destroy without something better to offer. The sterility of Castalia marked to its fullest by the requirement of celibacy, which Knecht finds no burden at all, is rooted in a tradition to which it cannot add. Its traditions and forms may not provide a self-sufficient and complete life for its members. But as a part of Knecht's preparation, they reveal the importance of traditional values in forming new ones. The seeds for transcendence are found in the past. Recognition of the values already ascribed to things would seem to precede necessarily the formulation of the newly valuable. If we recall that Knecht eventually leaves behind all these goods in the name of something more important, two points come to mind forcibly. One is that tradition, however beautiful it may be, is never self-sufficient or complete. The second is that the very seeds which produce something new and different are rooted in the tradition of art, science, and philosophy upon which Castalia rests. If the tradition prepares Knecht, it prepares him for its own repudiation.

### 3.  *Plinio Designori*

The role of this counter-character in Knecht's life cannot be overestimated; and if we are inclined to treat him lightly at first, Hesse warns us of his role by a very portentous name which suggests the Roman Pliny thus great political fame—and an emissary or ambassador; though the name cannot be translated literally. Plinio is the son of a ruling family, thus defined in his role in society. He is quite unfree in fact, showing how untrue are Knecht's earlier remarks on the outside life. He is destined for great things and exposed to Waldzell for the furtherance of this role. Oddly, Plinio may well be one possible construal of Plato's conception of the philosopher king: the king made philosopher. And Plinio's total inadequacy in *both* roles because of their conflicting natures marks Hesse's own bitter pessimism about solutions such as Plato's. On the other hand, Plato too recognized the danger here, and suggested that only the philosopher made king would really do. We watch Knecht for the test of that particular thesis.

A deeply pessimistic view is expressed in Plinio's inadequacy in both the world of Castalia and the world outside. Indeed, if we consider the nature of the ideal and its remoteness from immediate concerns, we can see that Knecht is too much the stranger, too much the perfect man far from exemplification in ordinary life. Let us instead of imagining a man like Knecht in whom the entire spiritual history of man finds a place, consider a real man in whom the intellectual and spiritual play a role, but for whom real concerns and genuine ties are also compelling. May we not be speaking of the men upon whom the future of mankind rests in fact, far more than it does on its spiritual leaders and teachers—the worldly and political, yet genuinely idealistic men for whom the great human possibilities have vivid appeal? Where are we to look for peace and fulfillment but to men of action whose vision includes the beautiful and the good, the excellent and noble? Perhaps all action corrupts. Perhaps no solution exists for man's tormented and alienated soul; for the man of action is corrupted by the power he achieves, while the man of soul is alienated by the ideals he discovers. But surely the possibility exists of the reconciliation of these two elements, as Plato sought a philosopher king of both vision and political capacity.

Plinio is terribly important to Hesse's purpose. Indeed, he may be truly the man about whom the novel is written, the man for whom we may find genuine sympathy and identification. Knecht is too much the spiritual leader, the man of perfection. We readers feel the call of the beautiful and the needs of the present. Teachers of today require decent salaries at least as much as they seek the perfect and ideal. Hesse clearly points out the dependence of the world of the spirit on the good graces of men like Plinio: support is provided for Castalia when necessary by statesmen who were first scholars in their youth (ML84). The ivory temples of the soul depend on earthly roots. The arts have been supported in times past by the wealthy and aristocratic; the sciences too require individual support. Today, the government has assumed the greater burden in education and science, art depends still on private contribution, while the university depends on legislatures with some vision and understanding of their nature and needs. Only by revealing some of itself to men of action can the world of mind expect to be propagated and maintained. Whether it can do so without corrupting itself or weakening them is the crucial question.

In Plinio, Knecht meets the outside world for the first and again for the final time. Plinio represents the "real world," on whose behalf he takes up cudgels. The great split between the urgent and the ideal is represented at first by arguments between Knecht and Plinio. Although Knecht represents the Order to Plinio, and argues vehemently and well on its behalf, he is torn and swayed by Plinio's appeal. He is still subject to the genuineness of the dilemma facing Castalia, one which few other Castalians appear to recognize. Plinio attacks the Bead Game as useless, the Castalians as "a castrated hoard of children tied to their mothers' apron strings." (ML88) Knecht is quite disturbed: perhaps there is a grain of truth here. He had wondered before about that possibility himself. To help him cope with both Plinio and his own uncertainty, Knecht is given the task of replying to Plinio's arguments, which strengthens his own conviction of belonging to Castalia and reveals to him the nature of his responsibility therein. He found that he was a true Castalian, but couldn't stop worrying about the nature of Castalia's isolation: "Why did the two worlds live presumably apart from each other in hostility and discord? Why could they not both unite and cherish each other?" (ML92) The great problem of the novel, that which his life itself must serve to answer, is thus posed to Knecht. At this point in his life, Plinio functions only as the gadfly to call Knecht to his responsibility: to preserve the values of Castalia against attack, yet to heed the necessity of reconciliation. (See the theme of responsibility below for further discussion of this.) Knecht's awareness of the need to affirm ties to the outside world mirrors both Freud's view of the irreducibility of the primordial id in man and Nietzsche's conception of the fundamental nature of striving or the Will to Power in *all* men. Plinio represents the irrational and perhaps the ugly: but also the very real and inescapable. To use older categories than these, in Knecht is found the Apollonian or beautiful—the commensurate, with its harmony and order, its ideals and virtues. In Plinio is found the Dionysian—the brutal and violent, the physical, the frenzied and vital, the strong and vigorous. Isolated, each is sterile and unfocussed: strength without order is chaos; order without energy is impotent.

Unfortunately for Plinio, he has been transformed by Castalia. He will return to the outside world, yet always carry with him what Castalia has taught him. Knecht finds in Plinio the seeds of unification of the two worlds, the overcoming of the dualism. (ML99) A man of action can, through education, learn the importance and beauty of the life of the spirit, and incorporate it in his principles of action. Would that it were so, that in Plinio could be found the escape from the dilemma that has plagued man for so long. When Knecht meets Plinio years later, although the latter is an influential person in the financial affairs of Castalia, he is also a man torn asunder to the roots of his very being. Here then is marked for us Plinio's very human soul, one that resides in the world amidst its responsibilities and cares, yet yearns for the ideal and beautiful which its worldly ties cannot permit it. The being of man once tied to the material elements that surround on every hand loses its wings but not its yearning. Where can the possibility of escape be found? Plinio laments "were I to have had a task and an ideal in life it would have been to incorporate in my person a synthesis of the two principles, to become an intermediary, interpreter and mediator between the two. I have tried it and failed lamentably." (ML268) What is impossible is to recognize the ideal and yet live like finite and corrupt man. Plinio, in particular, is in a terrible position, for as a political leader he must understand and work with ordinary men. And that can be accomplished only when he becomes like them. (ML269) It is in the person of Plinio, not Knecht, that the plight of man is to be found. Plinio is the noble soul with feet of clay; the soul caught in what Augustine called "original sin," what Sartre calls "absurdity" and the "nausea of being-in-itself." Without spiritual values, Plinio would be but a blind and ignorant animal seeking satisfactions without hope of recognizing them when achieved. Yet once the greater possibilities are revealed, either he must relinquish life itself, or he will be forever tortured by the irreconcilability of the real and the possible. In short, the beautiful is the ideal and the possible; it is not now the real. If it were to become so, the great chasm in man's soul, his alienation from the world he lives in, would be overcome. Hegel, Marx, Dewey, and Fromm offer paths to this achievement. Hesse offers the pessimistic vision found in Ortega, Schopenhauer, and Sartre that this may well be impossible, shown by Plinio's failure.

## 4. *Tegularius*

The other side of Knecht's character and being is revealed by the comparison between him and Fritz Tegularius (again, the name is significant, for *tegularius* means "ornament" in Latin, signifying his utter adherence to Castalia). Tegularius is a brilliant student—perhaps as much or more so than Knecht himself—but poor in health, and weak in mind as well. The unending battle between the mind and the body continues here, not to be escaped even in Castalia. The intellectual or aesthetic life is still human. Bodily and emotional frailty do not cease to exist, whatever the pretences of Castalia. Though brilliant, Tegularius cannot be trusted to teach. Knecht declares him, "the most talented and brilliant Bead Game player that I know. He would be an obvious choice for Magister Ludi were not his character completely unsuited to the post on account of his delicate health." (ML133) Bound to the ascetic, regulated, and safe life of Castalia, he is unable to leave even to visit the monastery. It nearly makes him ill. New experiences are too much for him to bear. His balance is assured only in a particular environment. In one sense, with all his strengths he is the truly enslaved man—slave here to art and the mind, not the body. Either extreme can destroy the union that is the whole man.

Tegularius represents the highest achievement that can be expected in Castalia—the brilliance of mind, the ingenuity of artistic insight that the weak and poor in spirit often achieve (driven perhaps by their very weakness of body). Yet indeed, in his melancholy, his self-doubt, he mirrors Plinio Designori: human, weak, lost, yet "he is a jewel and a quite irreplaceable treasure." (ML133) The great in the world of man are often so displaced and isolated, dependent on special circumstances to provide for them, yet capable of great achievements once so secured. One of the strengths of the spiritual world found in Castalia is its ability to offer a place to a Tegularius—a brilliant but weak man who would not survive in a cruel world very long. Yet in fact his weakness reveals the poverty of Castalia's solution to the human condition. Can it really be said that man will be saved through dependence and admission of weakness, rather than through the discipline and self-mastery Knecht achieves through meditation? Particularly since what Tegularius lacks most of all is the responsibility that becomes Knecht's whole life.

In the deepest sense he was totally unhierarchical and individualistic in outlook and mode of life . . . rather an indifferent [Castalian] in character and in his attitude towards the hierarchy and the morality of the Order. His greatest vice was an incorrigible casualness and a neglectful attitude toward his meditation. (ML243)

The perfect Castalian, Tegularius lacks precisely what Castalia needs most of all—inner strength and awareness of responsibility. It follows, then, that the solution Castalia offers to men who need it most of all may be its source of destruction; for these men will not be able to provide Castalia or themselves with the discipline necessary to preserve and sustain it. He is the pure scholar—the man who needs the life of spirit the most yet who can offer it least in a historic or enduring sense; though he does provide it with great achievements (Games) by its own standards. If Castalia is to be saved, it cannot be the purely spiritual and needy who will save her.

## 5. The East

In line with Knecht's role in representing the total spirit of man, and to support his mastery of the internal order of the soul found in meditation, during his early years he not only withdraws into a solitude that the narrator confesses that he does not understand, but becomes an acolyte of an "Elder Brother," from whom he not only learns Chinese, but self-sufficiency as well. Perhaps Knecht is withdrawing in the face of his impending responsibilities and obligations. But it is far more appropriate to recognize that the strength he needs is to be found precisely in the meditative and internal, the restoration of his inner soul in the face of external obligations.

The Elder Brother is a great student withdrawn into solitude, reticent and inarticulate—as are the masters of Zen and other ways of living rather than speaking—either a sage or a fool. To Knecht, he marks both personal order and individualism of a noble sort—the rejection of community for individual peace. In a way, he possesses a spiritual harmony that Castalia seeks but cannot find. Yet this is achieved by a degree of isolation and rejection, a retreat from activity, that puts even Castalia to shame. Knecht learns much from the Elder Brother—in particular, to bring Eastern elements into the Bead Game. Yet he is told "one can build a pretty little bamboo garden in the world, but whether the gardener could succeed in incorporating the world into his bamboo garden seems to me to be questionable." (ML120) Perhaps in fact the achievements of peace and harmony can only come from withdrawal from the world, and Knecht's quest for reconciliation is but a vain dream. Knecht is offered once more the strengths of meditation and peace, but the utter denial forces him to return to Waldzell. He has to continue his quest for the highest.

## 6. *The Church*

Surely the center of Western man's spiritual authority cannot be neglected, even in the context of a society dedicated to the aesthetic and scientific, the intellectual and philosophical, rather than religious. Knecht, who already has given indication of seeking a unification of the tormented halves of man's being, is not only given the tools for effecting such a unification in his exposure to all the pure and holy aspects of human life, but *becomes* in fact such a unification, though only from the point of view of teacher. Embodying all the strengths of man that can be derived from acquaintance with the ideal, Knecht is indeed the full and saintly man in his awareness of the needs and hopes of man, without being weakened or tormented by this knowledge as is Plinio. On the other hand, his ability to persevere in the task that he sets for himself is as doubtful as is Plinio's.

Knecht is sent to Mariafels, revealing a further tie to the outside world—for Mariafels is not so isolated as is Castalia. The power and function of the Church has always been unquestionably worldly, however spiritual its final goals are taken to be. In addition, this mission reveals the hardening of his responsibilities in tasks set for him. Knecht faces obligations which indeed shadow his whole life, and which are realized in political ways even in Castalia. So long as Castalia exists in this world rather than in memory or imagination only, it must face political realities. In this sense it faces, whether it would or not, the same accommodations the Church continually makes. In Mariafels Knecht becomes for the first time a teacher, representing to the Church the body of wisdom it may once have preserved but no longer can lay claim to, and which it requires for its sustenance. Knecht wonders at the fact that the monastery possesses only one true scholar—as if even the worldliness of so unworldly a place as Mariafels prevents true self-discipline and concern for the ideal: a brutal commentary on the esoteric remoteness of Castalia. On the other hand, he does discover Father Jacobus, in whom the spiritual and political meet to a degree never before encountered by him. The Church does in fact rule over a worldly realm, though whether it achieves a fusion of its real power and spiritual goals is not easy to determine. In theory, however, it should do so, and has done so in its greatest men. This Knecht learns and comes to respect.

The political side of the spiritual realm is stated explicitly to Knecht by Father Jacobus in his claim that Castalia is "completely lacking in historical sense." (ML152) There is a real and historical side of human life, but Castalia only distills from it the Apollonian elements of order and beauty it desires to find. There is much more, and neglecting it will only result in the eventual destruction of all the order and beauty Castalia holds dear. Understanding requires order and reason. But there are ways of ordering that repudiate disorder, while other ways imply willingness to face and conquer it. Here again are the rational-irrational Apollonian-Dionysian poles in human life. Here we may discover Hegel's objections to the rationalist age prior to the discovery of real history—that men lose contact with the real and particular in their formulation of ideals which exist only in thought. True and complete understanding is reached only in the union of the universal and the concrete, through reason in (not beyond or above) human life and history. Ultimately it is the concrete and particular that surround us, although we seek order in principles of beauty and cognition. The greatest achievement required is the union of these two strains. The singularity and incomprehensibility of history marks its challenge to men, one which can be ignored only at dire peril.

To Jacobus, the fundamental quality of the Church is *endurance*. He contrasts the momentary nature of heroism, the transitory nature of certain ideals, with the persistence of the Christian Church. The implication here is that the valuable must become a part of history where it can persist and retain its qualities and values. This recognition marks one of the fundamental distinctions between the ideal and the real: the concern with Time, with effect in a span of existence, through history. The real is marked by *power,* the ability to influence and direct. The eternity of ideals is but the timelessness of possibility, not the permanence of effect and power. The question becomes one of rendering ideals something more than empty shells, by giving them life and influence as well as remote appeal. The need for vitality and power is thus found by Knecht in the remarkable establishment of a Church that has persevered through transformation after transformation in the real history of man. More than kings or empires, the Church possesses great political wisdom, marked by nothing more than its endurance. Contrast with this Plato's words about his ideal state: "Hard as it may be for a state so framed to be shaken, yet, since all that comes into being must decay, even a fabric like this will not endure forever, but will suffer dissolution." [20] And Castalia too, we discover later, is in peril because of events in the outside world. "Many of our parliamentarians speak openly on occasions about Castalia's being somewhat of an expensive luxury to our country. . . . The breakers are ahead, and one day they will capsize us." (ML322)

Knecht's success with Father Jacobus reveals to us that the latter's words do not fall on deaf ears, as they might with any other Castalian. Knecht is already sensitive to the other dimensions of the human predicament. Father Jacobus only strengthens and defines his resolve, which is further clarified by the task presented to him—that of unifying Castalia and Rome, the spiritual and the religious, which until the Romantic period were virtually identical. Over and over Knecht is represented to us as the principle of unity, if one can be found at all. The endurance of the Church Jacobus claims is based on its recognition of the bestial side of man, which Castalia cannot but overlook as it is constructed. The controversy between Knecht and him is *unending*, for there is a fundamental schism at its heart: whether order and the ideal alone can fulfill man's needs. Castalia itself can recognize history only in a schematized and unreal form. Knecht, in order to convince Jacobus of the value of Castalia, must learn himself about real history, so that on the one hand he accomplishes virtually the spiritual regeneration of the Church, but on the other can do so only by relinquishing his isolation from mundane and political matters. Great effort is needed to overcome the division between the ideal and real. Knecht accomplishes it so far as he does only by uniting the elements in his own being. The pure esthete or scholar can never reach any degree of communication with those who most need him.

## 7. *The Bead Game*

Little need be said of the importance to Knecht of the Game. In one sense it is his whole life; in another it is but a background against which he reaches sufficient consciousness of himself and his task to depart from it in the name of its values. What seems most important is his utter success in playing it, although he hesitates in learning its principles and forms when young. While others are playing the Game during apprenticeship, Knecht studies the Game in all its aspects, especially its origins and history. He engages in the task of "learning to the full the content, principles, workings and system of the Game plan and in tracing a way back through the different cultures, sciences, languages and arts of centuries; . . . the most detailed verification of the system and possibilities of expression in the art of the Bead Game." (ML114) His mastery, then, is not the fruit of inspiration, but the sheer control of every element, for he has sought understanding of every aspect of it. Here again we see Knecht's utterly complete mastery of the life of Castalia, against which his departure gains such importance.

While at Mariafels, Knecht enters the annual competition, one in which inventiveness and originality are of prime importance. And he wins with a game "which was above all rigidly symmetrical and of a crystal-clear classical composition, although highly decorative, old master-like and graceful in execution." (ML178) Here again we see Knecht's capacity and superhuman qualities revealed to us most strongly, for instead of utilizing the original elements of his own studies which no other Castalian could have matched, he wins in a completely pure and formal manner. He does not release his unique abilities until he becomes Magister. Discipline and control come first in the ideal. Here is represented the attitude of the perfect scholar, whose mastery of the formal qualities of his field must precede his inventive designs—as must the composer of new music achieve a mastery of traditional forms before he strives to perfect his idiosyncratic talents. Anything else is unformed and chaotic. Hesse portrays Knecht's development to Master of the Game as virtually the most perfect that that development could be—in the terms of Castalia alone. Thus when Knecht chooses to leave, it is not as a slight misfit, but as a man who has surpassed the heights of Castalian life, toward something greater. He chooses to depart out of a compulsion toward something even higher in the spiritual life of man than the ideals represented by Castalia. If *Faust* is the story of man striving toward ever-new experiences, *Magister Ludi* is the realization of man striving toward ever-higher ideals, even at the apparent expense of those ideals themselves.

## 8. *Responsibility*

This is a major theme of the novel, second only to that of the dichotomous nature of man. It has already been pointed out that Knecht's first encounter with the ideal and beautiful, in the person of the Music Master, is a "call"—an obligation which the recognition of values as ideal automatically creates. Knecht is again "called" when he meets Plinio Designori once more after many years and feels the obligation to depart from Castalia. (ML280) And upon his departure, we are told that Knecht has viewed such "awakening" "as a gradual progress toward the heart of the world, into the center of truth, as something to a certain extent absolute, as an advance along a path which could only be traversed step by step, but which in idea was continuous and direct." (ML341) The Hegelian conception of the merging of reason and its ideals and the particular acts necessary to fulfill them is expressed here—one which Knecht has always felt obligated to pursue. And the quest is eternal, for truth is found within the particular steps which are taken. "He now found himself, at the end of this path, by no means at the heart of the world and in the centre of truth, and saw also that his present awakening was only an eye opening, a reorientation and an adaptation to new conjunctions." (ML341)

The same theme is embodied in the Greek sense of the Good, which is not necessarily the Right, but which automatically compels service by its very nature. Every man seeks his good: it need not be good that he *should* do so—that would be redundant. If the average Castalian is but seeking escape or personal satisfaction in the Bead Game, his action represents no capacity to recognize the *Ideal*, which beyond gratification and pleasure offers at least as much responsibility and compulsion as it offers satisfaction. We are on a higher plane of the Good immediately when we recognize the difference between gratification and the ideal, which offers yet compels at the same time. The highest life is that which asks the most, not that which merely appears to offer gratification. For it is in meeting obligations that the greatest achievements of men are found.

The theme of responsibility continues in Knecht's appointment as respondent to Plinio Designori's criticisms of Castalia. Not only does he serve the social function of repudiating Plinio's attacks, but he develops through the fulfillment of his task into a person of even greater social and moral responsibility. Surely we can imagine that most Castalians, like most men, would ignore challenges that call for a reevaluation of their whole way of life. Fundamental choices usually bring a kind of blindness concerning themselves. To face them squarely often risks one's whole being in the discovery that one has chosen wrong. Moral consciousness and true responsibility may well require the strength not to be fearful and blind on this level. Indeed, such strength would appear to be precisely that which Nietzsche describes the superior man to possess—the strength to challenge oneself and thereby the world surrounding one, on a fundamental rather than superficial level. And it is precisely this strength which Knecht reveals that he possesses again and again. Hesse seems to imply that this strength comes from an inner repose reached through meditation; and the fact that he even offers a pathway to it should be compared to existentialists and nihilists who call for strength without either defining it or explaining how to reach it.

In his years of "free study," prior to his mission to Mariafels, Knecht speaks of the *happiest* time of his life. Yet the irony of this remark is clear, for he chooses not indulgence but discipline, not frivolity but even greater regimentation. It is now that he examines all the elements of the Game in the fullest detail. By now the necessities of his life and being have been formed, to the point where an irresponsible or arbitrary act is unthinkable. This fact about Knecht is essential, for without it the nature of his final decision is obscured. Unless his choice to leave is viewed as the *responsible* act it is, we may wonder if perhaps Knecht has chosen either foolishly, wantonly, or haphazardly. Only if Knecht's very being is seen to be suffused with the obligations and needs that compel his actions can his final decision be viewed as fully ideal—in intent, if not in execution. What Knecht is striving for is not explained or even set forth. If it is not to be rejected out of hand, this must be because of his nature and the responsibility which can be taken for granted in everything he does.

Knecht's mission to Mariafels is, of course, another form of responsibility, one which forms part of his development insofar as he executes a diplomatic task well, learning to use real power in a real setting. In a brief return to Waldzell, he feels both a release and something else: "it was the responsibility, the embrace of the General and the Higher, which made many young men appear old and many old men young, which held one fast and at the same time supported one." (ML162) Perhaps it may be thought that such responsibilities curtail one and limit his freedom. But Hesse recognizes here that such restraints may enhance and provide freedom. The old are made young by their dedication to tasks of great import. Only the young resent responsibilities which indeed magnify one. As the rest of the quotation points out, a young tree would fall and wither if not supported. Only in a context of well-defined alternatives (constraints) can a man choose well; otherwise he chooses but arbitrarily and blindly. The nature of human life renders men afraid of the very responsibilities which would provide both strength and purpose for them. Particularly where the responsibilities are for something higher and more ideal do they literally imbue consciousness with value and meaning that capriciousness and arbitrariness (sometimes called "freedom") cannot provide. Of course, the satisfactions Knecht achieves within the framework of responsibility are almost beside the point for him. He would no doubt act properly whatever the cost (perhaps that is precisely what he eventually does); but nevertheless the satisfactions of bondage to the noble may well be the most rewarding of states of being.

Finally, Knecht becomes Magister Ludi, the pinnacle of personal success in Castalia, and discovers that his role is far less that of one whose success can be savoured than that of a pure servant whose duties know no release. He of course conquers the elite and becomes truly master, discovering that what Castalia wished to make him was "a master, a regent and servant, a perfect tool." (ML209) Service is absolutely essential.

However, Knecht is not just a tool—perhaps it may be that service to the Ideal cannot properly be performed by a mere instrument, but only a man of responsibility who nevertheless is something in his own right. Knecht finds the position arduous and tasking, a continual service to others—for his primary function besides administration is that of teaching. The latter becomes his great reward. He finds that his freedom is curtailed by his office; his responsibilities are enormous and time consuming. Yet he is left with enough liberty to turn toward the only activity that interests him— teaching. The role of Magister is completely that of service; still, this service becomes the fulfillment and satisfaction of Knecht's life. It is but a minor step (not in fact minor—rather earth-shaking from all other points of view) to recognize that his role as teacher calls him to break with Castalia and to offer his gifts and endowments to those who need them most, the men who live outside Castalia, and who may never really come in contact with it. The greater call than Castalia exists.

Upon his departure, the theme of responsibility arises for Knecht with even greater emphasis. He ponders the rule

Should the Higher Authorities summon thee to office, know that each promotion on the ladder of office is not a step into freedom but into bondage. The higher the office the heavier the bondage. The greater the official power, the stricter the service. The stronger the personality the more expressly forbidden is wilfulness. (ML340)

Hesse represents this theme again and again to make sure that we understand that Knecht is not capricious or willful, but fully responsible for his actions, and just because of that forced to leave Castalia. An act which to others of narrow vision appears to be a subjective decision for personal needs may be truly something far more—an acceptance of a greater responsibility—to one who sees further. Put another way, Knecht *must* leave if he accepts the standards and values of Castalia—leave to preserve Castalia, to fulfill its mission and purpose. It is precisely because he is a pure embodiment of all that is valuable in Castalia that the obligations of his office compel him to abdicate it. In this way Hesse shows that the purity of spirit of the intellectual and artistic life is weakness and personal gratification alone unless accompanied by service and responsibility. Castalia is truly beautiful only insofar as its obligations, which it indeed proclaims as part of its fundamental concern, are met. It is not that Knecht discovers values external to Castalia which he considers higher: such a discovery would indeed be unlikely and arbitrary. Rather, he takes the values essential to the Castalian way of life and pursues them to their conclusion.

> Would he be able to convince others and prove to them what seemed so clear to himself—that the 'wilfulness' of his present behavior was in truth service and obedience, that in reality he was not pointing toward freedom but towards new, unknown and strange ties, not a fugitive but one who had been called, not obstinate but obedient, not a master but a victim. (ML342)

*          *          *

Knecht's preparation is complete, and he has become Magister Ludi—the highest achievement a man of mind and spirit can attain. Yet the novel itself portrays—it does not explicitly tell us—how insufficient this pinnacle of success must be to Knecht. The narrator tells us that "he had grown weary of office and had already turned his face toward other goals," (ML258) as if it is but dissatisfaction and lack of gratification that motivate Knecht. On the other hand, in the next line we are told that he "had reached the point where great natures abandon the way of tradition and obedient compliance and with confidence in higher, unnamed powers feel themselves obligated to attempt and make themselves responsible for the new, the uncharted and the unknown." (ML258) Must we remain satisfied with this appeal to unnameable higher powers, as Nietzsche implies? Must we turn from the rational—exemplified in Castalia—to something different, irrational, or suprarational? Does this not take us back to the Dionysian or the arbitrary?

Here it becomes plain that despite his reverence for Knecht the narrator's place and circumstance limit his understanding of the Magister's final actions. The narrator is a Castalian, albeit one who responds to Knecht's uncommon nature and value, and who simply cannot reach understanding except in terms available to the rational hierarchy—in terms of ideals that cannot but be timeless.

The lack of intelligibility of Knecht's obligation to a Castalian mirrors the fact that the obligations built into the realm of Spirit seem only to involve pursuit and support of the Ideal in intellectual terms. What Knecht sees and cannot really communicate to those who do not for themselves is that the Ideal must actually be given up if it is to be strengthened and made secure. This seems quite paradoxical and absurd to them. He never expects to be understood by men whose lives are devoted to what may be called the ideal preservation of the Ideal, if he feels called to render the Ideal in fact and reality. We are told explicitly of Knecht's utter obligation to the task ahead: but to everyone else he has "been long tired of office or of Castalia, and been tormented by a desire to lead a worldly life," (ML347) something quite impossible for Knecht, as the reader cannot but recognize. Even Magister Alexander recognizes his own implausibility by the line, "how then was it possible that, harboring such thoughts, desires, and resolutions, already a deserter in your heart, you could remain so long in office and apparently continue to conduct it in a faultless manner?" (ML348) Moreover, he remembers when Knecht became Magister Ludi: "I was content with both you and myself to a degree that very seldom happens with me." (ML354) How though can he understand Knecht's words: "I desire that there should be hazards, difficulties and dangers to face; I am hungry for reality, for tasks and deeds, and also for privation and suffering"? (ML353) The call to Life may transcend that of the Ideal, but to one who sees the Ideal in its purity as more beautiful than in its reality or concrete manifestations which always fall short, Life's appeal is unintelligible.

Alexander can only understand that Knecht is disloyal to the master he swore to serve—not realizing that Castalia itself is not important, but the principles for which it stands and to which Knecht is utterly faithful. In an earlier tradition, though devoted to very different purposes, it was taken for granted that existence was a perfection—that ideals in concrete existence are worth far more than ideals of the pure or withdrawn imagination, that the true seeker after the Ideal will abandon it wholly if it cannot be realized and will pursue what is enactable: that truth cannot be grasped by one whose devotion is to the untrammeled and uncompromised ideal. The gap here is fundamental, concerning what is truly ideal: the pure or the achievable.

The greatness of the novel is that it takes the reader one step beyond the narrator and Magister Alexander, who cannot understand. The utter necessity of Knecht's step—to endeavor to reconcile Castalia with the world it has abandoned but of which it is still unavoidably a part; the *obligation* to unify if at all possible the divisive elements in the world of man—has become clear to the reader. Of course, we may abandon hope and despair of any solution to the needs of man: but even despair does not vitiate the obligation. Knecht has reached the recognition that his very status as Magister Ludi obligates him to preserve Castalia: and he can only do so by abandoning her. His status as a man requires him to achieve the good and the beautiful; and he can only do so by bringing the ideals of imagination into the lives of men through teaching, and by becoming a *man,* not a disembodied contemplator of the Beautiful. His status as a virtual embodiment of man's intellectual and spiritual heritage obligates him to fulfill this heritage in man's real (historical) life, not in the dreams of a few. His status as a man obligated to acts and deeds for other men and their ideals prevents him from acting out of sheer self-gratification. His preparation has led Knecht to the realization, not that there is something higher *for* him, but that something higher is demanded *of* him, an obligation he feels is built into the very position he holds in Castalia.

His preparation has also led the reader to the realization of Knecht's state long before he makes his decision and speaks his mind in the circular letter. Perhaps Hesse could even have omitted that letter altogether without weakening our conviction that Knecht has chosen to act in the only way he possibly could, as well as the only way which is the salvation of all that is dear to him and the other Castalians. Surely if we are not already convinced by the time of the letter of what Knecht must do, his words are a waste of time. The force of the argument rests upon the compulsion of the events of the novel, our conviction that this is just how they must be. If an alternative remains for Knecht, if a way out remains which is either as worthy or as likely a path in terms of what Knecht is, then his final decision becomes capricious and arbitrary, rather than necessary in both senses. Hesse's argument is indeed that no man capable of acting to reconcile the divided soul and life of man can (morally) remain content with doing nothing: that abdication is but the mark of a weak or impotent man. The nature of the argument rests in the character of Knecht; and if the forces within that character do not satisfy our desires for conviction, no words uttered can possibly do so within the framework of the novel.

Nevertheless, some consideration of the circular letter, Knecht's explanation of his decision, is necessary if only to point out the repetition of the major themes already clearly expressed. It is remarkable that Knecht makes use of the talents of Fritz Tegularius in composing the letter, signifying both the role of the pure scholar in great works and the degree of irony in even attempting the task of explanation within the framework permitted by Castalia. For Tegularius is probably the last person who could understand the nature of Knecht's mission, hampered as he is by the desire for but his own self-gratification. The form of the letter, its appeal and argument, are so much more Tegularius' qualities than Knecht's. Yet we cannot discount it: we can only wonder at all that remains unexpressed.

The burden of the argument is that Castalia is threatened, to the point where Knecht "feels called imperatively to other spheres than those which I now occupy." (ML312) The security and peace of Castalia depends on a denial of Castalia's place in the world, its reliance on an external world it yet ignores. It is thus, however noble and beautiful, parasitic and self-centered.

Yet it is not only Castalia that concerns Knecht, but the world outside as well; and here he begins to fail to reach the average

Castalian. He emphasizes that it is impossible for human beings to withdraw from history—they are responsible for it and affected by it; yet Castalians pretend not to know this. The common attitude of the ordinary academic scholar in the United States today, not to mention Germany of the past fifty years, is so susceptible to this criticism as to need no further justification of Knecht's position. Only in France have intellectuals and artists accepted any degree of social responsibility by virtue of their position. Knecht's comments here mark not only a profound truth about the nature of man, but a shallow and obvious truism about the academic community, especially in the Germany of the last fifty years, but applicable throughout the Western academic world. Castalia counts itself safe and pure, but historical facts do not support this view. Knecht is proclaiming, that is, the need for Castalians and intellectuals to recognize that they can be assured of the integrity that is necessary to their being only by actively seeking it—even at the risk of compromising that very integrity in the acts necessary to secure it. Yet the paradoxical nature of this last remark is precisely the point at which Knecht's position is no longer clear to even the Castalian hierarchy. For is the intellectual really still an intellectual of integrity when he becomes politically partisan? When he leaves his specialty and ivory tower, is he anything other than ordinary—perhaps even less able than most to reach out and communicate with the majority of men?

The answer Knecht proposes is not the Platonic—that the philosopher should rule the State. That is a vain hope; but a dream. There remains to the scholar only the role of teacher, a teacher not withdrawn or hidden from view in mystical clouds, but who represents in the world directly the truths that remain the only ideals worth striving for. And so Knecht is obligated to a task of education of monumental proportions—though for which no one has been better prepared.

The response to the letter is typically academic: discussion is provoked, but acceptance of action is quite impossible. Perhaps the attitude necessary to scholarship prohibits action even when necessary. As Kierkegaard recognized, action often takes place at a point where rational considerations are utterly beside the point. He proposed an irrational leap of faith necessary to surmount the absurd. So too Nietzsche glorified the mask, the hidden, the inarticulate. On the other hand, need we readers rest content with dumb acceptance? Is it not clear that Knecht is simply demanding action in the name of

urgency? The hierarchy can do nothing but "take up a patient attitude of waiting." (ML331) Here is the desperate nature of the split
between the active and intellectual lives. Does it truly follow that
only inarticulate and mute—absurd—remarks can be made about
men who fail to recognize the urgency of action even where all the
alternatives do not permit rationally decisive choice among them?

There remains only the "legend," by which Hesse tells us of
the tentative nature of his view, embodied in Knecht's death. Here
we are no longer *sure:* and if Knecht represents man's spiritual life,
then Hesse is asking a question—whether it can persevere to the
point where man is saved by it, or whether its fruits can only survive
in a world isolated from man himself. If the fundamental problem
is the divided world in which man is alienated and forlorn, then we
have already seen the impotence of the pure scholar and the ordinary man of action who has tasted the fruit of the Ideal. If salvation
exists, it can only come through the realm of the Ideal itself, in what
it can teach to ordinary men. Knecht has become the perfect representative of the Spirit, the embodiment of all that is beautiful and
valuable as well as its complete master. Can he then succeed? If not,
Hesse's view would appear to be the bitter and pessimistic one that
man is doomed.

Knecht's return to life is that of a walk in which the natural
once again affects him, for the first time since he returned to Waldzell from Mariafels. "It was all perfectly new again, mysterious and
of great promise." (ML367) He is refreshed and restored, for now his
service and his independence become one. Nature and its joys—its
strengths and vitality—are lost in the sterile world of mind with all
the pains and extremities of life. The weakness of Castalia is thus
symbolized by what Knecht discovers as he leaves it. The energy of
life is regained, with its exuberance as well as its dangers. Knecht
brings to life all the control and value that the world of spirit can
provide, to pit all that man can develop of order against exigency
and urgency.

Yet it is the beauty of the country, the starkness of a mountain
world, in which Knecht acts out his final scene. He has succeeded in
reaching Tito and commanding his respect. Tito

felt an exciting intuition that to belong to this type of nobility and to
serve it could perhaps become a duty and an honour, that perhaps here, embodied in the figure of this teacher who in his gentleness and friendliness

was a perfect aristocrat, was something that approximated to the essential meaning of his life and was destined to be his goal. (ML378)

But Knecht is weary: for the reality of nature and its demands are not so easily to be mastered by the scholarly strengths he has gained. Tito is a child of nature and its vital inner forces however much Knecht appeals to him. Out of something deep inside him—the feeling of danger and shame at succumbing to the wild, the vital, the Dionysian—Tito challenges Knecht to swim to the other side of the lake. And Knecht, recognizing the need to meet the challenge if he is to retain Tito's respect, swims and drowns. And that is the end.

Thus the dangerous and only slightly hidden forces within man destroy Knecht at the very beginning of his entry into life proper. Relations among men are often shameful, guilt-ridden, and irrational. The coolness of thought is quickened by urgency and vitality. Even Knecht is destroyed at his first brush with immediacy of decision—even by an encounter with a young boy: flesh is very weak, however strong the spirit. The violent pessimism embodied here is realized in our awareness that Knecht's end is so necessary, so likely. The holy man cannot withstand the forces of reality that surround him. There seems no hope for man but the torment with which he lives every day. Against the vision of a unified life for man, Hesse presents the starkness of a view without hope, for the greatest strengths men possess from a powerful spiritual tradition are impotent. Only the faintest glimmer of hope remains in the very last lines about the young boy's realization of what has happened. "A feeling of sacred awe took hold of him which foretold that this guilt would change him completely and would make more demands upon him than he had hitherto ever demanded of himself." (ML384)

But the novel is not over—only the life of Knecht. Beautifully realizing the possibilities of Knecht's teachings, in poems and tales presumably written by him years ago, Hesse takes us back and yet forward, into themes which portray again Knecht's consciousness of the urgency of restoring the unity of the human soul, yet take us on away from his death to renew the necessity of his endeavor. The incarnations and poems are presented as an appendix which we may read to learn of Knecht's wisdom after he has died. The pessimism is thus accentuated by our feeling of what has been lost, yet transformed is thus accentuated by our feeling of what has been lost, yet transformed and perhaps mitigated by the realization that the possibility remains, without Knecht's person. For Knecht is the true work of art, and his life and thoughts remain for our consideration. The novel proper is transformed into one of four incarnations. The starkness and despair of the novel proper is held in suspense while the urgency of man's plight is repeated, earlier themes are asserted once more, and the desolate vision becomes instead a question: must it be? May it not be that Hesse's vision of the direction life is now taking may be changed, somehow, some way? The revelation of possibility, insofar as we are awakened to its horror, *may* bring with it the seeds of its own prevention. Perhaps.

I shall not repeat the earlier themes which are exemplified in the poetry and incarnations. Hesse portrays the danger of life and the obligations of responsibility and service, the ever-recurrent need for personal sacrifice before which only the weak quail. The strength provided by spiritual discipline and education too is repeated, in visions of the possibilities in which men rise to something higher. Fear and desperation are inherent and inescapable in the life of man. Hesse simply portrays ways of meeting them. Above all, the incarnations represent spiritual nobility from which we can learn, and through which we can be restored, if we are despairing at the plight of man revealed in the novel proper. Surely mere fatherly advice could not so provide as can Hesse's tales. Through great visions of the human spirit, gathered from three poles of human experience, Hesse repeats the elements of the novel proper. And through all runs the main theme: that the true art is that of forming human life itself—in living beautifully. All spiritual achievement is a means to that end.

# 9

## *The Trial*

## *by Franz Kafka*

What are we to make of this hauntingly disturbing, yet quite dispassionately-written book? We see Joseph K. traduced, arrested, investigated, perhaps persecuted, and finally killed, in a strange and peculiar manner. Nothing in the novel really makes literal sense. Yet the novel makes altogether too much sense if it is a novel about man and the world he lives in, particularly, though not only, the world of the twentieth century. There are many deeply symbolic novels—such as *Finnegan's Wake*—which arouse in us the response "what does it mean?" What does the novel mean as a whole? What do the sentences mean individually? What is the author getting at? *The Trial* too compels us to ask for an explanation— but what is remarkable here is that we do indeed know what is meant and we can explain what is happening. Here our difficulty is not that we cannot make sense of the novel, but that it makes *too much sense,* it means too much. And we wonder if its ability to evoke so many moods and interpretations does not at once provide its enormous power and effect, yet render its content opaque and unintelligible, even inconsistent and paradoxical.

*The Trial* possesses a unique kind of ambiguity in meaning —one which may well be called "conjunctive" rather than "disjunctive" ambiguity. Like all great works of literature, it is many things at once, means far too much to be translated into any other form without great loss. Most symbolic novels function on different levels, and in reading a work of literature we are called upon to recognize these various levels and to interpret the work by considering all of them. But these different levels are *alternative* ways of interpretation. For example, one may read William Golding's *Lord of the Flies* as an adventure story of boys on an island, or as a Hobbesian-Freudian revelation of the impulsive and destructive in man, or as a parable of modern society and the forces within it. It is indeed all of these at once, but we can only read it as making sense on each level individually. The interpretations are perhaps consistent with each other; but each of them is quite apt on its own. One is led to interpret the novel in one or another mode, but not all at once. In short, one need not be interested in the adventure story, and yet lose almost nothing of the content of the novel. The boys and the literal events that concern them are in a sense the vehicle which Golding uses to reveal something more profound. The latter, however, if it exists on different levels, does so disjunctively: the novel means one thing *or* another.

*The Trial,* however, is very different. Its meanings come together, and cannot be separated. All of them together comprise the "meaning" of the novel, the philosophic position Kafka wishes to reveal to us. And just in case we are inclined to be bewildered by the multiplicity of possibilities within the novel, the seemingly disparate and incompatible images evoked by it, Kafka goes out of his way to warn us that much more is going on than appears on the surface. For in the only scene that seems superfluous, recondite, and overly intellectual—that of K.'s encounter with the priest at the very end, just before he is taken and killed—we are very carefully instructed as to what the mode of multivocity of the novel is. Oddly enough, just because we are told so late, we must reread the novel directly if we are truly to understand it. For until this moment the reader has been able to make sense of the novel only in the usual way—by thinking through fairly coherent modes of interpretation one at a time. It is bewildering to be warned that this approach, so satisfactory elsewhere, is quite inappropriate here.

The parable which Kafka uses to tell us of the peculiar multivocation of *The Trial* is virtually self-explanatory, and I shall touch on it very briefly. What I wish to do is relate the parable to the novel as a whole, finding within the novel interpretations which fairly closely parallel those given for the parable. I will conclude by explaining just what these multiple meanings imply, and shall show as well that Kafka has indeed a very profound point to make about man and the condition in which he finds himself—one which virtually no other mode of expression could have captured so well.

A word of warning must be given, however, before proceeding. Many highly persuasive interpretations of *The Trial* can be found in critical literature. In general, the critical articulation of a work of literature is a valuable and aesthetically rewarding achievement, and is usually enhanced by forthrightness and conviction. Ernest Jones's interpretation of *Hamlet* is to my mind all wrong; but its narrowness, idiosyncratic vision, and dogmatic repudiation of alternatives is its very strength. It is wrong, but *Hamlet can* be read that way. My own reading of the play has been enhanced by the personal force of Jones's view.

However, just because *The Trial* offers not alternative possibilities of interpretation, but multiple interpretations to be grasped together, a given interpretation, however persuasive, can suggest a unity of understanding that is utterly alien to the novel. The response, *"perhaps* Hamlet does indeed covet his mother" can only enhance the richness of the play. The "perhaps" has positive force here. I wish to suggest that there is no such "perhaps" in the modes of interpretation appropriate to *The Trial*. All of them are indeed proper to the novel. It means them all at once, together. In short, beware of the disjunctive notion of "perhaps" in interpreting this novel, where new possibilities of interpretation add to the richness of aesthetic response. I shall explain why.

### *The Parable* (T267–269) [1]

The priest is trying to tell K., without great success, that he has failed to grasp his situation and the function of the Court. K. does not understand or believe the priest. Finally the latter, in order to reach K. as he has not been reached before, tells him of a tale pertaining to the Law which characterizes K.'s delusion. A man desires entrance to the Law and is denied it by a doorkeeper, who warns him that he will prevent him from entering. The man tries to bribe the doorkeeper and fails, and spends his life waiting for the restrictions to change. Finally, he asks "how does it come about, then, that in all these years no one has come seeking admittance but me?" (T269) As the man dies, the doorkeeper replies: "no one but you could gain admittance through this door, since the door was intended for you. I am now going to shut it." (T269)

Since it is quite clear that *The Trial* is itself as a whole a parable, we have here a parable within a parable, one we need to guide us to an understanding of what Kafka is getting at in the novel itself. We must then look very closely at the interpretations of this smaller parable to determine which are applicable to the larger one, and how.

K.'s response is immediately, "so the doorkeeper deceived the man." (T269) [Interpretation I] [2] And indeed this has been his continual response to the strange situation in which he has found himself during the novel. "The doorkeeper gave the message of salvation to the man only when it could no longer help him." (T269–270) The priest, however, replies: "don't be too hasty. . . . He was not asked the question any earlier." (T269–270) And goes on to defend the dutifulness, integrity, and generosity of the doorkeeper. The suggestion, of course, is that if the doorkeeper was honest and even kind to the man, then it was the latter's complete responsibility for having waited and wasted his life without putting his final question earlier. In short, it is the latter's responsibility for failure; he was not deceived. [Interpretation II]

But this is not the definitive interpretation, the priest continues, only an opinion on the matter. "There even exists an interpretation which claims that the deluded person is really the doorkeeper." (T273) [Interpretation III] K.'s response here is remarkable, for he admits "I am inclined to agree that the doorkeeper is deceived. But that has not made me abandon my former opinion, since *both conclusions are to some extent compatible.*" (T275) [my emphasis] "The doorkeeper's deceptions do himself no harm but do infinite harm to the man." (T276) I emphasize K.'s recognition that the different interpretations are not incompatible with one another because that reveals the kind of multivocation Kafka is employing. K. recognizes this, but is not capable of drawing the appropriate conclusions from it. Finally the priest concludes, "many aver that the story confers no right on anyone to pass judgment on the doorkeeper . . . to doubt his dignity is to doubt the Law itself." (T276) [Interpretation IV]

K. does not understand what he has been told. Perhaps, however, we who are not so personally involved as he is can do so. I shall present now interpretations which fairly closely—though not perfectly—parallel the ones given above. At the end I shall explain what this all adds up to.

## Interpretation I: K. Persecuted

"Someone must have traduced Joseph K., for without having done anything wrong he was arrested one fine morning." (T3) What an incredible way to begin the novel, immediately confronting us with the impact of accusation, betrayal, arrest, and the question of innocence. The key words here (in this interpretation) are "without having done anything wrong." K. is innocent, a very ordinary man (a bank clerk) who has bothered no one, behaved like everyone else, but who suddenly is singled out for accusation. All of our fears at unjust accusation are aroused in our identification with K. Can we not imagine ourselves caught in a web of circumstantial evidence, "framed" for a crime we did not commit? Mystery writers love to work with this theme, just because of its natural appeal. Our hackles rise when we hear of the rare, but unfortunately quite real cases of men who have spent their lives in jail for crimes they did not commit. The themes of guilt and innocence resound in the opening line of the novel. We are put on the alert.

The twentieth century offers us another mode of approach to the problem of persecution and injustice. The rise of massive bureaucracy frightens us with the very real possibility that we will become numbers on a card, ciphers dealt with in mechanical and unfeeling ways. Errors once made will circulate forever within the system, dooming forever the individuals concerned, with undetectable and unredeemable accusations. The man whose credit card is denied is not told why. The man whose references are poor is refused a job without comment or explanation. The whispered allegation of sexual or political deviation condemns without chance of public hearing or confrontation. Totalitarianism, we all know, condemns the innocent without concern or rationale. The Jew taken to a concentration camp, that faithful Bolshevik purged for political deviation, could not have grasped the reason for their persecution. The mighty talons of a State indifferent to the individuals who live in it descend without animosity upon occasional individuals to destroy them, often without reason, without purpose, almost indifferently.

The huge modern State, democratic in its gross processes, can be as indifferent to the lives of some of its members, and can take its toll without thought or feeling. K. is but a solitary man in a world indifferent to individuals, and may well be crushed by it without concern. Of course, the forms must be and are preserved. He will be accused and tried. But the absurd trials K. faces are not more absurd than those found in Nazi Germany or the old witchhunts in Salem, Massachusetts—to the innocent. One of the qualities of innocence in the face of accusation is the utter absurdity, irrationality, and despair which surround the attack. "I am innocent, so why am I persecuted?" But there may be no answer to that question; the whirlwind denied one to Job.

One of the remarkable qualities of the Nazi concentration camps was their capacity, by virtue of unintelligible and inhumane procedures, to degrade their victims and render them incapable of genuine moral disapproval and opposition. Once they were arrested for unknown crimes—and however loyal and patriotic they might have been—herded into cattle cars like animals, stripped naked of all their possessions, how could Jewish prisoners have retained any sense of themselves as men capable of withstanding a powerful state-machine devoted to destroying them? Many of them were only one-half or one-quarter Jewish, not so by choice but birth, based on long-forgotten records. Many were local Germans. At least political prisoners could understand why they were incarcerated, an understanding that could provide the strength to resist. K., like the politically loyal quarter-Jew, cannot comprehend what has happened to him. And his decline and resignation at the end are quite natural consequences of his persecution.

It is crucial in Interpretation I, then, to recognize K.'s innocence of anything that would count as a human crime. He has broken no laws, intentionally or otherwise—that is, no laws that anyone could have been expected to know of or understand. No one explains to him just what he is guilty of. He is innocent, and condemned for something unreal, imaginary. Lost in a bureaucracy of the most overpowering kind, K. seeks to comprehend what is unintelligible, for he has been picked for destruction without rhyme or reason, to suffer without concern or care. Utterly without malice—even with occasional pity or compassion—he is destroyed by a bureaucratic machine that works according to inhuman rules.

How else can we understand the first confrontation with the Law, in the person of menial and empty-minded men who are all too ordinary, rather than dignified officers of the Law? In general, policemen are usually very ordinary, although their circumstances often call them to be something more than average—in incorruptibility, courage, and responsibility. The men do not understand or condone his arrest; they are only doing their duty. (As the German soldiers stationed in concentration camps explained: they were only carrying out orders.) Remarkably, Kafka has the warders appropriate K.'s underwear, an omen of the total appropriation of all vestiges of personal property among concentration camp prisoners.

Furthermore, K. claims that he does not know this Law, prompting the reply, "he admits that he doesn't know the Law and yet claims he's innocent." (T10) So too, the "unfit," condemned to sterilization by Hitler's proclamations of law, might not have found it possible to know the Law, yet were guilty nevertheless. Under totalitarian or bureaucratic persecution, one can always be found guilty.

We are told that "K. lived in a country with a legal constitution, there was universal peace, all the laws were in force; who dared seize him in his own dwelling?" (T7) Yet is it not precisely our discovery in the twentieth century that the price paid for a national state large enough to function in peace and with a secure legal system is that an occasional individual vanishes into the bureaucratic maw to be devoured without notice or outcry? The remarkable thing about injustice is that, individually speaking, it can occur almost in spite of law, peace, or courts of justice. Statistically speaking, we may live in a country of order and justice. Few innocent men are convicted of crimes. Yet to the remaining few, the general peace and order must seem all the more irrational and cruel. The larger modern society becomes, the easier it is to lose a single individual in the morass of respectable statistics and general well-being.

I have described K.'s condition as one of innocence, where he is persecuted by a cold and inhuman bureaucracy. But the key issue is not the source of the persecution, but its very existence. Surely the parents of a kidnapped child feel as strongly: why did this happen to me? The statistics of crime, their own possession of wealth, though seemingly quite relevant are still completely beside the point so far as their feelings are concerned. They know that some innocent men are unjustly condemned; they know that some innocent people are murdered; they have heard of kidnapping for ransom. Still, when it happens to them, it is not "explained" by any statistical facts. It is the sheer lack of a particular reason for it happening to a particular individual at a particular time that is so debilitating and paralyzing. After all, K. is not imprisoned; he is arrested but allowed to go about his business freely. How strange! And how remarkable that this does not diminish but enhances the feeling of persecution. What can he do? Where can he turn? Something very important has happened to him, and he cannot understand how or why. Nor is there any way out.

From the point of view of this interpretation, K. alone in the society in which he finds himself is aware that he is innocent. Most other people are too apathetic, resigned, or confused either to care or to believe him. The adage "where there is smoke there is fire" seems to be their maxim, though not to the point where they articulate it as a gossiping woman might, but rather in their empty and unquestioning way. In modern bureaucratic society, we leave the workings of the Machine to those in charge of it, and seldom worry about the details except during a major breakdown.

K.'s first interrogation takes place absurdly on the top floor of a tenement building, but only K. within the novel recognizes its absurdity. The participants in the drama accept the sequence of events without hestitation or demur. Though nothing concrete has yet been revealed, we see how accusation will come to cause K. great confusion, how it will render him incapable of doing his work at the Bank, bewilder him, and break him down. K. tries to explain to the whole audience in court how innocent he is and tries to make them understand the irrationality and absurdity of the whole proceeding, as a sane man might have tried to reach the master of the Inquisition, with utter failure. He is told nothing but "today—you may not yet have become aware of the fact—today you have flung away with your own hand all the advantages which an interrogation invariably confers on an accused man." (T60) No wonder all K. can find to reply is the shout, "you scoundrels, I'll spare you future interrogations." (T60) No one really can see that the proceedings are a farce; no one will believe his innocence.

He looks around him and sees nothing but corruption. The woman he finds in the courtroom the next week gives herself without question to the Examining Magistrate. Her husband tolerates this without objection. Surely K. is in the right, and the entire system, with all its degradation and corruption, stands against him to crush him. The very atmosphere of the offices of the bureaucracy suffocates him, as if to tell him that protest is of no avail. The usher who takes him in has already told him "as a rule all our cases are foregone conclusions." (T77) How can K. possibly fight back and win? The very air he breathes seems no longer to sustain him.

It is not necessary to dwell on the details of Interpretation I. A persecution takes its toll; and K. is a broken man long before his final murder. He discovers that though he is at first quite innocent, everything he does to save himself rebounds to his guilt. His protest against the warders who first arrest him leads only to the accusation that he caused them to be beaten. Utterly dismayed at this unexpected further accusation, K. casts about to save them, almost coerced into accepting his own guilt. Absurdly, though there seems to be no alternative, he hires a ridiculous and useless lawyer, who talks about great work and tasks but accomplishes nothing. The lawyer makes no definite claims, talks of pleas and rejoinders which are never read, and demonstrates clearly to K. his own ineptness and uselessness. How else can an innocent man's advocate appear to him when he is confronted by hidden charges which everyone, including the lawyer, accepts as true? K. looks about and sees nothing but a man, Block, like him accused, whose life has become a vain pursuit after the will-o'-the-wisp of his case. In frustration, K. dismisses his lawyer—his empty, posturing, and inept lawyer—and we see that he is doomed. He was doomed from the very beginning.

For has he not been told very clearly by the painter Titorelli, who is part of the Court in some inexplicable fashion, that there is no genuine hope? There are but three possibilities for an accused man: definite acquittal, ostensible acquittal, and indefinite postponement. If he is innocent he will be definitely acquitted—according to the Law. But Titorelli has never heard of a case of innocence. So everything is prejudged, and K. is doomed. All he can do is find a way within the bureaucracy to postpone the judgment of his guilt —to play along with the System, as it were, though he cannot understand how it works. His fate, as it was in the beginning, is in the hands of others. And since he cannot bring himself to trust what he cannot grasp, he eventually dies, a broken man, incapable of resistance, incapable even of suicide, incapable of functioning in the affairs of his life.

## *Interpretation Ia: K. as Hero*

Interpretation I stresses K.'s helplessness and decline before the amorphous and monolithic bureaucracy which seeks his destruction. He may well be thought of as a mediocre, ordinary man, caught in the toils of a persecution without reason or intelligibility, which crushes him. We are horrified at K.'s fate because we fear it for ourselves, insofar as we recognize our own lack of heroism, and the possibility that we too can be crushed by our surroundings at any turn. Anyone may be so destroyed, indifferently as only a modern State or Nature herself can, quite dispassionately, in a manner befitting nothing more than an insect—as in Kafka's *Metamorphosis,* perhaps. The great machine of society crushes in its maw the ordinary, without hatred or malice, without regard for personality or individuality. It is K.'s utter anonymity—even namelessness—that makes us sympathize with him, and take his fate to be our own.

But *The Trial* can be read somewhat differently, within the context of the same general interpretation. For despite the hopelessness of K.'s fight against the forces arrayed against him, however vain his abortive efforts, however inevitable his doom, he is not content to go along with the absurd just because others do so. He refuses to conform to what he cannot understand, though others urge him to. He does not accept his fate at the hands of the System without fighting back, albeit hopelessly and vainly. In other words, K. deserves more of our respect than Interpretation I suggests. It implies only that we pity K., an ordinary man destroyed so cruelly and irrationally. Like the man of the parable of the doorkeeper, who remains for all of his life waiting for an opportunity to enter, who tries his best, even to offering the doorkeeper bribes, K. fights back to his utmost, affirming his innocence to the end.

Thus we may notice that K. protests quite directly the heavy-handed manner of the warders. "How can I be under arrest? And particularly in such a ridiculous fashion?" (T9) He "felt he must put an end to this farce. 'Take me to your superior officer.' " (T11) Where an ordinary man, like Block, would be cowed and frightened from the very first, wondering if he had indeed committed some awful crime without knowing it, K. has great conviction of his innocence and demands his rights as best he can. He fails, not as a mere insect, but as a man must fail, beaten by superior forces.

At his first interrogation, he is quite sarcastic about the charge, the court, the whole proceeding; he notes the corruption in the Law and the "misguided policy which is being directed against many other people as well. It is for these that I take up my stand here, not for myself." (T53) How can we but respect K. in his denials, his reproaches, his pursuit of justice? How can we not esteem his search for understanding far above the self-abasement of Block and the others who accept what they do not understand? What we need in a bureaucratic and indifferent world are men who demand understanding as their right, and we honor them if some are tragically destroyed by that which refuses them.

K. seeks to save the washerwoman from her corruption and tries to make her oppose the man who covets her disgracefully. An undistinguished, passive, and unresisting tool, she will not heed him. Surely here he represents strength of mind and resistance to tyranny, rather than acceptance and fear. The bureaucracy functions irrationally and mercilessly; K. is the hero who seeks to make it face itself. His failure is one of ability, not of effort or will. He is even compassionate in seeking to stay the whipper from his task. He demands that his lawyer be clear and rational, though the Law according to Huld is strange and his own efforts beyond the comprehension of the ordinary man. Finally, not afraid to stand alone, where everyone else capitulates and accepts the world with its absurdity and senselessness, K. fires his lawyer and will prepare his own case. He will not bow before what does not deserve his respect.

And in the end, still sure of his innocence but broken in spirit by the failure of his efforts, he dies. But they cannot bring him even here to condone what is being done by killing himself. He will not testify against himself, thus justifying the system. They may kill him; but they will have to do it themselves.

## Interpretation II: K. Guilty

It is possible to defend precisely the opposite of the above interpretation—K. is no hero but quite to blame for his misfortune. For as he is clearly told, over and over again by everyone who seems to know something about the Law, innocence will persevere, and he will be acquitted if he is not guilty. It would seem to follow, then, that many paths could be found along which he might escape his doom, and that his final death is but a form of capitulation, not the tragic end of a hero or the destruction of a man of ordinary accomplishments. But perhaps I should not oppose this interpretation to that in which K. is viewed as a mediocre and common individual in a modern bureaucratic society, for it is precisely the average man who suffers the passivity and emptiness of vision that leads to an empty and useless death.

Thus K. at no time formulates a coherent and forceful reply to his accusers. Rather, he wanders through the novel expending his energies furiously but to no avail. He protests his innocence at the beginning to the warders, who can neither help nor are interested, and when he could not possibly know of what he is accused. He feels persecuted when he is treated quite fairly and straightforwardly, if a bit strangely. He is not taken into custody, but allowed to pursue his own affairs, to prepare his case if that is what he desires. His feelings of outrage may be legitimate, but they are premature and even destructive under the circumstances.

At his interrogation, he prepares no defense of any sort, fails to seek out the grounds for his arrest, and simply rails at the court. He is quite uninterested in the truth of the matter—that he might have committed some lapse without being aware of it—and endeavors only to win over the audience to his side. He is late, perhaps because he is unable to find the Court under those peculiar circumstances, but definitely late. Yet it doesn't disturb him at all. His speech is mostly irrelevant, and quite hostile to the Court—which if legitimate deserves some respect—and quite maliciously cruel to the warders who arrested him first. He doesn't understand what is going on, *and doesn't really want to*. He sticks to his own preconceptions of what justice should be, and nothing can change him. No wonder the Magistrate tells him: "today you have flung away with your own hand all the advantages which an interrogation invariably confers on an accused man." (T60)

Worst of all, K. expends his abilities uselessly, seeking approval where truth and guilt or innocence would seem to be of major importance. He pursues all the women he encounters, somehow taking them to play important roles in his case. Here it is plain to see that he refuses to take the arrest seriously. It is not the truth of the matter that concerns him, but whether these women hold him attractive or not, persecuted or not. His most active phases occur in confronting Fräulein Bürstner, in whose room he had no right to be; the washerwoman, who is another man's wife; and Leni, who loves him only because he is an accused man. Whenever he faces his accusation directly, he becomes paralyzed—as in the offices of the Law, in confronting the whipper, before the painter Titorelli, and finally at his death. And he well knows it, for his last thought, that he has died "like a dog!" is quite true. He has met his end no more forcefully or directly than a dumb beast.

The painter tells K. that if he is innocent he will be acquitted —though implying also that no one has ever been acquitted. What follows from this is that K. is guilty; but he never faces that possibility, and simply goes through vague, insignificant motions that occupy the time till his death. In a way, he is given all the rope necessary to hang himself, while there lurks throughout the sense that if he is only wise or brave, if he accepts his lawyer or the rules of a Court he doesn't even try to understand but which everyone else accepts, he will prevail, and even learn something. It is not that he is caught and killed, but he kills himself by his lack of patience, lack of courage, and unwillingness to face the possible truth about himself.

### Interpretation III: Internal Confrontation

The door in the priest's parable has been kept open for the man only, and will be closed when he dies. Moreover, the priest offers us one interpretation of the parable that it is the doorkeeper who is deluded. Can we read this without raising the question whether the entire confrontation between the man and doorkeeper is not a very strange one, perhaps not even between two people at all, but a personal, internal confrontation? Perhaps the door is open only as a possibility for the man; only he can enter it or keep himself from entering it. In short, it is possible to view *The Trial* as an internal dialogue, in which K. fights with no one but himself. This surely is suggested by the dream-like quality of the writing, the black and white, yet very clear imagery, the relentless and consistent illogic of the events.[3]

The beginning now takes on a very different tone. K. is "arrested" on his thirtieth birthday *in bed*. The place of this arrest is surely very important, suggesting to us that all the ensuing events take place in a dream, and that the entire novel takes place in K.'s mind, while he remains in bed. The word "arrested" can mean official apprehension—but K. is arrested quite peculiarly from that point of view. He is not really charged with anything or taken to jail. The point is that the word "arrested" can also mean "stopped." On his thirtieth birthday, in his sleep, K. discovered (perhaps unconsciously) that he had ceased to develop, ceased to grow, that he has somehow been arrested in development, that he has become a stagnant personality. Here his thirtieth birthday is very important, for this is just the age where a man is too old to be considered a youth, and yet is not too old to change, to recognize whether he has lived up to his hopes, aspirations, and ideals.

After all, what kind of man is K. at the beginning of the novel —not to mention later on? If his reaching thirty brings him to look closely at himself to discover what kind of man he is, what does he see? He is unmarried, childless, apparently friendless as well. He has no home, no family ties, lives in a rooming house. He knows no one well, has found nothing of great significance which gives character to his life. A cabaret girl is the only woman in his life. He has no apparent ambitions—to be rich, famous, even to share his life with someone else. At most, he wishes to be Manager of the Bank— a rather sterile ambition for a man of thirty with the whole world to choose from.

K. is thus an empty shell of a man, and at thirty years old. He has no great ideals—though we could forgive him for that if he had some vital or magnificent passions, great drives, perhaps a bit of eccentricity. He is, however, a mere cipher. There is nothing in the world that depends on him, no one who loves him or needs him. Perhaps the only place he accomplishes something is the Bank. And what we discover in the course of the novel is how even here he is quite dispensable. He could vanish without a ripple and no one would care. The world is for most men a cold and indifferent place, and some find ways of marking within it a place that is unquestionably theirs. Otherwise it is unbearable. K. has appropriated nothing of it to himself. He is in effect utterly alone and bereft of any ties. And he has discovered this in himself at the age of thirty.

All that follows, then, within the novel, are events within K.'s consciousness as he seeks to discover some genuine and vital basis on which to be related to the world he lives in. He has confronted himself—has found something of great importance wanting—and must find something that can justify his life. Put another way, the title of the book—*The Trial*—means not only an investigation or inquiry, but a *test*. There comes to most men a moment of doubt in their being, their value, their reality. Here K., on the surface without any value at all in the world, even to himself, is tested by some part of him: can he find a way of relating to the world meaningfully? Is his life worth living?

The nature of the events of novel marks the dream-like quality of K.'s self-confrontation vividly. Kafka's style of writing is drab and colorless, quite dispassionate and dry, extremely detailed without being vivid. Most dreams possess this very quality. Events occur, with their own logic, often in great detail, yet without color or vitality, as if noted rather than felt. Kafka's style retains these elements completely.

Moreover, the events of the novel seem quite matter-of-fact, yet from a normal point of view they are absurd and ridiculous. K. is arrested in his bed; the warders steal his clothing; the court of inquiry is at the top of a tenement building; the air of bureaucratic offices, found in the attic of the tenement, causes K. to become faint, unable to move in the oppressive atmosphere of the place—though others function quite well there; and the warders are whipped in a back-room of the bank—though no one knows it but K. The last scene mentioned shows most vividly that what is occurring must be thought of as internal, not taking place in the public world, and I shall examine it in detail.

The entire whipping scene has the quality of a full-scale hallucination, or at the very least, the edge-of-consciousness forebodings that mark an utter nervous collapse. Walking down the corridor, K. hears sighs *in the Bank*. How absurd! Yet he opens the door of a lumber room and confronts a scene utterly incompatible with the reality of a cold and austere financial establishment. If this is not a dream itself, it is nevertheless some psychic manifestation, a hallucination to be found nowhere but in the mind of K. Whether dream or insanity, this scene reveals that K.'s mind is breaking down. Something is coming to the fore that he has up to now refused to confront.

The warders are to be whipped because of K.'s testimony in court that they took his underwear—and there is no doubt at all that he did so accuse them. Have we not here found something for which K. is indeed responsible? No: "I never complained, I only said what happened in my rooms." (T104) K. simply refuses to accept responsibility or blame, though he is willing to admit that he did what these men say. "I had no idea of all this, nor did I ever demand that you should be punished, I was only defending a principle." (T105)

K. thus is confronted, in his own mind, with consequences of his own real or imaginary actions. He might have faced himself and taken responsibility for what he had done. He might well have agreed the warders deserved punishment, for he had accused them. But K. only blames the organization. He does try to bribe the whipper; but afterwards thinks only "it was not his fault that he had not succeeded." (T109) He does wonder if a higher bribe might have not prevented the whipping. Still, "at all events, he could have done nothing but slam the door." (T110)

These phrases, "it is not my fault," "I couldn't help it," and the like, marks K.'s willingness to rationalize everything, and his refusal then to face himself and the character of his life and actions. He has been *arrested*—but it is everyone's fault but his own. He couldn't be guilty. Why then does he need a lawyer? Yet the remarkable thing about having a lawyer is that one must live continually with one's case. Block, after all, has six lawyers. As he puts it: "I daren't ignore anything that might help me. . . . I've spent every penny I possess on this case of mine. . . . When you're trying to do anything you can to help your case along you haven't much energy to spare for other things." (T216) What a warning K. is given by some secret part of himself: over and over he is told to face himself, commit all his energies to his case and save himself. Yet we notice that he becomes as passive and exhausted as Block, without the strength of the conviction that he is helping himself. His end is no murder, but the expiration of a mere cipher who has no ability to be vital and human. He challenged himself and lost.

K., deep within his own psyche—in a dream or not, it doesn't really matter—finds himself an utter failure, a man whose development has ceased, and who is warned by some hidden source of energy that he must find the strength to return to life, to find meaning, to succeed according to some lights, or he is lost. Amidst the normal affairs of his life, which continue without cease or change, K. discovers confrontation after confrontation, all of which he fails to meet. His encounter with Fräulein Bürstner is his first direct encounter with a woman—and almost an insane, delirious one. He throws himself upon her, quite without her approval or consent, in the middle of the night in her room. Here is a perfect indication of the breakdown of K.'s defenses, his irrational and absurd—perhaps insane—behavior. The strains deep within his personality have become too much to bear. Everything he does or witnesses is a warning to him that something is very wrong—*in him*. A man collapsing under nervous strain—going insane, as it were—must have the same sense that everything is wrong around him, incapable as he is of seeing that the illogic and irrationality is in himself. K. seeks a rational accusation, something he is truly guilty of, and fails to find one. But surely he is guilty of *something;* and when we look at him closely, which he never does, we see clearly how empty and meaningless his life is.

K. begins to break down on all other levels as well:—for example, he is incapable of doing his work at the Bank. The emergency signal of his unconscious warns of something seriously wrong, and warns as well of an impending total collapse. If K. cannot meet that warning, it is inevitable that he will collapse. He feels some enormous compulsion (though it may be but a dream) to face the accusation, but so absurdly that he really faces nothing—only exhorting and ranting against his accusers, who in this case are but himself. Finally, when all else has failed, when he has given up the fight and is virtually a broken and defeated man, he is told by the priest quite clearly and straightforwardly, if only he can try to understand, just what is happening. But even here, he fails to grasp what he is told. For he is bewildered and disjointed, suffering a nervous collapse, unable to muster the strength to survive. Everything is opaque and enigmatic to him, though not to the others. He knows something is very wrong, but cannot grasp it. What his lawyer tells him is obscure and unintelligible—somewhat like the interpretations told a very sick man by a psychiatrist must sound. Kafka succeeds in creating a perfect atmosphere in which a true paranoiac would live—persecuted and beset by others, yet without rhyme or reason. And as in the case of the paranoiac, the real problems and persecution come from within, not from the world that has become so strange.

Here, then, K.'s final end marks his utter failure. He cannot choose to live or to die. He is killed, knowing that it is "like a dog," for he has lost the ability to live like a man. Some kind of strength—to fight himself, the world which oppresses him, to face his wasted and empty life—is required if he is to persevere. And his failure is due precisely to the lack of this strength.

## Interpretation IV: The Hidden Source of the Law

If *The Trial* is viewed as an internal confrontation, it may be understood in a wholly different way from the one given above, in which K. is accused by some inner voice that he has lived an empty and wasted life, and is an utter failure. The key to this other interpretation is to be found in the words of the priest: "the story confers no right on anyone to pass judgment on the doorkeeper. . . . It is the Law that has placed him at his post; to doubt his dignity is to doubt the Law itself." (T276) This utterly monolithic conception of the sanctity of the Law and its officers suggests two modes of interpretation, one an internal authority, in which the irrationality of the events of the novel retains the quality of Interpretation III above; the other the most complete external authority—that of a Divine Will.

*A.* Interpretation III views K.'s life from without, and recognizes the emptiness of his choices and the sterility of his accomplishments and goals. Here K.'s failure is real one, one he is incapable of coming to grips with. The most horrible thing about psychic conflict, however, is that there is no simple way to tell if one's self-accusation is legitimate or not, for the very internalization of one's guilt renders it opaque to rational considerations alone.

Imagine, then, that we accept the Freudian conception of an utterly irrational set of desires and impulses—the *id;* a principle of rationality and reality, which seeks to oppose those desires of the id that are destructive to the person involved—the *ego;* and a mechanism for transfering external sanctions and punishment into internal guides to action—the *superego.* The latter is what concerns us here, for it alone is related to guilt and innocence. Parental disapproval, according to Freud, is internalized as principles of right and wrong, utilized to control the dangerous instincts of the id. A mechanism like a conscience, though often working unconsciously and quite as irrationally as the id, acts upon the powerful instinctive impulses to harness and control them. And the energy the superego works with is guilt.

The ordinary person is thus a composite of various elements, one of which is a repository of parental and social sanctions from which flows guilt inevitably. Every man is at least partly a creature of frustrated desires and anguished hopes, and only guilt and shame can control the unintentional and dangerous release of hidden passions. Thus some degree of guilt and shame is necessary in any civilized man. Freud speaks in his early writings of a workable balance of the parts of the personality—one in which id impulses are redirected or *sublimated* into useful channels—and in his later writings of the danger of too-powerful a superego. But it seems clear that in all men the price paid for functioning in society and among other men is fear, shame, and guilt.

Let us, then, think of K. as perhaps an average man, but whose superego is of great strength—a likely hypothesis for a German Kafka might have in mind. In other words, imagine K. to be a man who experiences shame and guilt, as do all men, but to a somewhat greater extent than many. Here it may be said that *The Trial* takes us into the phenomenology of guilt and shame, the peculiar byways of feeling that are the working of the civilizing aspects of the human personality. This interpretation is justified by Kafka's own enormous involvement with his father, and his perpetual sense of shame at the kind of person he himself was.

The remarkable thing about the superego's authority is that it is quite irrational and unalterable—except perhaps in psychoanalysis. A man who feels guilt may know only that and no more—not its source, its object, or its justification. In fact, since all men covet their mothers in orthodox Freudian psychology, a fundamental degree of guilt for this unacceptable lust is necessary to all adulthood. It is no wonder that K. seeks in vain to understand the source of his arrest, the nature of his accusation, the right of this Law to judge him. The Law is the law of the human psyche; its rules vary with time and circumstance, yet are utterly binding on the personalities upon which they work; the accusations are often relics of parental authority, indefensible yet utterly powerful. It is perfectly true that if K. is innocent he will be acquitted, for one feels guilt and shame only if one has indeed done something shameful. The point is, however, that the nature of the human condition is such that no one can avoid guilt entirely, and thus complete acquittal is quite impossible. Man is therefore doomed to guilt and torment by life itself, without any real hope for peace of mind without guilt. K.'s arrest is but a condition all men share—an amorphous anxiety without definite object upon which to retaliate, without rationale to which to reply. The trial that K. experiences is life itself—the cost of being an adult. He, however, either has not the defenses to resist or is condemned by his early life to too powerful a set of superego sanctions. The word "condemned" here is fundamental: though not *originally* his fault, K. is condemned anyway, by himself, for being what he is.

*B.* This condemnation without appeal, a condemnation for what one is though in some sense one is not the cause of one's own being, is a form of *original sin*—one from which there is no escape. It is extremely plausible, then, that we consider as a last interpretation of *The Trial* the sense of belonging to a world created by a Divine Will whose word is Law, whose understanding is beyond comprehension, and from whom utter damnation or eternal salvation flow. This would explain the omnipresence of the Law, its appearance in weird and wonderful places. God is omnipresent, and His will can never be escaped from. That is how a tenement can be a Court, and a painter part of it. Here we must set aside the Catholic sense of the Church as intermediary, which can provide salvation for men if its teachings are followed. We need here a personal sense of the confrontation of God and His will by a particular individual, doomed through the doctrine of original sin, unable to *earn* grace, yet who is offered it as a genuine possibility though he will be doomed without it.

In fact, let us carry the interpretation one step further—to that of a man doomed to eternal pain and torment for what he is, yet aware that he has not sinned particularly often or maliciously, that his failures are but weakness, and that he is not really to blame for lack of strength. We can imagine a defiant Lucifer, doomed to eternal Hell, taunting God by all the sins he can commit. But K. is considerably less daring than that, and much more compliant. He seeks no great sin, is not malicious or evil. He is an ordinary man, with ordinary desires and tastes. But he is, like most ordinary men, weak enough to commit some sins, and may be doomed forever for them. Is he really guilty? Is he to blame for not having been given the strength to resist temptation? How can the world, in which guilt and sin have so fundamental a place, be grasped rationally?

What will the Day of Judgment feel like to those sinners cast off on the left? They see their neighbors saved, but they are damned forever, though both have lived pretty much the same kinds of lives. This sense of dismay and injustice is very much the same as that feeling which accompanies all personal catastrophes: why have I been singled out? Why did this happen to me? Normally, there is no answer possible; the futility we feel is bad enough. But where the world is viewed as rational, governed by Law, its events are too much to bear. Utterly incomprehensibly, the Divine Will fashions and molds. We cannot defy, so we whisper. A priest tells K. that he doesn't understand—exactly as the whirlwind told Job. But it *cannot* be understood, we want to cry out: except that if there *is* a God, perhaps it can—though not by man.

The focal point of all these interpretations is the problem of guilt. Through the creation of a parable that has not one, but many interpretations all dealing with guilt and responsibility, Kafka not only achieves a very powerful aesthetic creation, but points out some very important facts and judgments concerning guilt. The point is that if all the interpretations are correct simultaneously, then when put together—something that can only be accomplished in a novel like *The Trial*—they add up to something of great importance. I shall try to express this, however awkwardly, in a nonliterary form.

All of the interpretations touch on the notion of guilt. Let me put forth Kafka's thesis as something like: "Life is hell; and guilt is its primary torture. But without guilt, life would be impossible." The novel itself shows how guilt functions and the difficulties that arise concerning it. What Kafka actually achieves in the novel is a fusion of multiple visions of human guilt and innocence in which can be found attitudes and feelings central to the problems of life. On the one hand, in the search for the Good Life we find the suggestion that guilt (the willingness to accept responsibility and blame) is a quality of life that provides strength and vitality, that through the possibility of moral failure and subsequent guilt one can be a morally praiseworthy person. On the other hand, we have the claim that guilt is but a form of torment, one which certainly will be eliminated in a perfect world.

The latter view can be put in more modern terms. Guilt today, for example to psychoanalysts, is often thought of as an emotion accompanied by the worst excesses men are capable of, one which exists in the human psyche only at enormous cost. The neurotic individual is one who experiences guilt for everything—for forsaking his parents and their values, for desiring a woman, for being guilty, for being a failure, even for being alive. What he has to learn to do is *not* feel guilty, to be able to be angry at injustice without guilt, to live without feeling blame for everything that he does, ashamed of being what he is. The human psyche is so much a function of guilt that the psychoanalyst can very plausibly propose that a healthy man is not a guilt-ridden one, but a self-assured, comfortable (I hesitate to say "adjusted") one.

However, without recognition of past failures, and the awareness of the possibility of future mistakes, an individual has no capacity to change and develop. If one's failures inspire nothing but indifference, they cannot possibly be the source of deliberate moral action. Yet if one cares deeply about one's failures, one can only come to feel some species of guilt for them. To have failed to help a man who needs it is to have harmed him. If he actually dies, that lapse was indeed a grievous one. How can a man respond to his deeds with concern and evaluation without the realization that he will indeed commit some such lapses, with the consequence of feeling guilt for them? The remarkable quality of German soldiers who assisted in the atrocities committed in concentration camps was the fact that even when they disapproved of the camps and the practices that went on inside them, they felt so little guilt for their own contributions. The ability to find excuses for one's conduct, at the expense of guilt, is the ability to avoid moral confrontation. If they had experienced more guilt for what they did, they might have possessed the ability to fight the orders they disapproved. Guilt is remarkably close to the vital energy a hero needs to resist.

Guilt, then, is an extremely dangerous emotion, one which causes pain and suffering, even personality disintegration in extreme cases. But even more horrible are men incapable of feeling guilt, for they become incapable as well of moral judgment in any but routine ways. The ability to change, to give up an older mode of behavior for a new, to admit to past mistakes, depends upon the ability to experience guilt or remorse. Only the mediocre, the empty and passive, can exist without the capacity to feel guilty for their mistakes. Adam and Eve ate of the tree of knowledge and felt shame. Before that they were pure innocents, quite without genuine moral capacity. Guilt is the horrible feature of the human condition without which man is incapable of moral judgment and righteous deliberation—either because he is too innocent or too depraved. It may well be that the greatest human incapacity is that of being incapable of experiencing guilt. For then one is bereft of grounds for moral judgment.

The Trial, then, exposes K. in all the complexity of his position—a position all men share with him. He is accused on all sides by forces completely out of his control—his society, his God, his inner self—of crimes he cannot understand, for they may be contradictory, irrational, part of an infinite scheme of perfection beyond his capacity to understand, or hidden deep within his own psychic mechanisms. He cries out his innocence, and we sympathize with him, for in the face of such unreasonable demands, defiance appears the most noble course of action. His doom is from this point of view a genuine tragedy—of a Promethean hero who defies the gods, the world, the limitations of his own mind.

But when accused of crimes which are not precisely stipulated, is any man innocent? Surely the judgments of others are central to a man's appraisal of himself. However much we seek individuality and idiosyncrasy, inner-directedness or heroism, these must not be confused with license, with sheer defiance of social norms, with rebellion and nonconformity for its own sake. Human beings grow and develop within social contexts which provide them with rational standards by which they can judge their own actions. No one can isolate himself entirely from the language and judgments of others. Tools of language, rational analysis, and of moral appraisal, come from a social context, and that social context cannot be abandoned entirely. It is not possible for everyone to be wrong—at least not in the world we live in. K. must be wrong, perhaps insane, if everyone understands something he is quite unable to grasp. He is a heretic, damned without hope if he defies God—and what is his defiance worth if it is of a true and genuine God? Finally, if one is confronted with one's own breakdown, given internal messages and warnings, is not one going insane? How can a man tell if his internal crises are a development or a disaster? How can one stand alone without feeling shame, and wondering if he is insane? Yet is it not quite imperative that men be capable of doing so?

One cannot tell the difference between insanity and heroism —that is the impossible problem involved here. The human capacity to feel remorse is both man's greatest asset and his most monstrous infliction. And it is never really possible to find perfectly clear indications which of these it is any concrete case. One's most sacred convictions—the source of moral heroism wherever it appears —may be nothing but the fruits of a diseased mind. One's self-development and growth may be nothing but a rebellion against parents or even God. We are called upon both to be heroic where necessary, *and* to recognize the continual possibility of being totally in error; to be humble before divine authority but to defy those who oppress us; to recognize deviation as an evil or a weakness, but nonconformity as strength of will. When all is said and done, man is trapped in a context of guilt and shame which provides no standards of any ultimate kind. He is tested, yet everything he does counts as a failure by some standards. Shame is his companion; guilt his closest friend and most hated enemy; anguish his continual scourge.

*The Trial* is a novel of mystery, and thereby touches on the inarticulate, the unintelligible, the mysterious in life. Among the deepest mysteries of all is the mystery of guilt and responsibility, for we are always being held to account for transgressions we do not understand, for deep-rooted motivations we know not of, for feelings we cannot control. Guilt is a continuous torment for men; yet without it, how can they be responsible for their deeds? That mystery has no intelligible answer, which is why men have turned to religion when confronted by it. Yet Kafka finds that the solutions of religion are quite as mysterious as that which they propose to resolve, which leaves us, from the standpoint of the novel, we know not where.

Something should be said in conclusion about the philosophic level *The Trial* functions on. Earlier (p. 24), I referred to Kafka's writing as "metaphysical," by which I wished to suggest that the generality of his concern, and the pervasiveness of his insights, are of great metaphysical significance. Perhaps a few more words on this notion would be appropriate here.

Most novelists of philosophic aspirations portray ethical values embodied in persons and events of their novels. *The Brothers Karamazov, Magister Ludi, The Stranger,* and *The Princess Casamassima* all emphasize problems of value or responsibility, of decision and deliberation, evil and sin. This is by no means a trivial matter, nor is it a narrow or overly particular one. Value permeates man's world, and every moment of life is filled with the need for choices and deliberations. Insofar as novelists concern themselves with man and life—the central elements of literature to be sure—ethical matters are inescapable. Human life is indeed a matter of evaluating and judging, and an exploration of the possibility of a unified order in the values of life (*Magister Ludi*), the nature and inescapability of judgment (*The Stranger*), the fundamental irresolution in moral confrontations (*The Princess Casamassima*), can have consequences of the widest kind within human life. There is nothing narrow or shortsighted about novelistic exploration of the ethical in human life.

Philosophers have often, however, dealt with more general issues than these—more general in that they concern not man alone, nor particular *kinds* of moral judgments, but the nature of Being itself, or slightly less generally, the nature of man, of life, of consciousness, perhaps of judgment. I am referring to what is usually called "metaphysics"—the investigation of the most general and pervasive characteristics of what is, either most generally as in Aristotle's analysis of Being in his *Metaphysics*, or somewhat less generally as in Locke's *Essay on Human Understanding*, insofar as that concerns the nature of understanding and what can be understood, rather than what simply *is*. Metaphysics continually strives for the most general traits it is possible to discern, and may be found within fairly narrow and specialized domains just insofar as they seek the general principles upon which the specific rests. Metaphysics is more of an impetus than an achievement—an impetus toward the most pervasive principles of order and explanation, rather than satisfaction with a settled and circumscribed subject matter.

In this last sense, Kafka's *The Trial* is without doubt a metaphysical novel, not *about* metaphysics—the display of others' views —but *in* metaphysics. It explores some of the most pervasive characteristics of human existence, perhaps those upon which value and judgment rest. It is sometimes said—by Aristotle, for example—that metaphysics is the study of First Principles. *The Trial* (and *The Castle* too) are in their own way analyses, exhibitions, or portrayals of the fundamental elements in human consciousness out of which the more specific traits arise. Where Dostoievski explores the suffering of men and their desperate inability to live well, where Hesse investigates the resources of men to be found in the spiritual life and all its contributions to man—both highly important, but fairly definite and specific characteristics of life—Kafka reveals the primordial condition of man, the welter of need, accusation, authority, disorder, and alienation that underlies the more specific elements of human life and consciousness.

It might be said that *The Trial* has little or nothing to say about ontology—Being in itself—in its most general aspects. Like all novelists, Kafka is fundamentally concerned with the human aspect of existence. Yet it may be pointed out that his emphasis on the human is no more restricted in generality that Sartre's *Being and Nothingness* or Hegel's *Phenomenology of Spirit.* In the latter, Hegel reveals the condition of existence to be the adventures of Spirit in things—where Spirit is nothing but consciousness aware of itself for itself. To Hegel, the moving force in history, in time if you will, the rational aspect of Being, is self-consciousness or embodied Spirit working its way to complete awareness and mastery of itself, thereby transcending the fundamental dichotomy between consciousness and its object. Hegel's metaphysics, which is the discovery of Reason in things, is nothing but the revelation of the order things have within and for the consciousness of man. *The Trial,* it seems to me, is not only general in many ways just as is Hegel's *Phenomenology* (though I grant, by no means as synoptic in its vision, nor as comprehensive in its analysis), but also like it emphasizes phenomenological awareness—the being of consciousness to itself, the fundamental elements of human judgment. Both explore the constituent elements of human consciousness: authority, freedom, order, the relation of the individual to the more general. (And I might mention again Sartre, whose fundamental metaphysical category too is Being for itself or consciousness, and who also seeks to analyze the unique and general characteristics of that mode of Being under the guise of metaphysics.)

In fact, a case might well be made for the claim that *The Trial* marks a metaphysical critique of Hegel's metaphysical system, on the level of generality necessary for such a critique—perhaps even a critique of all rationalistic conceptions of being which find an ordered relation of man to Nature. Unlike most rationalists, who sought a permanent and intelligible order in Nature, Hegel saw whatever order existed to be an order in becoming, not being—a pattern could be found in the evolution of things, a pattern within which dichotomy, conflict, and schism have a place. Thus to Hegel, order always exists *amidst* disorder, Spirit works its way to fulfillment through the most spasmodic, chaotic, and violent events. Hegel's repudiation of the classical tradition was based on its acceptance of a static and unchanging Reason, which had thereby to be opposed to the irrelevant and spasmodic events of life. Still, Hegel assumed an order in things—in history rather than in permanent Being—which man should and would become part of. He replaced a static sense of the Ideal by a developing Spirit working through history. But he maintained a sense of order amidst disorder.

What Kafka shows in reply, however, is that consciousness is fundamentally and apparently quite irrevocably torn asunder by its primary elements. What is wrong with human life is not the simple alienation Hegel speaks of—the desire for what is forbidden, the awareness that what is lacking in life is forever unrealizable, even the fundamental alienation of the civilized and natural elements in man. Such dichotomies, Hegel argues, can be surmounted by a proper development of philosophical awareness (a difficult enough thesis to accept). *The Trial,* however, reveals human consciousness to be not so much dichotomized as fragmented, not so much torn asunder as utterly inconsistent with itself. It is not that man is an ambivalent and fragmented creature, who yearns for incompatible alternatives. A change in conscious awareness might ameliorate that situation. Rather, it is the nature of being human itself, its very demands and fundamental limitations, that is chaotic, disorderly, and unresolvable. It is not a failure *in* man, that he fails to meet the demands of some ideal. It is a failure in any and all ideals—that they necessarily either make impossible demands on men, or lose their capacity to function as ideals. To exist as human is to strive toward something—be it divine or simply some natural ideal of self-realization. But the very existence of such goals is and must be a torment to consciousness—thus contradicting their very purpose of existence. And if the ideals are eliminated, then men cease to function humanly, and life becomes devoid of meaning.

More specifically, human consciousness is a perpetual awareness of, coping with, and attempt to escape from guilt, remorse, and confrontation. And it is not weakness in men that makes guilt so terrible: it is the nature of guilt itself. For either one triumphs over remorse and shame—and becomes incapable of self-confrontation and challenge, isolated from social values and judgments (like Meursault in *The Stranger*)—or one becomes party to guilt and suffers the torment of failure. Hegel's optimistic solution to this condition depends on self-conscious awareness of one's being. Kafka's revelation of the true nature of that self-conscious awareness is utterly the most frightening thing possible to contemplate.

# 10

## The Brothers Karamazov
## by Fyodor Dostoievski

*The Brothers Karamazov* is, as the title tells us, a novel of a family, a father and three or four sons. Other characters influence them and are influenced by them, and in some respects represent some very important aspects of Dostoievski's views. Nevertheless, I feel that the most illuminating presentation of the philosophic aspects of this novel can be reached through the consideration of the members of the Karamazov family individually. It is, of course, true that Dostoievski puts in the mouths of some of his characters very long and important speeches of great philosophic import—the most famous of which is the Grand Inquisitor tale Ivan recounts to Alyosha. However, I shall discuss such speeches not isolated from the body of the novel, but within the context of the kind of man Ivan is. For what is remarkable about Dostoievski's literary technique is that the philosophic remarks of some of his characters are at times less to be taken as representative of some intellectual position than they are to be viewed as indications of the kind of men who utter such words. Put another way, Dostoievski is capable of such intricate and subtle construction that the position the reader is led to is often radically different from that of any of the explicit philosophic and moral speeches given in the novel—all the more remarkable when one considers that Dostoievski often worked incredibly quickly to produce serialized versions of his novels.

### Father

The novel begins with Fyodor Pavlovitch Karamazov, a natural beginning providing the history of the family and giving us the background of the novel. This history, however, is a remarkable one in the picture painted of a father whose sensual lusts are enormous, and whose corruption is virtually endless. Fyodor Pavlovitch is horrible enough in himself, a man most of us could do very well without encountering outside the pages of a novel. But he is also the father of a number of sons (I regret the hestitation with which I state the size of the Karamazov family, but it seems to me that the ambiguity of Smerdyakov's parentage is a genuine one, despite all the hints given by the narrator, and I prefer to preserve some element of doubt in exposition), among whom we may find a richness of alternatives coupled with a common background and nature that can well justify a reader tentatively viewing them as representatives of mankind. In Alyosha the gentle and saintly, Ivan the intellectual, Dmitri the passionate and noble, and Smerdyakov the ambitious and selfish, we see a wide range of kinds of men, children of a common father of the worst possible kind. From the very beginning the Karamazov family represents in concrete form one version of the doctrine of original sin, without the theological paraphernalia. Man is not doomed so much because of a sin in a distant past, but because men are born of fathers and mothers, and *the sins of parents are indeed visited upon their children,* from generation unto generation. Once given the desperate plight of man in any generation, and once we recognize that any new generation will be born of the flesh and raised to the values of that older one, then we are led to the desperate possibility that the plight of men will never be overcome. The lusts and passions of Fyodor Pavlovitch are passed on directly to his children, and they cannot escape them. We are all human, and if our ancestors could not find a way to peace and righteousness, how are we so very different as to expect that we can? *The Brothers Karamazov* begins with this very bitter sense of human life, and in most respects never forsakes it.

I have spoken of the Karamazov family as representing mankind. But that is an oversimplification of a very important kind. Surely the four types represented by the sons do not exhaust all human possibility. Most human beings are not as brilliant as Ivan, as nobly passionate as Dmitri, as gentle and saintly as Alyosha, or as self-interested as Smerdyakov. In fact, the Karamazov family is writ quite large, far grander than life-size. Their lusts are greater than an ordinary man's, as are their torments and their insights. Perhaps this was the quality of Russian life at the time Dostoievski wrote, though it is very difficult to believe this when we consider Dostoievski's secondary characters, who are often pale and unreactive by comparison (though they too suffer from a milder version of Dostoievski's sense of human torment). No, it would seem that the Karamazov family is at once all men in their suffering and pain, and also men of extreme and extraordinary qualities. In his own way, Dostoievski is seeking a hero, a solution to the desperation and anguish of life (if there is one, and there may well not be). Such a solution is not to be found within the weak and cold, the prosaic and ordinary, for a number of reasons. First, though the common man suffers pain and torment too, the small size of his passions does not require a "solution" of any extraordinary kind—while where his passions are indeed grand, he too becomes uncommon and vital. Second, ordinary men sway with fortune and circumstance, sometimes content, sometimes anguished; they do not carve out solutions to human problems, but are more controlled by history than in control of it. It is the great men of passion, intellect, and ambition who create history, who are driven by their needs and mold the world to meet them, who qualify as the heroes upon whose shoulders mankind climbs to the stars. In his quest for life and peace, man is always larger than ordinary. The ordinary man only sits and waits.

It is clear that *The Brothers Karamazov* is a book concerned with fundamental moral needs and goals. Within it one can find most great moral options set forth and evaluated. Plato rests the Good Life on the control of passions by reason, but Dostoievski's characters *cannot* subdue their powerful emotions; that is their desperation. Ivan, the man of intellect if not of reason, is perhaps the most desperate. It is of no avail to recommend a policy that men cannot adopt in the weakness of their natures. Epicurus seeks escape from confrontation, in a peaceful life of rational pleasure. But Dostoievski shows that withdrawal, as in the monastery, only displaces human passions; it does not eliminate them. Stoics and utilitarians advocated radical social participation, to render human society fit for man, worthy for him to live in; Dostoievski replies to that with Rakitin, the selfish and ambitious reformer. In short, other philosophical alternatives are set aside by Dostoievski as *external* to man, as attempts to put men into situations within which they would find peace of mind. But men are not able to *find* peace, at least not in external circumstances. The only hope for man is within himself, in an inner resolution or strength that brings fulfillment and happiness with it. When all is said and done, of course, this is Plato's and Epicurus' view also. The point is that until man is viewed without blinders, programs offered to save him are always vain. And when we so view him, we may suddenly realize the possibility that programs *cannot* resolve human difficulties, for men are too anguished and twisted to be saved so simply.

There is one alternative which Dostoievski never takes up explicitly: that of creating by education and psychological conditioning a *new* man, free from the lusts and passions, desperation and anguish, hatred and jealousy that ordinary men suffer from. Perhaps it is because he cannot believe that men *can* be so changed. Perhaps the Karamazovs do represent a necessary condition of mankind in that sense. But perhaps there is something far more important at stake here: that the nobility, passion, and brilliance of the Karamazov brothers is the price to be paid for a new man, and that it is not worth paying it, even for peace and contentment. In short, to those who propose a solution to human ills that depends upon radically changing the nature of man, the reply may well be not that it won't work—for it just might—but that the price to be paid is all the glory and beauty of man, and that it is too great a price to pay. This point will be pursued further in discussing Alyosha.[1]

Fyodor Pavlovitch, then, is father to the brothers Karamazov, and in a sense the original source from which they come, the heritage of flesh and lust that belongs to all men. Granted, he is an extreme version of life's temptations and cruelty, but not so extreme as to be wholly inappropriate. When Ivan discusses the torture of children subjugated to cruel parental whims, when Dostoievski portrays the humiliations and pain men heap upon one another in their desperation in the chapter entitled "Lacerations," we see that the picture of Fyodor Pavlovitch is not false or out of place, but an illuminating caricature of the world we all live in. It is not so much that Fyodor Pavlovitch is at all inhuman, but that too much evil is laid upon one head.

Yes, Fyodor Pavlovitch is certainly evil, if evil exists at all. By ordinary moral standards, he is contemptible and hopelessly corrupt. As Dostoievski (or the narrator, who is not really the author) tells us, he "was a strange type, yet one pretty frequently to be met with, a type abject and vicious and at the same time senseless." (BK3) [2] A toady, yet a miser, "one of the most senseless, fantastical fellows in the whole district." (BK3) He married a beautiful heiress, appropriated her dowry, was beaten by her—surely the depths of weakness and degradation in a man—and was finally abandoned by her. He immediately gave himself up to orgiastic drunkenness, coupled with tearful explanations of his abandonment. She died of typhus or starvation —and we feel pity for her having met so miserable an end as this man's wife. We are told by the narrator, who is never certain about some of the most revealing aspects of character in the novel, that upon his wife's death Fyodor Pavlovitch probably "ran out into the street and began shouting with joy," and *also* "wept without restraint like a little child." (BK6) What a loathsome and disgusting man is this. How degraded! How evil!

But if this is evil, what a manner of thing it is! The problem of evil has long assailed philosophers who sought rational visions of order and harmony in the universe. What of evil? The traditional reply has been that what appears evil to men is only that from a narrow and finite point of view. From a wider perspective, all is for the best. This is the best of all possible worlds, in which good and evil balance each other. To Dostoievski, however, evil is real and important. It assails Ivan and drives him to despair. Pity and suffering permeate Dostoievski's novels. More, perhaps, than any other author, Dostoievski reveals a sympathy for man and his feelings that generates pity for the worst excesses and deepest degradation.

Dostoievski certainly shows us Fyodor Pavlovitch as an evil man; but when the picture is completed, we are left with far less revulsion than pity, less hatred than sadness—an awareness that if all men share something of Fyodor Pavlovitch, the latter is kin to even the best of men. One of the themes of Dostoievski's writing is precisely the exploration of evil, a profound study of its nature and characteristics. Svidrigailov, in *Crime and Punishment*, is surely a corrupted and loathsome seeker of young female bodies, driven by insatiable lusts. But he possesses as well a strength of character and a yearning for goodness amidst the imperative demands of his worst side that leads him to commit suicide before he has wholly abandoned himself to degradation. Fyodor Pavlovitch—unlike Svidrigailov

and Milton's Satan possesses no grandeur, no defiance, and is virtually beneath contempt. He is without redeeming qualities of any
kind; but he is nevertheless human, with human complexities and
needs. Loathsome as he is, he wept at his first wife's death. As abomi-
nably as he treated them, he desires his sons' affection.

In the most telling scene of all, which takes place right at the
beginning, just after the introductory history, we see this disgusting
old man in action before his three sons and Father Zossima. And we
gain great insight into his character, an insight that cannot but
modify our judgment of the nature of the defects of this old man.
Fyodor Pavlovitch starts execrating himself before Father Zossima:
"I always say the wrong thing. Your reverence, you behold before you
a buffoon in earnest." (BK44) He goes on babbling quite repulsively
and embarrassingly, yet insulting himself quite readily: "I am an
inveterate buffoon, and have been from my birth up, your reverence,
it's as though it were a craze in me. I daresay it's a devil within me."
(BK45) "I play the fool, Pyotr Alexandrovitch, to make myself agree-
able." (BK46) As the narrator tells us, everyone who visited Father
Zossima before this did so with the greatest delicacy. Fyodor Pavlovitch, however, is indelicate, even horrible.

But the nature of his evil is explained to us at the same time.

> I always feel when I meet people that I am lower than all, and that
> they all take me for a buffoon. So I say, "let me really play the buffoon. I am
> not afraid of your opinion, for you are every one of you worse than I am."
> That is why I am a buffoon. It is from shame, great elder, from shame; it's
> simply over-sensitiveness that make me rowdy. If I had only been sure that
> every one would accept me as the kindest and wisest of men, oh, Lord, what
> a good man I should have been then. (BK47–48)

And if we look ahead to Book IV, called "Lacerations," we can understand that Dostoievski is showing us that evil and malice, destructiveness and cruelty, are always the result of an inner desperation that
men cannot cope with. This is probably more a psychological claim
than a philosophical claim, and not a novel one, though Dostoievski's
insights into the mechanisms of defense and hostility have not been
supplanted by psychoanalytic theory. It is the claim that men are
driven to cruelty and hatred only when they cannot live with themselves; that malice is an outgrowth of desperation and internal tur-

moil; that the malicious and cruel are often the men who suffer the most.

Thus in "Lacerations" we find Fyodor Pavlovitch nasty and vituperative toward Ivan and Dmitri, for he fears the loss of the girl he lusts after. We see a group of schoolboys furious at the boy Ilusha, viciously throwing stones at him. And we later discover just how miserable the boy is, how his own unhappiness drives him to attack everything he holds dear. Alyosha visits Lise, who clearly loves him; but we discover much later that even she is compelled by her own internal needs to drive him away. We see Ivan and Katerina in fury and hatred; for they too are unhappy. And return again to the boy whose father is forced out of desperation to beg, then hates himself and the world.

In brief, evil and destructiveness are not so much cold and rational qualities, but desperate outbursts from desperate men who find no inner peace. And since their own destructiveness can inspire others and render them desperate in return, we have the vicious circle that is life, from which there appears to be no escape. Here there is no genuine evil, no devil to blame, only misery and despair. Fyodor Pavlovitch, the worst of them all, is but a buffoon, desperate for respect and approval, and driven by this need to act in ways that make all respect utterly impossible. The novel does not lead us to condemn him so much as to pity him and regret his misery—though we do not by any means forget his destructiveness to everyone with whom he comes in contact. The point is that Dostoievski reduces his malice to corruption, his hatred to degradation, and we feel not so much righteousness as pity for the natural forces at work which create so much misery and pain. It is easy to be revolted by what Fyodor Pavlovitch does; it is not so easy to censure him—for that would amount to condemning him for suffering.

Dostoievski accepts so much of the doctrine of original sin, as found in Christian theology, to preserve the *dualism* at the heart of that world-view. Man is a creature torn by spiritual yearnings and physical corruption. Beset by lusts and passions of the most irresistible power, men nevertheless strive for something higher. At the heart of the worst men are elements of the best; and the best of men are bound to the physical corruption which is the heritage of mankind. Even Fyodor Pavlovitch is cognizant of the spiritual elements in life—and therefore cognizant as well of his own feelings toward them—and recognizes them for what they are. He denies God's existence, yet recognizes that what God represents is everything beautiful and good, even to himself. His own life is a failure by his own standards. To Dostoievski, all men share an essential goodness; they differ only in how much the other side of their dual nature is in control. Even Smerdyakov, as self-interested and malicious as he is, seeks truth above all else, and upon discovering how vain was his act of murder—as Raskolnikov discovers in *Crime and Punishment* too—kills himself.

The recognition of the dualism at the heart of man cannot but transform our conception of evil. Particularly where love is central, as it is to Christianity, the predicament of man caught between two incompatible forces within himself compels our sympathy more than our hatred or contempt. Dostoievski's sense of man torn asunder by competing elements is not new; like Plato and even Freud, he reaches a similar position on human responsibility and freedom. The Grand Inquisitor, who seeks to save men by eliminating their spiritual conflict *at any price,* represents one genuine aspect of this view— that men suffer all too much to be condemned for their failures.

Fyodor Pavlovitch is the worst of all men: the worst of fathers, lovers, friends, companions, the most debased of men. Yet as human, he arouses only pity: for he too pays for every crime by his despair and longing. What he desires he succeeds most in making unavailable to himself. Though we are not really shown his heart, we can guess it fairly well. If we ask, ready to condemn him, "is it not his fault?" we must hesitate in answering: how could it be; is he not incapable of any degree of self-control? Evil and responsibility fall to nothing beside such a vision of man.

For we can hold men responsible for their deeds only when they are in some genuine sense in control of them. Fyodor Pavlovitch and Dmitri are men whose passions are beyond coercion, to whom self-control is utterly meaningless. To hold Fyodor Pavlovich responsible for his actions is as rational and justified as holding a stone responsible for its fall, a tidal wave for its devastation. It takes a cold and unpitying regard for mankind to disregard the despair from which malice flows, and judge the malice independently. We cannot read Dostoievski with so dispassionate an attitude.

## Alexei Alexandrovitch

We are told explicitly that Alyosha is Dostoievski's hero, in the introduction and many times in the text. The novel begins with him in the introduction, continues with him immediately after the history, and ends with him. Yet Alyosha remains throughout a pale, unbelievable character—particularly by comparison with his brothers. This is a very important fact about the novel, and one which merits careful analysis. If Alyosha is Dostoievski's hero, then it is rather clear that he marks Dostoievski's solution to the human plight revealed by Fyodor Pavlovitch and his other sons. We must, then, determine what kind of solution Alyosha represents.

Alyosha is the younger legitimate son of Fyodor Pavlovitch and Sofia Ivanovna. His mother is "A meek and gentle creature" (BK10), married at sixteen, innocent and beautiful. Fyodor Pavlovitch "took advantage of her phenomenal meekness and submissiveness . . . and carried on orgies of debauchery in his wife's presence." (BK10-11) She "fell into that kind of nervous disease which is most frequently found in peasant women who are said to be 'possessed by devils.'" (BK11) Now this possession to Dostoievski was very close to a divine gift, at once a prize and a curse, an illness and a sign of great purity. Prince Myshkin of *The Idiot* suffers from epilepsy, a mark of his purity and a source of his persecution. The simple and loving, the meek and the humble, are persecuted and destroyed by the passionate and corrupt men among whom they live. This most of all seems to be Dostoievski's sense of Christ—that the pure will be destroyed. Possession was to Dostoievski at once a curse and a gift—for it marked the purity and innocence that made the possessed victims.

Alyosha and Ivan were this gentle creature's children; they inherited her innocence and meekness. But Alyosha was also his father's son, with his passions and lusts. To Dostoievski, this union of purity and corruption, of gentleness and passion, of submissiveness and lust, is the source of Alyosha's enormous strength. In this union he finds the salvation of man, at least so far as that salvation can be said to exist. Alyosha is not a simpleton as was his mother, no meek and cowed shell of a human being. A passionate Karamazov, nevertheless his passions are transformed from the lusts and self-destructiveness of the other Karamazovs into love for them and peace of mind. In effect, Alyosha represents not the sheer humility which Christianity makes so much of, but a love that is self-affirmation and passion, though not of the destructive kind. In an extremely Nietzschean conception of saintliness, Dostoievski portrays humility and submissiveness as in reality dependent upon great strength. To Nietzsche, humility was but one form of the will to power, and he praised the saints for their will, but condemned their hypocrisy. Alyosha represents another version of that will—humility and gentleness dependent upon passions and feelings, not their absence.

Perhaps it may be said that most moral alternatives to desperation have been dependent upon either an unrealistic—because psychologically impossible—conception of goodness, or a heroic one which only very few men are capable of achieving. Thus Plato, despite the care with which *The Republic* is constructed to provide a place for all men, ultimately finds the only truly good life in philosophy: other men can only achieve that kind and degee of happiness appropriate to them, but the philosopher experiences the highest pleasure—of knowledge—and has his soul in perfect internal order, controlled by reason. Very few men are capable of philosophy, in Plato's sense. Although Aristotle, in Books I and II of the *Nicomachean Ethics,* conceives of happiness for man as a "life in accordance with perfect virtue," in Book X we discover that because the natural function of man is the exercise of reason, happiness is really contemplation—again, a way of life few men can achieve. Epicurus' saintly withdrawal from life depends on an ability to set worldly cares aside. Stoicism demands the ability to invest emotional energy solely in what is in one's power—a form of discipline that most men lack. Epictetus and Epicurus possessed a saintly nobility that simply cannot be expected of lesser men. In short, moral visions generally depend on the subordination of passion to something higher, in that way transcending and controlling the passions which render life so harsh. And to men whose passions rage fiercely, such visions are remote and empty.

Alyosha, however, represents a different conception of moral goodness, one not at the expense of passion, but dependent upon it. Dostoievski tells us of Alyosha's violent nature many times, and we are to understand that his purity is not a heroic or exceptional one, but one which arises from the same stock as the lusts of Dmitri, the bitterness of Ivan, and the selfishness of Smerdyakov.

Although Alyosha appears almost continually throughout the novel, Book VII is entitled "Alyosha," and it is here we may look to discover Dostoievski's conception of his hero. The book begins, however, with the death of Father Zossima, and we may realize just how important the monk is to Alyosha, and to our conception of him. It is worthwhile, then, exploring the role of the monk in the novel before returning to Book VII.

Clearly Father Zossima is a holy man, a man of great purity and goodness, even a man capable of miracles; surely a man deserving of great respect, if not reverence. Throughout the embarrassing confrontation with Fyodor Pavlovitch at the beginning, he retains a simple dignity that is impressive. He tells Fyodor Pavlovitch "above all, don't lie to yourself," (BK48) maintaining remarkable self-control. Everyone is embarrassed by Fyodor Pavlovitch's performance except Father Zossima, who is capable of very clear vision into the inner hearts of men. Upon meeting Dmitri, he bows down to him, and later explains: "I seemed to see something terrible yesterday . . . as though his whole future were expressed in his eyes. A look came into his eyes—so that I was instantly horror-stricken at what that man is preparing for himself." (BK339) With all his unworldliness and withdrawal from life, Father Zossima sees further than do most men into what surrounds him. In response to Ivan's clever claim that if the Church became the State, the threat of eternal damnation would prevent men from crime, Father Zossima replies that men need not more threats, but love, and the Church offers that only so long as it remains separate from the laws of the State. Men need understanding and forgiveness, not threats and punishment, for the latter only fail and add more horror to human life.

Shortly before his death, Father Zossima tells of his life before he became a monk—in particular that he was a young and passionate soldier, ready to fight a duel for an unrequited love and an imagined insult. Suddenly, however, he realized the futility of such life, not with bitterness, but with love, and refused to fire. Remarkably, he is scorned by many of his fellow soldiers for cowardice, really because they fail to understand him. Love and humanity are so wondrous that most men fail to understand them when they encounter them.

Shortly thereafter, Father Zossima is approached by a successful and wealthy businessman, who had murdered a rich and handsome widow in his youth, and cast suspicion on her servants. The man told Father Zossima of his crime, eventually announced his crime publicly, and was thought mad but died happy. So, Father Zossima seems to be saying, love for all men, and a willingness to struggle with one's base side, can bring one to redemption. All men, however depraved, have a good side; and all men, however good, must fight their base impulses. But through love and suffering, salvation can be gained.

Unlike most monks, then, who enter a monastery very young and virtually as an escape from the ordeals of life, Father Zossima is transformed prior to his becoming a monk to the point where he no longer *needs* withdrawal. Alyosha is quite like him in this respect— a man of passions, suffused with a love that transforms them into goodness rather than destruction. Thus Father Zossima tells Alyosha to leave the monastery, for he does not require it. A monastery is a place for men who cannot survive in the outside world, who achieve goodness by resignation and withdrawal.

This is made particularly clear upon Father Zossima's death, for although he has been considered so holy a man as to be capable of miracles, by some remarkable trick his body putrefies immediately —revealing to those monks whose faith is dependent upon miracles, or who are envious of Father Zossima's fame, that he has always been an imposter. In this manner Dostoievski shows us that neither miracles nor withdrawal are solutions to the plight of man, though a few mistaken men can find satisfaction with them. God will not appear before us with miracles in hand to show us the path to Truth. Rather, as Ivan recognizes all too clearly, the world is an absurd, irrational, and evil place, capable of defiling everything holy, reversing every expectation, rendering void every miraculous happening. It is in this kind of world that men seek salvation, not the simpler imaginary one in which God reliably sends His Word to lead man to peace. The arduous nature of irrationality confronts men; and many of them seek refuge in escape, to a simpler mode of life. The death of Father Zossima and the decay of his body reveal, however, that even the holy monk, within the walls of the monastery, can serve as a temptation to the ordinary man. If withdrawal is a refuge, it is no solution—at best but a temporary one.

It is Alyosha's reaction, however, that concerns us. He too has been dependent upon a naive faith in an orderly universe with rewards and punishments given only to those who deserve it. How could the body of such a holy man decay so quickly (though why it should not is quite unclear)? Alyosha's immediate reaction is one of enormous depression and disillusionment. Partly it is "that the man he loved above everything on earth should be put to shame and humiliated." (BK408) But there is something more—revealed by Alyosha's desire to go to see Grushenka. For he is seeking humiliation. When internally desperate, all men seek to debase themselves —the same message revealed in "Lacerations." Evil is a form of desperation. As he puts it, "I came here seeking my ruin, and said to myself, 'what does it matter?' in my cowardliness." (BK427) But he discovers something loving in Grushenka, and he is restored and uplifted. He returns to Father Zossima's coffin and finds "rapture, yearned for freedom, space, openness." (BK436)

Thus Alyosha is saved by love, and not so much by his loving or being loved, as by an example of love for another. Moreover, it is precisely as an example of someone who can love that he gives strength to the boys and teaches them to love as well. It is not because he loves them that the boys grow, but by seeing his love for others, watching it in action. At the very end of the novel, as Alyosha leaves, he tells them to love and remember love, not badness; and the memory of love will keep them from badness, or at least can never be corrupted. And the boys respond: "Karamazov, we love you!" "Hurrah for Karamazov." (BK939–940)

The love that Alyosha possesses and speaks of is something that must be examined. It is by no means mere passion or lust. In a way, *The Brothers Karamazov* is a study of forms of love, an analysis of different ways of loving. Dmitri, for example, is a man of passion and lust (as is his father), to the point where his obvious nobility of character is powerless to assert itself against his violent emotions. Dmitri loves particular people—women—in such a manner as to destroy his life and corrupt him and them completely. Ivan, on the other hand, admits he dislikes particular people—but he loves mankind, cares for human suffering, and is desperate because of it. This too fails to suffice, for Ivan's love is nothing but an excuse for passivity. Love in the abstract, but not in the particular, is absurd. Katerina's love is one of utter self-sacrifice; but that wonderful martyrdom becomes an obstacle that Dmitri cannot surpass. The ability to give love is a very difficult one—for so often the giving of love is but a form of control, injuring the person loved.

The love that Alyosha gives, however, is very different from all the rest. It is a cool and restrained love by comparison with Dmitri's, neither lustful nor possessive. Dmitri must possess the object of his love, and will move heaven and earth to do so. Such possessiveness is a violently destructive force, to everyone involved. It is not until Dmitri gains his loved one that he can cease his desperate search and become cognizant of the nature of human needs. Alyosha's love is, however, quite particular, not an abstract "concern" for mankind. He responds to particular needs of men, tries to comfort them. He is completely aware of their desperation and suffering, yet is not himself made desperate because of it.

Alyosha is thus capable of sensitive response to particular individuals, a genuine concern for their well-being, a sympathy for their suffering, with neither possessiveness nor bitterness at the inability of men to improve themselves. And it is precisely at this point that a number of doubts may come to mind, for the conception of man presented through Alyosha seems at times unbelievable. If Alyosha were meek and humble, without feeling, we could understand his lack of hatred and anger; if he became disillusioned and bitter at the failure of men to better themselves, we could sympathize with him; but his unselfish concern for others seems to depend on his being not a Karamazov (a normal, passionate man), but a saint. And if he is so unbelievable, we cannot accept him as a model.

Kierkegaard, in *Fear and Trembling,* speaks of Abraham's greatness when God asked him to sacrifice his only son Isaac. The narrator, Johannes de Silentio (Kierkegaard's pseudonym), tells us that he could understand Abraham if he defied God and said that no father could be expected to kill his son; or obeyed God with "infinite resignation" and disillusionment. But Abraham is exceptional because he obeys God with joy, willingly. What kind of faith must a man have to survive in a world of irrational coincidences and cruel hoaxes? What hope is there for men in a world of paradoxical demands, of unintelligible lapses? To Kierkegaard, faith is an absurd leap, a transcending of the universal into the particular, the recognition that law and principle can fail us, and the skill to persevere in a particular case where we cannot find anything but intolerable alternatives.

Dostoievski's solution, embodied in Father Zossima and Alyosha, is very similar, if not as triumphantly absurd. Ivan is the great rationalist; yet he is indifferent, even cruel, in particular cases. Rakitin is the great reformer; but he is a selfish, egotistical little man. Alyosha, however, has the capacity to love mankind in each and every case, without destroying himself or others in the process. Surely it is not impossible to imagine such a capacity. It is not absurd like Kierkegaard's leap of faith.

Yet an element of mystery remains, quite intentionally, I'm sure. For this is not only an ethical, but a religious solution that Dostoievski is proposing (perhaps there is to him no difference between them). Father Zossima is not only a good, but a holy man. I have already mentioned that Dostoievski explicitly rejects the role of miracles in man's religious life. The need for miracles is not faith, but its opposite—a faith that can only persevere if continually rewarded. Alyosha's faith persists in the absence of reward, amidst denial and suffering. Such a faith is a far more glorious thing.

The problem of religion—as distinct from that of theology, which attempts to rationalize the religious and place it in a system of categories—is to reveal to us the mysteries that religion accepts without explaining or destroying them, and to show us what such an acceptance can mean to one who accepts them. Dostoievski captures many elements of the mysterious—for example, in the desperation of Ivan in confronting a world of so little order and sense, and so much cruelty. We must love our fellow man though he be degenerate and malicious. Two replies are given to Ivan's questions by Dostoievski in the novel, both of which preserve some aspects of mystery and faith. One is the realization that men, however destructive they are, are indeed more in pain than triumphantly evil. This permits us at least a glimpse of the possibility of loving them despite their destructiveness. The other is the realization that Ivan, paralyzed by the irrationality of existence, is incapable of acting as men must, *if* hope is to be found. Thus without in any way eliminating the mystery—for Ivan's sense that the world is utterly irrational and absurd is quite correct—Dostoievski shows us that there are better and worse men, actions of greater or lesser promise, even amidst ignorance and despair. Love and faith are the only alternative to the anguished withdrawal from life that Ivan approaches—surely a religious even more than an ethical conclusion.

Another way of describing the problem of religion is to find the bounds to the rational, and to explain what faith offers beyond these bounds. To Dostoievski, rationality alone, in the kind of world we live in, leads to nothing but despair and bitterness—exemplified by Ivan. Only a faith strong enough to transcend the rational, to love with no reason, to worship even an unreachable and unintelligible God, can offer man a hope of escaping from his plight. In short, the very goal reason is dedicated to—the improvement of the life of man—is to be reached by faith instead.

Yet Alyosha is not credible. Perhaps it is because when all is said and done, his faith appears to us as absurd as Kierkegaard's knight of faith. But I am inclined to feel that the difficulty lies elsewhere. Alyosha is *imaginable:* he is simply not credible as a *Karamazov,* as a normal man. He is more akin to a god—and we can understand the return of Christ. But we cannot be expected to become gods ourselves.

In the prefatory "From the Author," Dostoievski tells that he really has two tales of the life of Alexei Alexandrovitch: "the main narrative is the second—it is the action of my hero in our day, at the very present time." (BKxx) In his letters he explained that he would make Alyosha suffer, and be redeemed through that suffering. For he realized that Alyosha was too pale, too unreal a character to represent a solution to the human predicament that he himself had described so well. Often he mentions in the novel that the lives of the characters will be continued in some sequel.

Now it is possible to treat the preface as simply raising certain questions concerning the novel proper, without necessarily implying the writing of a sequel. Thus, as Dostoievski puts it, "Still, he has warned us of something," and "having become acquainted with the first tale, the reader will then decide for himself whether it is worth his while to attempt the second." (BKxx) Read this way, *The Brothers Karamazov* must be taken as the novel which sets the problems and begins the solutions. And if Alyosha is unbelievable here, it is impossible to see how he could serve in a sequel without radical change.

The problem, I believe, is that we are not so puzzled by Alyosha's *being,* as by his *becoming.* That is, it is not impossible to imagine a man like Alyosha, a man capable of love and humanity, yet strength of character as well. Nor need we deny that *if* an Alyosha existed, he would have great influence on those around him—though I suspect that he would eventually find that he would pay a price for that influence which would end by destroying him, like Prince Myshkin in *The Idiot*. Nevertheless, saintly men have existed at various times in history, in almost all traditions, and have had enormous influence on those around them. Perhaps Dostoievski is portraying a true Christian—even a semblance of Christ himself—and we can recognize the beauty of the portrayal, and be convinced by the presumed efficacy of his actions.

But Christ was God, and offers no true model for men. The problem raised by the Grand Inquisitor is not whether there could be a Christ, but just what Christ means to ordinary men. If Alyosha represents something all men need, it is only in two possible ways. Either he is a great teacher, who by living and loving those around him inspires them and teaches them love and the way to contentment as well, as Christ did. Here he represents a model who by his very being renders those close to him like him. Surely that kind of charismatic effect is conceivable. But the appearance of such an individual would then be a kind of miracle—as is that of God giving His only son to man. Father Zossima is that sort of miracle—his tale of his early life is simply unbelievable. Where is there a sign that he retains any element of man's dual nature? Must we believe in the possibility of transcending the evil part of the soul? Dostoievski may be thought to be re-representing the story of Christ in modern dress, revealing to those who cannot understand the effect of true faith on others just what this is. Genuine love and humility are contagious: that is Christ's fundamental message. But if we ask how Alyosha *came to be,* we are left without an answer. He is but a miracle, and though we can imagine miracles, Dostoievski himself tells us that they cannot represent any kind of hope for man.

The only other alternative is that Alyosha is to be thought of as man transformed, originating in deepest degradation, a man of passion and lust, yet transmuted into one of faith and love. Father Zossima too tells us, in Dostoievski's reply to Ivan's bitter desperation as shown in the Grand Inquisitor scene, that he was once a man of violent impulses, whose confrontation of nature, of the harm his actions caused, underwent a complete transformation.

That is what a man has been brought to, and that was a man beating a fellow creature! What a crime! It was as though a sharp dagger had pierced me right through. . . . In truth we are each responsible to all for all, it's only that men don't know this. If they knew it the world would be a paradise at once. (BK355–356)

And although we can believe in a once-in-a-lifetime conversion, we cannot quite take this unto ourselves. For we all "know" of our responsibility and concern for all men. And there are enough occasions in everyone's life to bring him to that awareness, if it were at all possible to do so. The problem is that immediate needs preempt the remoteness of "all," and in particular cases we lacerate and destroy those close to us.

Father Zossima and Alyosha are beautiful representations of God on earth. But they are not men. Or if they are, they are so extraordinary as to provide but another form of the requirement that we must strive to reach the ideal with dull clay. The Grand Inquisitor accuses Christ of demanding heroism from men, and men cannot be heroes. Alyosha is another kind of hero; he is as rare and as noble as the best of men. Therefore, we cannot accept him either as a valid model, or as a genuine possibility for ourselves.

Alyosha fails as a model because he lacks passion. Although Dostoievski tells the reader that Alyosha's love is genuinely rooted in passion, we cannot believe it. Rakitin tells him, "you're a Karamazov yourself; you're a thorough Karamazov . . . You're a sensualist from your father, a crazy saint from your mother." (BK91) But it is not credible. Dmitri tells Alyosha: "all we Karamazovs are such insects, and, angel as you are, that insect lives in you too, and will stir up a tempest in your blood." (BK127) But although we can imagine Alyosha *becoming* a man of sensual lust, he would have to be very different from the man he appears to be in the novel before us. What is unbelievable is that ordinary and passionate men can *become* like Alyosha, or that Alyosha, without radical change, can experience lust and violent passion. Where is his desperation and despair? Where is his selfish need? How can men who are so rooted in torment become free of their violent passions? And do they really desire to be free of them? For Alyosha is not really admirable: he is in many ways a watery, rather unresponsive character. Dmitri and Ivan are far more vivid and vital. Is it not worth the price, vitality at the cost of pain? Or would it be worth achieving peace of mind at the price of passionate awareness?

Dostoievski tells us, when Ivan is collapsed in a coma, that he will awaken and be transformed by his sufferings. This we can understand, for Ivan has learned the brutally hard way that his cynicism is intolerable, that his rational awareness leads to disaster. Through the greatness of his mind and the violence of his moral passions, will he not awaken a man of violence tempered with reason, firmly against evil, passionately aware of other men's needs, rationally capable of judging what they need, and aware that active generosity is the only reply to the moral chaos of human life? Perhaps—though it would take another novel, even another novelist than Dostoievski, to make that credible. The point is that it could be understood, while Alyosha cannot. Even suffering cannot make Alyosha live for us, since he has not the soul for true suffering and change. To what would he change; and what would it mean?

## Dmitri

Dmitri is the oldest brother, the son of Fyodor Pavlovitch and Adelaida Ivanovna Miusov—his first wife. Not unexpectedly, then, Dmitri is a man of violent passions, driven by raging emotions. It is unquestionably true that a genuine nobility of character shines through the torment with which Dmitri surrounds himself, but it is for most of the novel completely overwhelmed by his anguish and lusts. He *gave* Katerina Ivanovna 5,000 rubles to save her father who had been using army money for profit and lost it. This incredible act of generosity, however, is but a hairbreadth away from his telling her that she was worth perhaps 200 rubles, certainly not worth 4,000. This is the secret of everything Dmitri does. He is capable of the most generous and noble acts—if he does not choose to be utterly loathsome and passionately destructive instead. And all his violence and torment is but one step away from nobility and generosity. He, more than any other character in the novel, is a paradigm of a dualistic creature, caught almost midway between nobility and unbridled lust. He is utterly incapable of self-control. But if the better side of him triumphs, he will be a noble and magnificent man.

Dostoievski's sense of human life, however, is nowhere as clear as in his recognition that the lustful and violent passions, even when generous and self-sacrificing, are in reality deadly in their effects. Dmitri's nobility of sacrifice for Katerina is matched by her equal willingness to sacrifice herself to him thereafter. She not only repays him, but loves him madly. "I will be your chattel," she writes.

"I will be carpet under your feet. I want to love you for ever. I want to save you from yourself." (BK137) Such willingness to sacrifice oneself for others, when it is the only mode of self-affirmation available, is a devastatingly destructive act, particularly because it is offered in the name of generosity. The altruistic act becomes the chains of bondage. So when Dmitri falls in love with Grushenka, he cannot but be tormented by guilt, anguished by the dependence of Katerina on him when he cannot respond to her, and violently angry at the existence of chains in the name of love that cause him guilt and self-degradation.

The love of Dmitri and Katerina is a possessive one, however altruistically it is garbed. Katerina wishes to sacrifice herself for Dmitri—but that willingness to sacrifice is an obligation created in the object of sacrifice. Katerina does not wish to make Dmitri happy, but to be the instrument of his salvation; and her desperate need to succeed blinds her to the realization that she is driving him deeper into perdition by her "love." Compared to this possessive and controlling love, Alyosha's is both weaker and far more successful. It offers without expectation of reward, without a need to possess and control. Alyosha seeks to give to men what they lack, whether recognized or not. This mode of love is something wonderful to behold and, I suspect, even more wonderful to encounter when one is lonely and in despair. It is at once a complete acceptance of the person, great sympathy, and a desire that the person be both happy and good. Dmitri only wishes to possess, or to destroy himself in seeking. Katerina, too, can love only by acquiring.

One of the most tragic aspects of all is that Katerina's honor demands that she offer herself to Dmitri when he does not love her and, it seems, she does not love him either, but loves Ivan. She cannot admit it, for she cannot love Dmitri in any other way but possessively. She cannot love him enough to let him go. Honor is at stake, and enters into this mode of love in the most destructive ways.

Driven by desires he cannot control, Dmitri seeks to preserve some vestige of *his* honor and then to possess Grushenka, who it is true loves him, or comes to love him. He must return 3,000 rubles to Katerina, from whom he took them. Surely 3,000 rubles would be a small price to pay for Katerina to relieve her gratitude to Dmitri, and would not hurt Dmitri to accept in leaving her for Grushenka. *Surely* they could come to an understanding here—or they could if men were more rational and controlled. But they are not, and Dmitri's honor is too great to have taken 3,000 rubles from his fiancee to spend on his mistress. Katerina's is too great to let money repay her debt to Dmitri. They don't love each other; but Katerina's purported love wreaks devastation on all sides, even to Ivan who loves her but cannot approach his brother's betrothed (again a matter of honor).

Dmitri, like his father, acts quite irrationally—that is eminently clear. Just why an old man like Fyodor Pavlovitch has to become so desperately involved with a woman so much younger than he, who will only scorn him, is impossible to grasp rationally. And Dmitri's desperate need to keep a vestige of his honor by repaying Katerina, though he will break his engagement with her, elope with Grushenka, and even kill his father if necessary, is equally absurd. Yet both are perfectly credible as human beings; men do act from passions and desires, from mistaken notions of honor and respect that destroy themselves and others. Here Dostoievski makes a very strong case for the claim that solutions which depend upon a new race of men ignore the *real* human predicament, which stems from the nature of man himself. Evil is not so much malice as desperation, not hatred but guilt. Dmitri and Katerina could not hurt each other more if they hated each other. It is their very honor, nobility, and love that is the root of their destructiveness (and evil, if there be such). And yet, it is Dmitri's very nobility that is his ultimate salvation as well.

There is seldom in men a desire to wound or harm except from despair and anguish, which does not ultimately stem from self-hatred, moreover, self-hatred is often a consequence of the noblest of passions—honor, love, respect, even goodness misdirected: this is Dostoievski's great insight into evil. In a sense, evil is only the other face of goodness, the best in man unable to come to fruition. Surely we can imagine sheer malice. But what frightens us most of all is the way the noble motives in men cause such violent destruction. The best example of this is the damage done to children by parental love and concern.

This is Dostoievski's reply to Ivan, when in the chapter "Rebellion" Ivan protests that innocent children are tortured by their parents. Told by Ivan, such events seem utterly horrible, and we share with him a sense of the cruelty of a world containing them.

But Dostoievski shows us, without weakening the sense of torment and the horror of the acts, that men are not malicious, but frightened and confused, driven by passions over which they have no control. And on the other hand, these violent passions are not contemptible, but are often themselves noble and admirable. In reply to Plato's subordination of passion to reason, Dostoievski reveals the poverty and emptiness of reason in the domain of human action, and suggests that only a proper ordering of the passions can be man's salvation. Moreover, the worst passions are not radically different from the best ones—except for selfish desires which are rather less important than is usually thought (none of Dostoievski's characters but Smerdyakov is truly selfish). Pride, honor, self-respect, even love are the most destructive forces, and yet at the same time are the height of human feeling. They need transmutation not control, redirection not subordination to reason. Reason, as found in Ivan, is a tool of the desperate passions, not their salvation.

Driven by his need for honor and his desire for Grushenka, Dmitri is ready to kill his father, and approaches him with readiness to do so. Yet he does not, though it appears quite plain to everyone within the novel that he did. And a very large part of the novel is concerned with the question of Dmitri's guilt or innocence. However, since the reader knows of Dmitri's innocence, the problem is of guilt and innocence in general. This must now be examined.

The most obvious feature of the trial is that to all appearances, Dmitri is guilty. Considering all the evidence, it is impossible to come to any other conclusion. Yet we discover that he is in fact not guilty of the crime for which he is charged. What conclusion can be drawn from this but that human justice is limited in its applications, and fraught with danger? Above and beyond the realm of human judgment, then, we must assume some greater realm of judgment, within which truth and falsity, guilt and innocence, are clearly and unerringly located. It is not so much that we assume a Day of Divine Judgment, but that we recognize that truth can never lie wholly within man's grasp. Human justice is fundamentally limited.

The paper which Ivan has written before the novel opens (see pp. 144 and 162 ff.) argues that if the Church and the State became one, the threat of eternal damnation would support human justice, and that crime would cease out of the fear men would have for their eternal souls. Father Zossima replies that men need forgiveness, not punishment. That is one reply Dostoievski offers, and it is exemplified in Alyosha's love for Dmitri even when he thinks him guilty. Here is an active representation of the doctrine of turning the other cheek. Punishment is of value only in cases like Raskolnikov's in *Crime and Punishment,* as a means to redemption through suffering. Book XII of *The Brothers Karamazov,* however, represents a second reply: human justice often errs, and if that became the sole mode of judgment for men, they would have to give up the quest for truth and understanding. Human courts ostensibly represent reason in action. Dmitri's trial—which is by no means a travesty, but looks to the facts and reaches the only defensible conclusion on the basis of them—reveals the poverty of reason; it is a case where the rational alone cannot go far enough.

It does not follow from this that reason should be rejected. Dostoievski never asserts this. Rather, its limitations must be recognized. Alyosha represents love and passion—irrational solutions to man's plight. If we rely on human judgment—and we must—then that reliance must be tempered by an awareness as well of its limitations. Thus, the Church offers through revelation and the confession an alternative to human modes of judgment, an alternative men cannot do without. The domain of the religious, to Dostoievski, lies precisely within the domain of the anguished responsibilities of men and their guilt. Here the Church stands as a major alternative to the overly rational and principled, offering love rather than condemnation. Only God can offer final judgment. A world without God, which presumes to judge and condemn, sets itself up only as a secular religion, not as a repudiation of religion. The domain of the rational does precisely that—turning Reason into a god, making the State a Church. This is a criticism of most modern societies, by the way, for they presume to maintain their right to judge men in some final fashion. Dostoievski's main point is that mercy, forgiveness, and love are required above and beyond reason to save men. To him, only God offers these. Perhaps we might accept the former and question the latter. But where else are mercy and love to be found in modern life?

It is interesting that the speech of the defense attorney both coincides with this view and yet abandons it. Fetukovitch argues that Dmitri didn't commit the crime (which we already know, though the jury does not), that there was no 3,000 rubles to spend, and that Dmitri was innocent of the crime. But he also argues that Dmitri was unloved in his childhood, that his father was cruel and unfeeling to him. "He is uncontrolled, he is wild and unruly—we are trying him now for that—but who is responsible for his life? Who is responsible for his having received such an unseemly bringing up, in spite of his excellent disposition and his grateful and sensitive heart? Did anyone train him to be reasonable?" (BK901) And so on.

The defense attorney is taking the common but absurd position that Dmitri is innocent, but if guilty he is not to be blamed. Yet this is not absurd from Dostoievski's point of view: he is seeking a radically different conception of human guilt and innocence. The *fact* that Dmitri slew his father (which he did not) is not all that is of importance in matters of judgment. An awareness of his background, the nature of man, the kind of person he is, is necessary also. And then we would be able to see that factual guilt is not as important as forgiveness and understanding.

On the other side, factual innocence is also unimportant beside love and concern for all men. Dmitri is *in fact* innocent of his father's murder. But even he is aware that on the most important level he is quite to blame, and in two ways. First—the reason for which he is convicted by the court—he lived an uncontrolled and violent life, did indeed wish to kill his father, and easily could have without any violent changes in his character. He didn't—but mostly by chance. Motivation here is far more important than factual guilt. Smerdyakov, who did kill Fyodor Pavlovitch, is guilty more the way a tidal wave or avalanche is, not as a rational and controlled man, for he is none of these. Dmitri too, whatever he did, could call his action mere chance. His desires and impulses, his irrationality and violence, these are truly Dmitri, and these reveal his true guilt.

Far more vital than this, however, is Dmitri's recognition that true responsibility has little to do with actions and concrete facts. Dmitri has a dream of a starving and freezing child, and awakes feeling "that a passion of pity, such as he had never known before, was rising in his heart, and he wanted to cry, that he wanted to do something for them all, so that the babe should weep no more." (BK616) Over and over he speaks about the starving child, and about his own having received a blow on the head; perhaps he will be purified.

Dmitri has discovered a general love for all men, something more than his possessive and particular love for Grushenka. He has realized that particular judgments, punishments, and rewards, are really beside the point. What men need is a general responsibility, a love for mankind that takes all evil to be the responsibility of each of us. Only then can we escape our own desperate and particular desires, and be saved.

Thus Dostoievski offers, against human moral judgment and the threat of punishment, the forgiveness of the Church coupled with a concern for all men. Only this is truly love, and only this general concern offers a hope for man. Particularly, guilt and innocence are really irrelevant to man's needs—implying that no solution awaits man through improved courts and systems of legal justice. Only love can save men, a general and pervasive love for all men wherein everyone takes upon himself Christ's burden—the sins of the world.

Dmitri, through suffering and violence, has undergone a radical transformation in character by the end of the novel. All in all, even with this transformation, he remains far more credible than Alyosha. However, two reasons exist for us not to accept him as a representative of human salvation. First, although we accept Dmitri's transformation because we know some men *can* be changed by suffering, we know other men are not (perhaps cannot) be so changed—such as his father, Fyodor Pavlovitch. Here we can believe *in* Dmitri, but only as a representative of a lucky few. This is no different from Alyosha—both are in this sense unique, rare, and heroic types of men, offering no solace to the mass of mankind. More important, Dmitri is transfigured only *after* he has gained his loved one—Grushenka. If salvation waits upon ordinary success in life or love, men will wait forever.

## Ivan

The explicit philosophical polemic in *The Brothers Karamazov* is to be found in the words of Ivan, and these will have to be considered very carefully. It should be clear by now, however, that the philosophical aspects and positions of the novel are not to be found only in the explicit words of Ivan, but in the juxtaposition of events and characters of the novel. Ivan's words are not only to be taken literally, as assertions to be judged as true or false, but as indications of the sort of man Ivan is, and that sort contrasted with the other characters of the novel. The latter would indeed be far more important, except that there is a definite union of content and analytic psychology in the novel, which brings Ivan's words, his questions, and his being into contrast with Father Zossima, Smerdyakov, and Alyosha.

Ivan is Alyosha's full brother; they have the same mother and father. Dmitri and Smerdyakov have the same father (granting that Fyodor Pavlovitch has actually sired Smerdyakov in that incredible act of unbridled and degraded lust), but very different mothers. Ivan, then, is far closer to Alyosha in temperament, especially in his great care for the plight of man. Dostoievski finds in the simplicity of creatures like their mother the only hope for mankind; Alyosha and Ivan are two sides of the same quest. Dmitri, by comparison, is unthinking, even unmoral. His nobility, grace, and sensitivity are natural to him—as natural as his desires and passions. They are, until his transfiguration, not objects of thought to him. Other men are stimuli he responds to, sometimes graciously, sometimes cruelly. To Ivan and Alyosha, however, men are pitiful and sad. Both are terribly concerned with the anguish in men's lives, though in radically different ways.

Ivan is revealed to us mainly in three long speeches, though in a number of other scenes as well which enrich our conception of him as a person. I shall take up the three speeches first, and return afterward to Ivan himself and his relationship to Smerdyakov. This latter is one of the most crucial aspects of the novel.

In our first direct encounter with Ivan, after the family history, he repeats the position he took in an ecclesiastical article—one which we have already been told in the history was so strange that "many of the Church party regarded him unquestioning as on their side. And yet not only the secularists but even atheists joined them in their applause. Finally some sagacious persons opined that the article was nothing but an impudent satirical burlesque." (BK14) Why all this confusion? Because Ivan's position, while perfectly rational and very well-argued, lacks something essential to religion.

Ivan argues that, as has never yet occurred in the Western State, "every earthly State should be, in the end, completely transformed into the Church and should become nothing else but a Church, rejecting every purpose incongruous with the aims of the Church." (BK70) In modern times—and Dostoievski is not so remote from our time—the union of Church and State seems absurd. Modern society has advanced almost precisely in proportion to its separation of the religious and the secular. Perhaps this has been at the expense of the Church, but in many respects it has strengthened it, making it immune to the great social upheavals of recent times. It is clear that Ivan's position is an eminently religious one—and Father Paissy is overjoyed at the notion "that the State should end by being worthy to become only the Church and nothing else. So be it! So be it!" (BK71)

Ivan's argument is, incredibly, an anti-dualistic one. He seeks a rational solution to the dualism of human life. Like almost no one else in the novel, he understands the human predicament. But through him Dostoievski shows that understanding and rational analysis are not enough. His claim is that the split between Church and State renders it too easy for the criminal to divide his responsibilities and escape genuine guilt. He commits crimes against the State, but claims that he honors the Church. What a union of Church and State offers is the threat to a would-be sinner that "he would be cut off then not only from men, as now, but from Christ. By his crime he would have transgressed not only against men but against the Church of Christ." (BK71) If men can sin so easily by imagining that their souls are not at stake, we must make it very clear to them that their souls are indeed at stake. By combining Church and State, the greatest possible pressure can be brought to bear to prevent crime and sin, and perhaps men can hope then for some degree of peace. Ivan is espousing the principle that State laws do not deter men from crime, and that only the Church and its appeal to conscience and eternity can do so. It would seem to follow that the Church should become supreme, and that it would then give to men the leadership that they obviously require. This view, of course, is also the principle of the Grand Inquisitor tale, which will be considered in a moment. First, we must evaluate the position as initially set forth.

If we consider Fyodor Pavlovitch as an example of a sinner, we may well recognize that no civil laws could possibly restrain him. Nor can we imagine Dmitri being constrained by fear of punishment. There is great plausibility, then, to Ivan's position. And we can understand theologians being overjoyed at it. On the other hand, the union of Church and State would seem to imply the secularization of the Church insofar as it would have to take on the tasks of administration and control. Could it then retain its distinctly religious character? What are the atheists celebrating about Ivan's position?

It only requires a consideration of Father Zossima's reply to find an answer to this question. True it is that sinners cannot be restrained by thought of punishment. "All these sentences to exile with hard labour, and formerly with flogging also, reform no one, and what's more, deter hardly a single criminal, and the number of crimes does not diminish but is continually on the increase." (BK72) But this holds true as well for the threat of excommunication and damnation. As Father Zossima explains, "what would become of the criminal . . . if the Church punished him with her excommunication as the direct consequence of the secular law? . . . perhaps then a fearful thing would happen, perhaps the despairing heart of the criminal would lose its faith and then what would become of him?" (BK73) Fyodor Pavlovitch is perfectly willing to pay for his crimes—if there is a God. The Church's law would affect him no more than do human laws. Men who suffer such desperate drives, who are less evil than driven and tormented, and torment others less than themselves, need forgiveness, not further threats of punishment. "The Church, like a tender, loving mother, holds aloof from active punishment herself, as the sinner is too severely punished already by the civil law, and there must be at least some one to have pity on him." (BK73) The true mission of the Church is to generate love, not fear. Ivan speaks of the Church as a weapon, and although he is concerned about men and their problems, his solution is empty for it lacks the pity and love that are what men most desperately need. And so does Ivan as well.

Thus Ivan's rational temperament, though at least partially based on genuine moral concern, lacks the warmth and generosity of a true Christian. His Church-State can be Christian in name only, for it lacks the fundamental qualities of Christianity. In a sense, Ivan, by identifying Church and State, destroys the mystery of the Church; by making its punishments secular in effect, it destroys the wonderful mystery of guilt—that sinners may be saved and forgiven, that there is hope amidst despair. The rational and secular offers no forgiveness and no hope. Ironically, Father Zossima points out that eventually the State *will* become the Church—but only after love has triumphed, when men will not be excluded by that transformation, but have already become one faithful people. He replaces reason by faith—a faith that is not in content incompatible with it, for it too points to the same end, "a single universal and all-powerful Church" (BK74)—but one that nevertheless differs from it wholly in quality. The reply to Ivan is not that he is wrong: rationally he is perfectly correct, the dualism of Church and State must be overcome. But he is correct without insight, and seeks justice without love. He cannot really see what it is that men desperately require, and that the Church offers them.

This Church, by the way, must not be identified entirely with any particular institution. Dostoievski offers no concrete institution in *The Brothers Karamazov* of any value: the monastery is exposed as a haven for the weak, not a bulwark of faith. Alyosha and Father Zossima are the Church—for they possess the only true faith. Thus it is that Ivan seeks to render an *institution* preeminent, though he has no faith of his own, and sees no value to faith. The reply to his rationalism is: you have abandoned faith and are without hope.

And indeed he is, as his two later speeches show. In "Rebellion," Ivan weeps at the fate of innocent children, forced to suffer in this world. The world is so cruel and evil, how could God permit it to be so? If there is God (and Ivan says here there is, though he has denied it earlier to his father), he is to be defied, not obeyed, hated not loved. Ivan describes terrible atrocities visited as a matter of course on young innocent children—soldiers killing babies before their mothers, children mistreated by their parents. He goes into great detail to describe the role of the Church in punishment of sin, how a poor mistreated child becomes a murderer and thief in the most natural of ways, is caught and sentenced to death; how he is surrounded by Churchmen who convert him, educate him, show him the light, and then execute him for his crimes. In short, Ivan points out that men are utterly horrible to one another, that love and mercy of Christ are utterly alien to men, yet Christianity calls for forgiveness. Where is justice? Who is guilty? As Ivan cries, and means completely, "with my pitiful, earthly, Euclidian understanding, all I know is that there is suffering and that there are none guilty."

(BK289) and, "if all must suffer to pay for the eternal harmony, what have children to do with it, tell me, please? *It's beyond all comprehension why they should suffer.*" (BK290) [emphasis added] Ivan wants to understand *now:* the world is cruel and utterly absurd. Suffering now cannot be justified by harmony later. He will not wait for paradise if this world is the price that has to be paid for it. "Is there in the whole world a being who would have the right to forgive and could forgive? I don't want harmony. From love for humanity I don't want it." (BK291) And to make his point perfectly clear to Alyosha he asks, would you build paradise if the price were the torture of one infant? And Alyosha answers, no. How then can one bear with a God who does?

Here we have probably the most forceful presentation of the problem of evil ever written. We are asked to love God and await His justice in a world of wholesale slaughter, cruelty, and injustice. Can we really believe that anything of the future could justify the pain of men now? Alyosha, a saint on earth, would not condone the giving of pain now to promote harmony later. Why should we who seek to understand accept God's ways? Either there is no God—for if there were, He would not ask so brutal a price of men; or He is to be hated and despised for His irrationality and absurdity. As Ivan puts it, "it's not God that I don't accept, Alyosha, only I most respectfully return Him the ticket." (BK291) Explain if you can what life and religion are all about. Justify the world to us.

But even Alyosha cannot, for it is inexplicable. That is the fundamental mystery of the religious, the mystery that Ivan cannot understand—for it *is* a mystery. The problem is, however, to make enough sense of the mystery to show that it is a genuine one, and not to be evaded, while leaving it mysterious. Otherwise Ivan's "rebellion" is eminently justified. We look to Alyosha for an answer, and receive none. Ivan asks if anyone could forgive; Alyosha simply says yes: "there is a being and He can forgive everything." (BK292) This is no answer. Alyosha least of all has an answer to Ivan's despair—he is no articulate analyzer to offer a rational reply to Ivan's arguments. Ivan is the intellectual seeking in the world for something to understand —especially in religion—and finding none. For the world *is* absurd, and the ways of God are beyond man's comprehension. Yet the problem is, how can this orthodox reply to Ivan be made intelligible?

Before pursuing this, consider Ivan's own solution, which is to take from God the power to save, and to let men save themselves—

surely the only rational solution to misery on earth. Ivan tells a tale of the return of Christ in Spain in the Sixteenth Century, and the speech of the Grand Inquisitor to him. What Christ gave to men was freedom: but men are rebels, and with freedom they suffer and destroy each other. The plight of men caught in an impossible schism between good and evil, and influenced by external circumstances beyond their control, makes Christ's teachings irrelevant, even malicious and cruel. Continuing the condemnation of God given by him in the preceding chapter, Ivan points out that God has either completely misunderstood the nature of man—in expecting him to be able to follow Christ's teachings without a radical and miraculous change in his being; or He doesn't care at all about men.

What the Church has done is to take that freedom from men to make them happy. By the use of miracles, mystery, and authority, the Church rules supreme; men submit to the Church and are made happy and content. The rebellious spirit of men must be suppressed; and only an all-powerful authority can succeed in doing so. Taking the Karamazovs as examples of men enslaved to desires and emotions, we may imagine the Grand Inquisitor's thesis in action: take from Fyodor Pavlovitch and Dmitri their freedom to destroy themselves and others, and they may well be content, gain peace of mind, even behave more securely and productively. Men suffer the agony of choice: guilt and anguish are necessary consequences of choices made by men. Remove their ability to choose, and let men live in peace.

Ivan has selected from the domain of the Church and Christianity one facet—that of the authoritarian nature of the priesthood, and the role of the Church in guiding men to salvation. The Church does interpret and rule as to what is or is not sin. It maintains an index of books unfit for ordinary Catholics to read. It stands between the individual and his God as mediator; and it carries its burden so efficiently that it can be argued that within the ritualistic behavior of men under such a Church, God actually ceases to be of direct value. Ivan's picture is very extreme, but it is not by any means alien either to religious or secular society. It is based on the premise that men alone are too weak and debased to rise to the heights demanded by Christ, by any of the philosophical or moral saints, even by ordinary morality. They are doomed to despair and torment unless a supreme authority—a human authority—finds a way to bring them under control. The argument is presented in religious terms, but in today's world it would do as well or better in a rational secular garb. Men cannot bear to choose, for their bestial side often makes them choose the worst possible alternatives. Make men free, and they will seek some overriding authority upon whom to lay their freedom—just the position Fromm sets forth in his *Escape from Freedom*,[3] to explain the behavior of Germans under Hitler. The only solution is to take from them that ability. Let the national state control all facets of life, particularly those which raise the alternatives men find so difficult to bear, so impossible to choose among. Then they will be content.

This position, of course, is exactly the same as the earlier one presented as Ivan's article, discussed above. Ivan is interpreting the elements of authority and mystery in purely rational terms. How can one understand the mystery of religion—as the deprivation of an individual's right to analyze situations for himself, to make decisions, and to stand by his convictions, for men will be corrupted, anguished, even destroyed by the free exercise of their reason. Ordinary men need to be cared for and tended, and the authority of a Church or State, shrouded in mystery and secret, as well as in the garb of worship or patriotism, enables them to be cared for as they need, by the few men capable of heroic determination. In short, given human misery and destructiveness, it cannot be maintained that men should be free to destroy, maim, even kill each other. Men fly from freedom into new modes of authority when old ones fail. Modern society has simply replaced older with new and different institutions and authorities, but maintaining its fundamental control over most of men's basic choices and moderating their fears, so that they do not care to think for themselves any more than men have under the most outrageously tyrannical regimes. Of course, some men are individuals, self-determined, and self-motivated. But they are the rare few. There have always been a few saints or heroes. The mass of mankind needs control.

What rational answer can be found to Ivan's position? Perhaps it might be argued that men do not require quite the degree of control he implies they do, that men can make some choices without despair and torment, provided that the general social structure determines the general character of social order, the fundamental roles and choices, the rituals of life and death. Where the social fabric is strong, and definite and straightforward expectations exist concerning work, family, birth, and death, then men can be left alone in all other respects to make free selections—for these will be relatively small, insignificant, undestructive. But this is not to repudiate Ivan's claim, only to suggest that a secular and nonmysterious, even indirect, institutional authority can achieve the same degree of authoritarian control and resulting security as the Church. Perhaps: in modern times, when ordinary social institutions are in continual flux, it would seem that only some central and overriding authority can save man from himself. And such authorities depend upon the use of mystery as a tool.

Alyosha has no answer to give Ivan. Indeed, perhaps there is no answer to be found at all, except an unjustifiable faith in mankind, or in an unintelligible God and his commandments. Alyosha does see that the Grand Inquisitor does not believe in God: for a supreme authority like the Inquisitor's uses the mysterious as a tool, it does not respect it itself. The Grand Inquisitor loves mankind, and seeks to save men as best he can. If there is another rational alternative, let it be explained. Rakitin too is a social reformer, who seeks social means of control to relieve injustice and suffering. The principle is no different—institutional means must be found, through control and manipulation, to save men from themselves. There appears to be no other rational alternative.

There may be no rational alternative to Ivan's position, and we may also have to reject Alyosha as Dostoievski's nonrational solution on the grounds I have given above, but Dostoievski does succeed, it seems to me, in showing that an alternative to Ivan's position *must* exist, however difficult it is to explain what this is. Ivan's solution is impossible: rational social control is doomed by the men who make use of it, perhaps even by the rationality behind it. If Ivan rejects God for His absurdity, then it would seem that there are no laws that cannot be broken, and "everything is lawful" (BK312)—as Alyosha has him admit openly. But although Ivan admits to this utterly immoral position, because it follows from the rational defiance he has been showing, it is clear that he espouses the utterly unprincipled use of authority only for the purpose of justifying the creation of a human authority to give peace to mankind. He repudiates God because God demands heroism and freedom of men in an absurd world, and that demand only destroys and tortures men. Ivan's defiance of God rests upon the sense that God makes men suffer. Ivan concludes that "anything goes" if it creates less suffering and pain in the world.

It is time we turned to Ivan himself, rather than his words, and to his alter ego, Smerdyakov, for it is through these two aspects of the novel that Dostoievski reveals the poverty of Ivan's position, and thereby the limitations of Ivan's use of reason. Perhaps the clearest clue to Ivan's personality comes in two lines: at the very beginning of the "Rebellion" chapter he states: "I must make you one confession, I could never understand how one can love one's neighbors." (BK281) And when asked of Dmitri, he replies in a paraphrase of the words of Cain: "am I my brother Dmitri's keeper?" (BK275) Ivan is the rational man of great moral concern. But he is a tormented and unfortunate man incapable of direct personal love, except in the possessive sense (and he is even more unfortunate in that unlike Dmitri he doesn't seem capable of attaining his love, making him all the more bitter). He desires much, for himself and for others, and receives relatively little. Though angry, defiant, and even cruel, he is completely a moral man, and miserable because of his very principles that are so flouted in the world around him. His defiance and bitterness never overpower his moral principles, or general love for mankind. He lacks but two things: love for men in the concrete and particular; and awareness of his lack, and that it is important.

What is involved here is Dostoievski's criticism of abstract moral principles, given on an *ad hominem* level. Ivan is so genuinely principled and rational as to be quite in despair over the cruelty of men to each other, the failure of principles in actual practice. Abstractly, in temperament and wishes, he is a noble and good man. But goodness, Dostoievski shows through the comparison of Alyosha's successes and Ivan's failures, is always particular, never abstract. Rational principles are not wrong; they are simply beside the point in human life. It is never men as a group that need help, but particular individuals, whom one encounters before one in seeking great works. Ivan's own example, of a child to be tortured for paradise on earth, shows that the particular child is of greater moral value than all other men. Ivan knows this rationally; but he cannot live accordingly. And he is not different from so many other men, who give their lives to great and noble causes, but cause pain and sacrifice to those closest to them. The ability to love in particular is not a rational gift, but a mystery. Ivan cannot understand this kind of love, but he does eventually learn to. His collapse is due to his realization that he has failed precisely in his lacking the ability to love particular human beings, just as they are. He fundamentally lacks true goodness.

Ivan's words are incredibly persuasive. They are also based on a fundamentally moral stance—and that is very important. For it is clear that Smerdyakov, the most degraded of the sons, has adopted Ivan as a model without the faintest awareness of Ivan's fundamental integrity. Thus Ivan's first speech is a genuine attempt to relieve the world's misery, if by threats and punishment. It is a rational alternative to the faith presupposed in Christianity and exemplified in Father Zossima and Alyosha. Only one book later, Smerdyakov, also directly encountered for the first time in the novel, is found to be saying that since no one has the faith that moves mountains, and we may well be damned for that lack, renunciation of Christianity is perfectly justified. In short, like Ivan, Smerdyakov concludes from the nature of the world that faith is useless and absurd. But where Ivan does so out of moral despair, Smerdyakov does so from self-interest. To him, the line mentioned above, "all is lawful," is a justification of any and all criminal behavior which is to his benefit, while to Ivan it is a justification of moral expediency devoted to the improvement of man. Yet their mode of argument is very similar, for Ivan has been Smerdyakov's model, though Ivan is not aware, or refuses to be aware, of his responsibility for this.

Here we have reached the fundamental issue. Ivan's despair and rational arguments are purely academic: he takes no actions, and looks to no consequences. This is in line with his abdication of the particular for the universal: he studies but does not act in the concrete cases where action is imperative. His rationalism, then, is safe only because he is both passive and genuinely of a moral frame of mind. His alter ego, however, is unlike him in that he is concerned with what can be done to benefit himself, and uses exactly the same arguments to justify action. And when Ivan's abstract defiance of God is rendered concrete, it becomes horribly destructive.

As he tells himself in his dream (or as the devil tells him), perhaps Ivan's hope that in another time "Men will unite to take from life all it can give, but only for joy and happiness in the present world," (BK789) is the solution to the human predicament. But when? *Now* if God is overthrown, "all things are lawful" for man. And Ivan's rationalism becomes the source of the worst license—a "swindle." (BK789) Man needs faith until he becomes God; and yet he will never become a god if he is subordinated to faith.

Just before the murder, Ivan is depressed, apprehensive, aware something is wrong. He despises Smerdyakov, but stops to speak to him. He gathers something very strange is going on, but refuses to face it, or to ask what it is. The alert reader cannot but be aware, even on a first reading, that Ivan is being told of something of great importance—that Smerdyakov is even telling him of the impending murder. He agrees to go away without realizing (is it possible?) that Smerdyakov is asking him to set an alibi, and yet to remain near. Ivan later asks, "how could I guess it from that?" (BK779) Yet how can the reader not be utterly convinced that he should have guessed? He was being told quite forcefully, if only by innuendo.

But this is Ivan's greatest failing: he is rebellious and defiant without consideration of the consequences of his actions. He blinds himself to the particular cases which come before him, and pursues an abstract understanding of little value, which only paralyzes him further. He loves all men, but none in particular. And he discovers that his own moral stance is not adequate—in some horrible way he has become an accomplice in his father's murder. Here we return to the theme of guilt. For Ivan has all along taken a general attitude of concern for mankind—in appearance, much like Dmitri's sadness for the starving babe—which in every concrete instance is of no value at all. Contrasted with Alyosha, Ivan's love of men is empty and useless. Ivan learns that this is so and learns also that therein lies his guilt. He has been an instrument of murder, though he is a moral and decent person in the realm of ideas. He discovers that neither his intelligence nor his fundamental decency has kept him from being a pawn of the devil. True goodness in man depends on something other than these. Even in his conversation with the devil, in his dream, Ivan seeks *justification*—for example, in the philosopher who walked a quadrillion miles, and shouted that paradise was worth it. Ivan needs external justifications—loving alone is not satisfactory to him—and he becomes defiant when these fail. Can there not be an internal justification of love, independent of consequences and the absurdity of things?

Something more than abstract judgment is needed in life, something almost irrational, mysterious, unjustifiable. Perhaps it is a faith that all will turn out well. Or simply a love for men who need it. It is the ability to act and love in an absurd and impossible world—an ability Alyosha has, and Ivan lacks. It is the ability to move well in the realm of the particular while the domain of the understanding has collapsed that is required. It is a kind of faith.

Yet something must be said about the fact that the reader who comes to this conclusion, who is even brought to it by artistic means, has done so *rationally,* even philosophically, if not in the simplest and most intellectually satisfactory manner. It is possible to maintain that it is not reason in itself that is being damned in the novel (I am not speaking here of Dostoievski's own personal convictions, but the conclusion reached by *The Brothers Karamazov*), but that kind of intellectualism that breeds paralysis and blindness. Whatever Dostoievski was trying to do, he succeeded only in reaching Plato's position on the rational in things—that a vital distinction must be made between genuine and spurious candidates for the office. A truly rational man, who loves mankind and seeks through reason to help them, will realize (again rationally) that too much disputation, however brilliant and intellectual, may eliminate the possibility of gaining the goals desired. In Plato's words, rhetoric and true philosophy must not be confused. If Ivan comes out of his coma transfigured, it may well be in the quite rational understanding that *intellect* alone is not enough. The ability to use one's passions and to act on them may not be itself an intellectual gift, but its value can without any question be recognized by reason.

Thus Dostoievski's irrationality can be tempered, even within the context of *The Brothers Karamazov*, particularly if one recognizes the hope that Ivan offers, if he comes to understand his shortcomings and the nature of his failures—and *if* he can come to do so. Only if Alyosha, as unintellectual as he is, is accepted as a model for all men can *The Brothers Karamazov* be taken as a complete and utter repudiation of reason in human life. And since Alyosha comes off so badly just because there is no foundation upon which his goodness rests—such as wisdom can provide—it must be doubted whether Dostoievski has succeeded in making quite the case he wished to. Still, he has succeeded in making part of the case—that intellect in the name of reason can be as blind as passion without wisdom. More is needed in human life than academic knowledge alone, however brilliantly supported—that is, a moral responsibility and love for all men. It does not follow, however, that declaring responsibility for all men can be efficacious where unsupported by reason.

# 11

## The Stranger
## by Albert Camus

*The Stranger* is not an easy work to deal with philosophically. The very strength of the novel rests on its refusal to take a clear and definite stand, even when one seems to be necessary. Just as Meursault refuses to become involved in anything, to *care* about what happens to him and around him, so the novel reflects that quality in itself. The novel is in his words, and reveals his thoughts and attitudes. The reader is left quite puzzled about the moral significance of the events of the novel to both Meursault and the author, and quite intentionally. If moral aspects of the novel exist, they are left to the reader to find for himself. Even Meursault's great transformation at the very end of the novel is a definite enigma; it is up to the reader to interpret his remarks for himself, if at all. In fact, it may be maintained that *The Stranger* is in reality not philosophical, that its values are primarily literary, and that the long deliberations and monologues of Meursault toward the novel's end are simply a talky way of conveying the mood. Even Camus' essays are rather unlike technical philosophy: they are not profound, and often not well argued; often they are as literary in style as his novels. Why then seek within the novel for a philosophic point of view which may not be there?

It is well known, of course, that Camus was an existentialist. And to students who are appalled by the rigors of Sartre's *Being and Nothingness,* Camus appears to provide a far more congenial path to the existentialist viewpoint. But I shall argue that *The Stranger* is in some respects the last place to discover existentialism—though it is by no means incompatible with it. Nevertheless, the novel surely seems to represent *some* moral or intellectual viewpoint, if only we can determine what it is. I shall endeavor to do so: but my main intent will be to show that philosophic novels are often *not* to be read as if they contain their theses on the surface, in the words of some of the characters, or the comments of the narrator. In fact, if *The Stranger* has a thesis, it is generated within the reader by his reactions to the events of the novel, rather than by his being told directly the author's position, in explicit statements within the novel. The difficulty of interpreting the novel calls forth the reaction: "what do you make of it all?" In this case, taking the easy path and letting the novel speak for itself may well be quite inappropriate.

There is no way to avoid an interpretation of this particular text, rather than a discussion of the important philosophic issues which it raises. For the events of the novel are, though quite limpidly and clearly described, rather bewildering, and some effort must be devoted to a consideration of just how and why. Furthermore, the philosophic issues of this novel are really profound, as I shall show. The remarkable thing about *The Stranger* is that it appears very significant and profound, but that is partly because of its beauty as a novel, partly a quite intentional quality that the reader must endeavor to see through if he is to understand what Camus is up to, and partly because the novel does indeed explore some fundamental moral issues. It cannot be said, however, that it resolves them. In this case, I must state my opinion that that is a virtue. *The Stranger* is a far greater novel, being what it is, than it would be if it were to set forth a positive moral thesis.

It seems rather clear that the novel is concerned with only two things and their interrelationship: Meursault (who has no first name) and the rest of the world. Perhaps it seems odd to speak of these as two: all human beings operate in an environment comprising the rest of the world. But it is clear in *The Stranger* that what is significant is not Meursault *in* the world, but the continual disparity, occasional confrontation, and frequent dissociation of Meursault and the world he lives in, particularly other men. Meursault is continually contrasted to others, for example, in the kinds and intensities of emotion they feel, their involvement and understanding. All this comes to a head in the trial, but that is only an explicit representation of the novel's continual implicit comparison, brought out in direct confrontation—or at least, as direct a confrontation as Meursault is capable of, for he falls asleep during the trial, often pays no attention, and on the whole is completely uninvolved in something that is of fundamental importance to him, and will mean his life.

The novel begins with the words: "Mother died today. Or, maybe, yesterday; I can't be sure." (S1) [1] Meursault explains that the telegram is ambiguous; but the tone of the novel is set. He simply does not care. He does not care about his mother's death, about the people he knows, about getting married or not—at least, not beyond the immediate moment. It is quite true that he is extremely responsive to sensory stimuli—far more so than the other characters of the novel, far more so than are ordinary people. But beyond that stimulation he remains aloof, dispassionate, uninvolved.

The impact of sensations upon Meursault, by the way, is by no means always an enlivening or colorful one, but often puts him to sleep. The tone of his description of his mother's funeral makes it clear that he is merely there—not out of duty or grief, but just there. He tells us why he didn't often visit his mother, and we look for those kinds of emotions psychoanalysts tell us we all feel toward our parents. Surely *some* emotion would be appropriate at one's mother's death, if only relief, guilt, even anger. He doesn't wish to see his mother's body—not because of distaste or grief, but again just because.

Obviously Meursault is "The Stranger," and he is that precisely because of his unreactiveness to many things to which it is taken for granted that men react. Shall we ask if he is an *alienated* man? Not unless we examine this notion carefully, for Meursault is no ordinary man out of touch with social conventions. And his responsiveness to sensory stimuli is also an admirable trait, albeit one too rooted in the immediate rather than the principled and universal.

The term "alienation" has been taken by contemporary analysts in an incredible number of ways, all of which have been thought in some context or other to be of enormous significance. I believe, however, that it is possible to discover two primary modes of analysis: alienation from society or the world in general, and alienation from oneself, with some dependence of one on the other. In its initial conception, in Hegel's *Phenomenology of Spirit*, "alienation" referred to the severance of consciousness from its object, especially when essential to a particular kind of awareness—for example, in the Christian sense of man as torn forever between awareness of his own finitude and a desperate yearning for the perfection of God. This self-alienation could for Hegel be bridged only by man finding God, not externally related to himself, but in a sense part of himself—by becoming the particular embodiment of Spirit come to awareness of itself through history. Marx repudiated the religious aspect of Hegel's thought, and emphasized human *actions* rather than thoughts, conceptions, or sheer consciousness. He turned alienation primarily into an estrangement from one's labor, a dichotomy between man the producer of objects, and the objects which take on a life of their own, independent of human activity, and even enslave their producers. An alienated society here is one in which labor is invested in tasks meaningless to the worker, from his point of view aimed not at fulfillment, but at nothing but survival. To the worker, the product is not his, and he is uninvolved in what he has himself created.

Modern social thinkers, in rejecting Marx's economic and sociological theories, have nevertheless found great usefulness in the concept of alienation, not simply as alienated labor, but as social isolation. As societies have become more complex, as they have grown in size and complexity of purpose, individuals have lost their ties to a coherent social order. The feeling of alienation may be identified with a feeling of lack of belonging, of an inability to accomplish anything in modern society, the inability to identify with any particular segment of society.

The difficulty with this notion is that alienation is presumably something to be avoided (or superseded, in Hegel and Marx); yet social identification can become conformity and "other directedness." The identification with some societies—such as Nazi Germany—is itself a moral lapse, and can be equated with a form of alienation from the species man, or from oneself. Withdrawal from destructive and cruel societies can only be considered an act of self-affirmation—not therefore alienation, which seems always to have pejorative connotations. If we are to seek identification within a society, it must be with definite awareness of the nature and commitments of that society, to which we are proposing greater allegiance. If Meursault is to be accused of social alienation (his self-alienation I will take up later), we must consider exactly what it means to belong to the society of man that surrounds him. This is exactly what Camus shows us, in altogether too painful detail.

For contrasted with every instance in which Meursault is un-involved are the unfortunate involvements of other men, which seem as strange within the novel as Meursault's drowsiness and lack of concern. Meursault dozes over his mother's body—an indifferent act to say the least. The vigil kept by the other inmates of the old-age home is, however, quite peculiar also, especially in the cold and de-tached light of Meursault's gaze, who perceives their actions in in-credible detail. Meursault is indifferent and passive, but amazingly observant, and in his first-person descriptions of the events of the novel bares the emptiness and futility of the way of life he is estranged from, and which he supposedly should adopt. "One of the women started weeping. . . . At regular intervals she emitted a little chok-ing sob; one had a feeling she would never stop. The others didn't seem to notice." (S12) Tears are normal at a funeral. Only Meursault is odd because he has none to give. Yet surely it is as odd here for others to cry as for him not to care. Meursault's gaze is valueless: if he is estranged it is precisely because he doesn't have *any* values—he simply doesn't care. Beneath the gaze of such a man, human values seem barbarous and weird, particularly when one notes how they are manifested. Thus, the old men at the "vigil," "were sucking at the insides of their cheeks, and this caused the odd, wheezing noises that had mystified me." (S11) And in the morning, "to my surprise each of them shook hands with me, as though this night together, in which we hadn't exchanged a word, had created a kind of intimacy between us." (S13) Is it not as peculiar that people take the sharing of life and death as productive of intimacy, as that Meursault does not?

Suppose a being from another planet landed on Earth and without personal reactions of any sort, investigated what was to be found here—as anthropologists study a tribe utterly foreign to them, noting in detail every ritual act and gesture, but without identifica-tion, which would interfere with their scientific dispassionateness. Would he not find human customs alien and strange, perhaps inter-esting, perhaps dull? We could forgive this alien for coming to ob-serve the natives if only he were able to react in some evaluative manner. If he too felt the horror of death, we would be very pleased. If he thought our customs were strange and bizarre, we would be angry—but we would then recognize his alienness. What would be unforgiveable, however, would be his utter unreactiveness, emotionless investigation, observation without reaction. We would then be to him nothing but objects of study, not beings with minds and choices, fears and passions, deliberations and decisions. It is living without valuing that is unforgivable. And it is that which marks Meursault's strangeness.

It is very important to understand this. Meursault is a stranger because he fails to belong anywhere, even to himself. We can understand the hero who stands alone. Violent rejection of social norms may be unjustified, even threatening, but it is intelligible. And we can understand also the man who belongs to another social group, with very different standards. In both cases there is genuine valuation, if different from our social norms; and the possibility exists that someone is right and others wrong, someone sees things more clearly than others. Meursault, however, has no values of any kind to offer, and is estranged and isolated because he neither accepts nor challenges anything. Since nothing means anything to him, he is capable of anything, provided it conforms to the pressures of the sensory moment.

I have so far continually juxtaposed Meursault to the rest of humanity, for that is what the novel does. But his anomalous character can be expressed without this comparison: it is that he never judges, even for himself, never evaluates courses of action, the behavior of others, or his own mistakes. It is not so much that he does not operate in the normal social context of judgments and norms, but that he has none at all. Surely any man would consider it a very important thing to get married, whatever his feelings about the conventional institution of marriage. It doesn't matter to Meursault at all, and neither does anything else except response to the immediate. This it is that marks him as odd.

Perhaps here it might be useful to reintroduce the notion of alienation from oneself. For Meursault is not only different from other men; he is devoid of the ability to judge or evaluate *anything,* even when vitally important to his future life. He lives only in the brief and present moment, a receptacle for stimulation and direct response, but utterly without the capacity to value and appraise what he encounters. Nothing is good or bad, right or wrong, to be sought or fought against. Things just happen to him. He is alienated not only from other men, but from himself and his own needs. He slides with events rather than molding them to his desires. He simply does not know what it is to value and prize, judge and formulate principles of action. He can only desire and dislike.

John Dewey, in his ethical writings, endeavored to make one major distinction which is applicable here—between what is liked and what is valuable, between the desired and the desirable. Liking and desiring are straightforward if immediate responses to things. That something is liked is a fact about it, taken in some present response to it. But for Dewey, something can be judged desirable only in the context of its consequences and antecedents, other likes and dislikes, and so on. In brief, the desired is just that, and desiring is an unconsidered, thus a nonevaluative response in a fairly brief present. Valuing something as desirable goes beyond any present, to other times, places, and consequences.

Without necessarily accepting Dewey's particular analysis of valuation, we may take cognizance of the important distinction between an immediate good or pleasure, and something *judged* good and valuable. Meursault rests content with immediate goods and pleasures—in a detail of response few men are capable of matching. But he simply has no idea of how to make value-judgments that go beyond the immediate pleasure or displeasure. He is a stranger to humanity and even himself not because he fails to share others' values, but because he fails to have any values at all. At least, according to Dewey's analysis, an immediate pleasure is not a valued good, only a candidate for one. A good is something that persists in being liked, that has liked consequences as well. Meursault never looks to consequences or future aims. He is thus without the most elementary moral capacity. He is thus at *least* (for moral values are only one kind of human value) amoral—meaning without any moral principles or alternative modes of judgment whatsoever.

It cannot but be realized, however, that Meursault's utterly objective and dispassionate regard of the behavior of others is in some fundamental sense a challenge—a challenge to any and all value that goes beyond the moment. Others in this novel act foolishly and blindly, irrationally and unjustifiably, cruelly and stupidly. In many respects, Meursault is by far the wisest (surely the most clear-sighted and perceptive) person in the novel: he has abandoned the foolishness of ordinary ritual, the emptiness of ordinary forms. The old people keeping their vigil seem foolish and ugly, especially in Meursault's eyes, and the reader cannot but share that point of view. "One of the old men woke up and coughed repeatedly. He spat into a big check handkerchief, and each time he spat it sounded as if he were retching." (S13) Old M. Pérez, Meursault's mother's "special friend," is described quite cruelly: "what caught my attention most was his ears; pendulous, scarlet ears that showed up like blobs of sealing wax on the pallor of his cheeks and were framed in wisps of silky white hair." (S17) Meursault's descriptions are horrifying because they are so accurate. Once we stop and look around us we too see the ugliness and futility of life. And so every old man must look at his spouse, and see her sheer oldness, her wrinkled ugliness? Can it not be that Meursault's very detailed observation of men misses something vital? Is the love of an old couple for each other stupidity and ugliness? Is M. Perez's grief but an empty ritual, a blind act committed in fearful darkness? Meursault can see in human beings what he sees in the sun, houses, or the landscape. That is why he is a stranger to man. At the end of the funeral, he tells us he remembers

the look of the Church, the villagers in the streets, the red geraniums on the graves, Pérez's fainting fit—he crumpled up like a rag doll—the tawny-red earth pattering on Mother's coffin, the bits of white roots mixed up with it; then more people, voices, the wait outside a café for the bus, the rumble of the engine, and my little thrill of pleasure when we entered the first brightly lit streets of Algiers [etc.]. (S22)

Everything is the same to Meursault; grief is no more interesting than looks, colors, or sounds—perhaps far less real to him.

When asking for leave to attend his Mother's funeral, Meursault says to his employer, "Sorry, sir, but it's not my fault, you know." (S1) And when he realizes that he will get four days "holiday" [sic] because of the funeral he thinks, "it wasn't my fault if Mother was buried yesterday and not today." (S22) This peculiar sense of blame Meursault feels here is equalled only by his utter lack of a feeling of blame when he has committed a murder. He simply doesn't know how to react to questions of blame and guilt, for without values to apply to situations in which he finds himself, he is bereft of guilt as well. Thus he is as likely to accept guilt for nothing as to deny it for a major crime. This is another aspect of his strangeness, rooted again in his dispassionateness and objectivity. He goes swimming, flirts with Marie, even asks her to go out with him in the evening, and sleeps with her that night. But he is in mourning, and she notices it. How can he be so gay when his mother had been buried only yesterday? Once again, he almost explains it was not his fault: "somehow one can't help feeling a bit guilty." (S24)

Two days after the funeral, Meursault sits on his balcony and watches the world go by, without feeling or concern, simply a passive observer. And he thinks to himself in the evening, "it occurred to me that somehow I'd got through another Sunday, that Mother now was buried, and tomorrow I'd be going back to work as usual. Really, nothing in my life had changed." (S30) Nothing has, for Meursault is aloof from the cares of ordinary men, and reacts only to the present and its sensory stimulation. It would take something far more serious than a mere funeral to change that.

What is remarkable about Meursault's reactions is not that they violate social norms (though it is that he is eventually accused of). We could understand a man who hated his cruel mother and who celebrated when she died—though we might not condone or approve. But such a son would not mourn, would not go to the funeral, and especially would not explain that it wasn't his fault (though he might feel guilty of wishing for her death). Meursault simply does not possess the tools for understanding ordinary moral judgments and the rituals based on them. He pretends to be human, though he fails because he cannot understand.

This "understanding" I speak of is shown by Camus not to be a *rational* understanding. Meursault lacks no rational grasp of what goes on around him; he is fundamentally only without *feeling*—at least those feelings upon which moral judgments are dependent. David Hume, in a celebrated analysis, argued that reason alone cannot provide us with moral distinctions, for reason takes us only from means to consequences, providing us with tools for deliberation *once we have made moral distinctions*, but has in itself no motivating force.

Upon the whole, 'tis impossible that the distinction betwixt moral good and evil can be made by reason; since that distinction has an influence upon our actions, of which reason alone is incapable. . . . Morality consists not in any relations that are the objects of science . . . it consists not in any *matter of fact*, which can be discovered by the understanding.[2]

We may know that unless we give to charity, others may starve. But only our feelings of regret and sympathy for others can then motivate us to act. Meursault is in some respects a man of pure reason: he can carefully observe, deliberate, and estimate prudential relations between means and ends. But he lacks the human feelings that render some things horrible and others good. Camus thus indirectly shows us that moral insight depends on feelings and passions. Without them, however rational a man may be, he is a stranger to humanity.

But what are the values of the rest of humanity, that Meursault is to be condemned for lacking? Camus shows a number of men in considerable detail, by comparison with whom Meursault comes off quite well. Consider Salamano:

> twice a day, at eleven and six, the old fellow takes his dog for a walk, . . . the dog pulling his master along as hard as he can, till finally the old chap misses a step and nearly falls. Then he beats his dog and calls it names. The dog cowers and lags behind, and it's his master's turn to drag him along. Presently the dog forgets, starts tugging at the leash again. . . . Every time they're out, this happens. (S33)

Surely it is no advantage to share with other men the hatred, futility, and self-abasement revealed here. Is Salamano a model of mankind that Meursault should emulate? He is revealed to be almost a perfect replica of his poor beast. Among the feelings that Meursault lacks are those that lead Salamano to his empty and futile existence, in which we can no longer tell who is the brute and who the man in the couple of them as they go walking. We find later on that Salamano's hatred for his dog is really a species of love: he is destitute when the dog is gone. Surely no love at all—like Meursault's feelings for Marie—is better than the love men like Salamano experience. And though rather an extreme portrait, Salamano's love is not so radically different from the destructiveness of many, many other human loves.

It is interesting, by the way, that Meursault has no normative reaction at all to Salamano's behavior. He tells us, "Céleste always says it's a 'crying shame,' and something should be done about it; *but really one can't be sure.*" (S33) [emphasis added] And there is a pimp, Raymond Sintes, who lives on Meursault's floor, whom no one else likes, but "I find what he says quite interesting. So, really I've no reason for freezing him off." (S34) Again, Meursault has no values to utilize here beyond the immediate. Of course, I don't mean to imply that one must scorn a pimp, only that most men have some values to offer against the ordinary values they repudiate. Meursault has nothing but an immediate pleasure, and quite disregards any other considerations. Interestingly, Raymond is disgusted by Salamano; even a pimp is more capable of moral outrage than Meursault.

Raymond is a pimp; but he does possess some fairly interesting human qualities: he fights for his honor, helped his opponent up even though the latter started the fight, and is eager to be Meursault's "pal." Meursault's reply is quite typical: "I replied that I had no objection, and that appeared to satisfy him." (S36) Later, when Raymond asks if they're "pals": "I didn't care one way or the other, but as he seemed so set on it, I nodded and said 'Yes.' " (S41) Even friendship is beyond Meursault's comprehension or desire, for it involves obligations and commitments beyond the present, and he cannot see that far. Raymond wants Meursault to help him teach his girl a lesson. Meursault once again has no moral reaction—"one could never be quite sure how to act in such cases" (S40)—in violent contrast to Raymond, who is furious and vengeful. Again, we wonder if the pettiness of Raymond's revenge is a worthwhile alternative to Meursault's passivity, except that Meursault has *no* reaction at all except interest and pleasure, while we are struck by revulsion at his acquaintances and neighbors. This lack of reaction is what is so strange: it would not seem that anything, however degraded or cruel, could cause Meursault to disapprove of it. He even joins in Raymond's revenge, writing the letter to his girlfriend. And here, too, he has no convictions whatsoever: "I didn't take much trouble over it, but I wanted to satisfy Raymond, as I'd no reason not to satisfy him." (S41) A third contrast is now beginning to appear: between Meursault and the reader. It is this contrast that is fundamental to the novel.

The problem, it is clear, is that except perhaps for Marie, who is quite straightforward and sincere, the characters we meet in the novel are far uglier than Meursault, distorted with their jealousies and hatreds, miserable with their fears and anger. It is easy, then, to take Meursault's side—to agree that if human passions are as sterile, destructive, and bestial as they appear to be, it is far better to give them up, to enjoy the moment and forget the wider meaning (which is useless and destructive anyway). The same theme is put in the mouth of the Marquis de Sade by Peter Weiss in *The Persecution and Assassination of Jean-Paul Marat as Performed by the Inmates of the Asylum of Charenton Under the Direction of the Marquis de Sade*. De Sade, in pointing out that Marat's Revolution has become a blood bath, offers as an alternative only the sensual pleasure of the moment. Some historians who celebrate the death of ideology also take the same kind of position: that ideologies lead men to death and misery, to ugliness and cruelty. It would be far better to have a world without ideology, without revolution, without values of that sort.

Such a position, however, is open to the criticism that it is itself a moral view, and must be based also on human passions and feelings. The alternative is not to abandon passions, but to change them. The ugliness of some passions only demonstrates the need to cultivate other, more worthy passions, not to condemn them all. To Marat, the blood of revolution is the price that must be paid to create a society that will not require revolution. Ideologies that have been shallow and destructive must be replaced by other ideologies, not none at all. The alternative to destructive love is not the absence of love, but a better one.

What Camus does that is so brilliant in this novel is to offer no alternative to Meursault's position within the novel itself. Let us take completely seriously a person—a Stranger—such as Meursault, incapable of moral judgment of any sort, bound to the moment and whatever it may bring. Let us not oppose Meursault with idealistic images of a more perfect world, but a harsh and cruel—though not unrealistic—picture of this one. Let us take Meursault's stance, and view other men without warmth or sympathy, without concern or love. Can we then conclude that Meursault is right and that all other men are wrong?

Perhaps men do make too much of death, perhaps funerals are silly, perhaps love and marriage are of no consequence, and even ambition is a futile run on a treadmill. There is much to be said for reforming human customs and redirecting human passions. Most men worship false gods and live with shallow and empty values. But senseless murder is another thing altogether, and it is to this that Meursault is finally brought. It is a very hot, blindingly bright day, a "red glare as far as the eye could reach." (S73) The light "was pounding as fiercely as ever on the long stretch of sand." (S74) Driven by the sun, Meursault approaches the Arab sunning himself, who flashes his knife in the brilliant sun. "Then everything began to reel before my eyes, a fiery gust came from the sea, while the sky cracked in two, from end to end, and a great sheet of flame poured down through the rift." (S76) Always very sensitive to sensations anyway, and completely unprotected by any moral principles or values, Meursault kills the Arab.

Shall we condone murder in the name of a new and better morality? Are we asked in reading a novel so to suspend our own judgment as to approve of Meursault's actions—or at least to withhold censure? It is incredible to me that so many people read *The Stranger* with no moral reaction whatsoever to the murder of the Arab. Completely captivated by Camus' style and Meursault's passivity and valuelessness, they become valueless themselves, devoid of moral attitudes, and almost become the same kind of stranger themselves. That is another brilliant facet of this novel—its seductive qualities which lead the reader to identify with Meursault and scorn ordinary human values. To reject Meursault is to identify with the rest of humanity as revealed in the novel, which is quite horrifying to imagine. There is, however, a major difference between Meursault's and the reader's moral position. Meursault really has none; the reader approves of him. There is all the difference in the world here, for that approval is an evaluation that Meursault is incapable of, at least in Part I. The reader, even if he judges Meursault to be correct, cannot abdicate judgment. He remains in the moral realm, rightly or wrongly. And it would seem necessary that he do so. His approval of Meursault, then, is in this respect quite absurd, and utterly indefensible. One cannot advocate valuelessness on moral grounds.

The second part of *The Stranger* marks a complete change of mood and significance. Meursault is no longer free, is in mortal danger, and is compelled by his own actions—which were so much a product of external circumstances even before, when he did whatever others asked of him, despite his apparent freedom—to face his own life and make some sense of it. He is tried and condemned to death, and in the confrontation with death gains some kind of insight, which must be examined very carefully.

We are exposed to the trial of Meursault for the murder in order to make the reader, with Meursault, examine the latter's life and attitudes. The world is on trial with Meursault, as well, for by comparison the two are held up to a merciless scrutiny. And incredibly we discover that even in the trial, society is egregiously at fault, by no means offering in its condemnation of Meursault a more satisfactory alternative.

Meursault is now a criminal, although he declares that being a criminal "was an idea to which I never could get reconciled" (S87) —another mark of his inability to grasp the nature of his act. To him, it was hot and fiery, so he fired five shots and killed a man. The possibility of guilt or remorse never occurs to him. Though he has been spared Christianity up to this point, now that he is a criminal he must confront the religious treatment of guilt. Meursault does not believe in God—again, not as a man carving out new values and opposing the old, but simply because he doesn't. To the magistrate, he is the most case-hardened man he has ever met. To us, he is less than that: he is a stranger to man.

Yet Christianity does not come off well here either. To the magistrate, it is a crutch which provides meaning for his life, not a greater or higher truth upon which the meaning of life rests. It is an escape from the realities of life, a false crutch to lean on, not a truth which gives meaning to life. Alas, how distortedly Camus presents society seeking revenge upon a criminal—yet how much truth there is in the caricature. Christianity is used to accuse Meursault of being an antichrist, not to redeem him or show him mercy. Society uses its mores *against* Meursault, not to find respect for him as a person, not to sympathize and perhaps pity him, but to find means to condemn him, however irrelevant or unjustified. Meursault's trial is much less for murder than for his inhumanity, his strangeness, his unwillingness or inability to care about others. Meursault is shown to be callous (literally unfeeling, we know) and unconcerned about his mother or her death. Certainly this is irrelevant to the murder, though it may be relevant to our understanding of the novel. Regrettably, Meursault's reaction is only "for the first time I'd realized how all these people loathed me." (S112) He still has no sense of failure or strangeness.

The defense lawyer finally protests: "is my client on trial for having buried his mother, or for killing a man?" (S121) We too wonder about this. Surely there is no room in Court for such irrelevancies. All that matters is the crime itself. Meursault is a murderer, but so is society, as inhumanly and with as little justification. Of course, Meursault has admitted the shooting, so the Court must determine his motives and attitudes. The Prosecution's reply is: "I accuse the prisoner of behaving at his mother's funeral in a way that showed he was already a criminal at heart." (S122)

The trial generates an ambiguous reaction in the reader. It is far too ridiculous to take seriously, yet is by no means wholly false to human life and practices. Meursault has committed a murder, and it is certainly important that, as the prosecutor alleges, "not once in the course of these proceedings did this man show the least contrition." (S126) Meursault agrees. "I didn't feel much regret for what I'd done." (S126) And goes on: "I have never been able really to regret anything in all my life." (S127) But the prosecutor also accuses him of being "morally guilty of his mother's death." (S128) And for *this*, it seems, he is found guilty. We simply cannot accept the plausibility of that accusation. Meursault is unfeeling, but he has not killed his mother.

It may be worth noting here just how central is Meursault's relationship with his mother to the novel and his life. The novel opens with her death, and closes with his "understanding" of her. And he is condemned to death because he has "killed her." Clearly the murder and Meursault's attitude toward his mother are fundamental to the significance of the novel, Meursault is indifferent to both. Completely moved by external circumstances, possessing virtually no feelings and judgments of his own, Meursault passes through his mother's funeral, the murder of the Arab, even his own trial, without care or concern. Yet the continual reencounter with his mother throughout the novel suggests that in fact, she is not so unimportant to him, whatever his overt feelings and awareness. Like the murder, once committed, works upon Meursault quite indifferent to his own reactions, bringing him to impending doom quite regardless of his own desires, so a man's mother in fact *does* have great impact upon him and his life, quite without regard to his feelings or wishes. Perhaps by implication a metaphysical principle is at stake here: that existence has fairly wide ramifications and influences, that nothing exists alone, isolated from everything else. In Whitehead's rather extreme formulation: "each entity pervades the whole world." And whether absurd or not, that world must be faced and dealt with by human beings who presume to be honest and responsible.

Meursault's utter lack of regret for anything he has ever done is a violent fault by ordinary moral standards. If he is not malicious and egoistic (and he surely isn't), he *is* devoid of feeling and concern for anyone, actually including himself. Still, the murder has been lost in a morass of accusations that are partly legitimate, yet seem wholly out of place in the trial. Surely a man should not be guillotined for lack of feeling—it is the crime that counts. Yet society does seek to kill Meursault, and the reader cannot but be aware that all too many cases of life and death are determined by irrelevant considerations. Amid all its moral affirmations, human society often acts mercilessly and without any consideration for individuals involved whatsoever. In fact, the lack of feeling and valuelessness of Meursault are reflected in the dispassionateness and lack of concern of society as a whole. Social institutions often are inhuman, almost exactly like Meursault, driven by inner forces to perpetuate themselves regardless of the human beings upon whom they work their influence. The murder becomes unimportant at the trial, only a means to Meursault's execution. When all is said and done, the Arab's death seems as unimportant to anyone else as it does to Meursault.

Thus Camus forces us to compare Meursault and the rest of mankind, and refrains from judging Meursault's passivity and emotionlessness as bad in themselves. Other men's feelings, need for revenge, and blindness are just as destructive and far more cruel. There remains, however, the reaction of the reader to the novel. The reader cannot forget that Meursault's lack of moral principle and response to the immediate has led him to an unnecessary murder. The reader can compare Meursault's coldness and lack of feeling with other men's fury and despair. Meursault can be content when others suffer; he is serene where others toil; he is also impossible to approve of—and so is the rest of society. Another alternative *must* exist.

It might be worth pointing out here that Meursault's strangeness is much the same as Smerdyakov's in *The Brothers Karamazov,* and that this rather short novel covers in depth one facet of the general problem of human misery and moral failure that Dostoievski explores in the larger and much richer novel. Smerdyakov is, in contrast to Ivan, quite without scruple or sympathy for others. He too is led to murder, and for very little reason. Dostoievski, it is true, portrays Smerdyakov as not without feeling or passion—of an extremely

self-interested, almost inhuman quality: Dostoievski couldn't imagine so passionless and inhuman a man as Meursault. But the absence of all moral standards and feeling for others in both of them is
similar, if the emotional quality is different. Dostoievski clearly
rejects both Ivan's rationality and Smerdyakov's lack of human feeling, and seeks an alternative to them within the novel. Camus offers
no alternative within *The Stranger,* but it does not follow that none
exists, nor that none is called for *within the novel.*

In the last few pages, Meursault undergoes a transformation—
he confronts the reality of death. Interestingly, when the priest comes
to see him in the death cell, Meursault is still the same, without passion or belief. "Whether I believed [in God] or didn't was, to my
mind, a question of so little importance." (S145) The priest tries to
tell him that only God can forgive sin; Meursault replies: "I wasn't
conscious of any 'sin'; all I knew was that I'd been guilty of a criminal offense." (S148) Here we can still admire Meursault for his refusal to accept the trivial and commonplace conventional norms. It
takes a definite effort to remain involved as reader with one's own
moral judgments and recognize that Meursault's conviction was perfectly justified: he killed a man and has experienced no remorse
whatsoever. Meursault's cool rejection of the ease provided by God's
judgment and an afterlife, his refusal to accept the view that gives
comfort to most men that all is well, in heaven if not on earth, that
God's judgment will finally bring justice to men—is quite powerful
and compelling.

The world of ordinary men is shown clearly by Camus to be
one of stupid and destructive norms. He offers us Meursault as an
alternative, a man who clearly sees through the shabby religious
hoaxes, the empty gestures most men live by, the myths and dreams
their lives depend on. There is no justice to redeem life's pain and
suffering, no afterlife to save man, no rational principle underlying
the flux and virtual chaos of everyday life—only men, their needs, and
their deaths. Ordinary men—and the priest in particular—live empty
lives, dead lives. As Thoreau put it so beautifully, in a very similar
context, though with sympathy rather than condemnation: "most
men live lives of quiet desperation." "None of his [the priest's] cer-
tainties was worth one strand of a woman's hair. Living as he did,
like a corpse, he couldn't even be sure of being alive." (S151) Most
men are half-dead, crippled by their fears and prejudices, stupid be-

liefs and blind dreams. Meursault is far more aware of what surrounds him than they.

We can see so far with little difficulty. Life for the ordinary man is a struggle—for meaning and purpose, even for life itself—hindered by foolish aspirations and outmoded beliefs. We can see how men should open their eyes, and turn from their blind prejudices to an awareness of life and its immediacies. They struggle so hard, for purpose and guidance, that they enjoy nothing of what Meursault enjoys in the immediate sensations of life. Yet is Meursault's savoring of the present moment the only way to do so? And is it any better? To him, at the end, "I'd been right, I was still right, I was always right. . . . Nothing had the least importance. . . . What difference could they make to me, the death of others . . . ? All alike would be condemned to die one day." (S151–152) And at the very end, "I'd been happy, and . . . I was happy still." (S154)

Thus, in the face of death, Meursault concludes that he has been right all along, and has even been happy. Since all must someday die, what does anyone's death mean in particular? He is obviously a murderer without cognizance of the nature of his act—who even finds justification for it in the common inevitability of death. How can we sympathize and approve of him? His view of mankind is clear and in many ways correct; but he is by far the worse, for he has nothing to offer of any value instead. At least men who go by ordinary standards of judgment abstain from murdering each other. That may be blind, irrational, even silly. But we as human beings must function with such values if life is to have any worth at all.

Death is the great leveler, the monumental condition of mankind. Yet even two pages before the end, Meursault has no concern at all for the life he has himself taken. In his violent explosion at the priest, Meursault only reapproves of himself. Because of death, nothing makes any difference. "What difference could it make . . . since it all came to the same thing at the end?" (S152)

Up to this point, Meursault has understood nothing of what moral judgment involves. He has moved only from an utter absence of judgment—the *inability* to judge—to a confrontation with death that forces him at least to approve of his own prior actions. At best, then, he has joined the accepting reader in approval, which is without doubt a genuine advance in moral capacity. But he has by no means resolved the difficulties his own clearsightedness has raised.

He has gained complete awareness of man's irrational condition and the futility of all rational judgment and planning. Death more than anything else reveals the poverty of that condition and the uselessness of any attempt to gain meaning through external forms of allegiance and loyalty. But he has failed, up to just before the end, to take the next step: to stand fast and hold to some meaning to life even though it cannot be justified in some absolute or final terms; to value and feel, to passionately care, although in some objective way everything is trivial and devoid of ultimate purpose. For otherwise one becomes a vain and powerless tool of an absurd and irrational world, an instrument of others' destruction. The irrational nature of the world in which man lives is not to be overcome by further irrationality, nor the view that anything goes for nothing matters. Rather, it calls upon men to carve out of their souls values to live by, though they may be unjustifiable by absolute standards.

There remains for consideration Meursault's last reflections, which do indeed seem to mark a genuine change, if a vague and indefinite one. And even more strikingly, we must consider the Christlike qualities of Meursault's imprisonment. For he has resisted three times the temptation to take comfort in religion and has refused three times to explain why he fired four additional shots after the first (one might have been explained as self defense)—reminiscent of Christ's refusal of temptation in the desert. While speaking to the priest, Meursault finds himself bathed in light, almost a direct representation of sacred light: "the chaplain gazed at me with a sort of sadness. I now had my back to the wall and light was flowing over my forehead. He muttered some words I didn't catch; then abruptly asked if he might kiss me." (S149) And the very last lines of the novel mark Meursault's own awareness of the Christ-like qualities of his role: "for all to be accomplished, for me to feel less lonely, all that remained to hope was that on the day of my execution there should be a huge crowd of spectators and that they should greet me with howls of execration." (S154)

In a preface to *The Stranger* written twelve years later, Camus remarked "I have sometimes said and still say paradoxically, that in the person of my character I had tried to create the only Christ we deserve," that "one is not mistaken in reading *The Stranger* as the story of a man who, without any other heroic qualities, accepts death for truth," and that Meursault "is animated by an intense, because stubborn passion, a passion for the absolute and for truth. It is still a negative truth, the truth of being and feeling, but without it, there can be no conquest of oneself or the world." Meursault represents Christ's famous principle: you shall know the truth and it shall make you free. But the only truth is the truth of death, of the lack of purpose and meaning in life, of the immediate feelings of things. Meursault sees human life as it is, a movement toward death, and refuses to be tempted by any of the hypocritical and delusory devices men use to hide the truth from themselves. He refuses remorse and religion, and will not lie or seek to excuse himself. To this extent, he does see truly. And up to the very end proclaims the *sufficiency* of truth and clarity of vision.

The ironic and consciously paradoxical nature of the last quotation is very clear. Meursault is not condemned for honesty, but for his actions—fundamentally murder, though *perhaps* his refusal to weep at his mother's funeral. The absurdity of society, and its condemnation of honesty, does not gainsay Meursault's genuine guilt—for an irrelevant and meaningless murder of a human being. Meursault does indeed represent a certain truth, but that does not sum him up.

Just as the Grand Inquisitor condemns Christ's truth as irrelevant to man, so Meursault's truth can be condemned, not as irrelevant, but as not all that there is. It is not the complete story. And though in enigmatic and obscurely suggestive words, Meursault seems to come to understand this at the very end. "I thought of my mother. And now, it seemed to me, I understood why at her life's end she had taken on a 'fiancé'; . . . With death so near, Mother must have felt like someone on the brink of freedom, ready to start life all over again. . . . And I, too, felt ready to start life all over again." (S153–154) Difficult as it is to follow what is meant here—for is only a portion of what is necessary—what seems clear is that Meursault's encounter with death brings with it a new grasp of life and its possibilities. His mother's "fiancé" is a ridiculous notion—but it does provide order amidst senselessness. To begin life here is not to collapse amidst the absurdity, not to capitulate to it, not even to become irrational in response to it, but rather to live within it. While facing death and its emptiness squarely, one must take from life whatever strengths and intensity it has, however one does this. Thus, though Meursault may die (who can possibly believe in the success of his appeal?) even here there remains the hope that the last few minutes of death too offer what they can—in a crowd to hate and execrate him.

If one reads *The Stranger* as a defense of Meursault's valuelessness and moral indifference, as a defense of momentary pleasure and hedonistic delight in life, then one must cope with that unnecessary and indefensible murder Meursault commits. The novel, which makes so much of a confrontation with death, would make nothing then of the death of the Arab. If Meursault is interpreted as a model, then one must defend superfluous and meaningless murders as ideal. And since Meursault never really quite grasps the nature of his act—with or without remorse—he can never be defended as ideal. His being is an implicit criticism of the rest of mankind, but he offers no solution to the problem he raises, even at the very end.

*The Stranger* is a very difficult book to interpret satisfactorily, precisely because it suggests so much, yet substantiates so little. Meursault is not defended, and is not really defensible. But his clarity of vision is. His sense of the futility and desperation of most men's lives is. Even the superiority of his honesty to the emptiness of others' lives is offered forcefully and persuasively. But he is no ideal.

The conclusion of the novel lies within the reader's understanding of the moral issues touched on by the novel—a reader who brings to the novel enough moral awareness to recognize that Meursault is an unrepentant murderer, however sympathetically he appears to us, and enough clearness of vision to see the absurd qualities of the rest of human life. All that can follow from this absurdity is a despair which eventually leads to approval of Meursault's behavior, the position he himself reaches with the priest—that there are no principles or standards of conduct, so anything is permitted. Or, there follows a triumphant reaffirmation of humanity in the midst of despair—the position he seems (though we cannot be sure) to reach at the very end. The shackles of superstition must be broken. It cannot be maintained, however, that *no* standards are left in the ruins.

The novel leads to no definite conclusion, except the awareness that Meursault's defiance is as indefensible as his prior life. For this reason, it cannot be read as an existentialist work from which one can learn of existentialistic solutions to the human predicament. At most, it marks the meaninglessness and absurdity of the world in which consciousness finds itself and to which it must bring value and moral principle. *The Stranger* reveals the poverty and despair of ordinary life, and the absurdity of typical norms and rituals in the face of annihilation. But it does not reveal to the reader any alternative but that of immediacy and sensual enjoyment, which cannot strike any moral reader as legitimate. In many ways, *The Stranger* generates nothing but despair, which can be triumphed over only by those men who find in absurdity and emptiness a challenge to self-affirmation—in short, existentialist or Nietzschean heroes. To those who seek an alternative or a solution to the difficulties of life, *The Stranger* has nothing at all to say, and may even be a great danger.

The fact that *The Stranger* only sets a problem, and offers but a hint at a solution—thus presenting at best a very weak, unclear, and undefined resolution—does not weaken it as a novel except in the last page or so. The immaculate clarity of Camus' writing, the utter truthfulness of Meursault's perception, and his bondage to external circumstance, form a perfect totality. What Meursault is and what he sees come together in a monumental condemnation of human hypocrisy—weakened perhaps only by the overdone parody of injustice which is so unnecessary. As the kind of alien he is to mankind, he represents a desperate challenge to human conventions and rituals. So far we are taken by Camus, and if we are not swept further into a clear and definite solution, it may be because the novelistic form has certain very real limitations. Or it may be that the absurdity of life is incompatible with any proposed solution. I mention such matters here to indicate the degree to which a novel—and this novel in particular—can succeed in developing and substantiating a thesis, and the point where the defense breaks down. Only one paragraph in *The Stranger* is devoted to resolution; only five pages to any overt moral awareness on Meursault's part at all. Surely Camus never expected so little a development—so unexpected and unanalyzed a development—to be conclusive to a thoughtful reader. This in no way affects the power of the criticism Meursault represents by his sheer existence.

# 12

# *The Princess Casamassima*
# *by Henry James*

In almost every one of his novels, Henry James takes up a problem of unmistakable moral significance. Usually a given novel deals with only one such problem—often a very delicate, subtle one—and explores it in great detail and quite deeply. Occasionally the problems presented are rather unbelievable—as in *The Wings of the Dove,* where Densher's decision to accept or refuse the inheritance is made quite unrealistic to the reader because of the incredibility of Millie. But sometimes they are quite genuine and realistic —as in *The Princess Casamassima.* It is precisely because of the importance and faithful realism of the problems dealt with in the latter novel that I have chosen it to examine here.

One point must be made clear before getting to the analysis of the novel. There are a number of ways of exploring a moral problem, many of which have little philosophical or moral significance. James's greatness as novelist rests upon his profound capacity to pursue human problems and concerns in all sorts of ways, from all kinds of points of view, interweaving them in a rich tapestry of human life. Above all, James possesses great psychological insight, revealing the dealings of men with others and themselves without elaborately reading their minds and exposing their inner thoughts, which no one but a novelist would presume to be capable of. His characters stand revealed in their words and deeds. Men caught in moral difficulties react to and are reacted to by others. *The Princess Casamassima* is a fine novel at least as much because James captures people and their behavior, their motivations and feelings, as much as he captures the moral qualities of the situations in which they find themselves. Emphasizing the latter exclusively will do some degree of injustice to the novel, but that is to be expected. James chose to be a novelist because of his wish to capture as much as possible of human life; the philosophical or moral elements of life may be constantly with us, but they are only a *part* of life nevertheless.

The background of the problem is very simple. Hyacinth Robinson is the illegitimate son of a Frenchwoman who stabbed a lord and died in prison. Possibly, he was sired by that very lord as well—though we and Hyacinth never really know. Raised by a dressmaker who is fascinated by the possibility that Hyacinth may be connected with the aristocracy, he is forever faced with the prospect of that beautiful world inhabited by the rich, the noble, the educated. In reality, however, he is quite poor and can aspire to no more than being a first-rate craftsman (a bookbinder). He becomes involved with a revolutionary organization dedicated (in its inner circles, at least) to violence in the name of a new order of things, and commits himself to aiding them by pledging himself, if they need him, to an act of assassination. But also *because* of this, he encounters two members of the aristocracy who are also interested in helping "the people"—as they are referred to throughout. His dual nature, then, is brought to the fore, and becomes the central concern of the novel. And he is faced with a moral decision that he cannot really make when so divided.

The general moral problem here is nothing less than the general problem of revolution—or more accurately, that of the destruction of an older order to bring about another, presumably better one. The difficulty, which is a genuine and inescapable one, is that the destruction of the old always necessarily destroys that which is beautiful as well as that which is ugly and reprehensible in that system, with nothing but a promissory note for the future that such destruction is worthwhile. Every revolutionary organization must seek destruction as a means to betterment of the condition of man. More generally, every action engaged in by human beings has all sorts of consequences, many of which are probably undesirable. In most moral decisions, someone will be hurt. Such harm, which is often highly destructive, is what Hyacinth Robinson must face as a price to be paid for the creation of a better world.

If this is the general problem, James refuses to leave it in such terms. If we have a moral problem before us, it can only exist within the domain of the comparison of the values of the two worlds at stake. Hyacinth thus represents to us a man divided and torn, a man who belongs to the poor and downtrodden, yet who lives, in a sense, among the wealthy aristocracy. He *feels*, as none of the others really do, be they workers or aristocrats, the strengths and beauties of the world that must be—indeed, will be—torn down. It is because of his divided nature that he can serve as the focus of the problem at hand. The others within the novel are either blind or self-centered, where he is sensitive and responsive to the circumstances surrounding him.

Hyacinth's divided nature must be examined in great detail, for it marks another kind of moral problem, one which may be thought to permeate every major moral situation. That is, is it possible for a human being to face a moral problem genuinely without becoming divided in two irrevocably by the competing issues at stake. Put another way, if we accept Hegel's conception of alienation[1] as a consciousness divided, torn by infinite yearnings and finite capacities, universal love and particular conditions, can one be a genuinely moral person without being at the same time, and for that very reason, an alienated one? In fact, is not Hyacinth Robinson's condition of ambivalence precisely that of all men who truly are concerned with ethical issues—a condition that is escaped by most men only by some version of self-interest?

I shall first examine the nature of Hyacinth's ambivalence before considering this last question. In a symbolic sense, Hyacinth is a man of two worlds—a struggling craftsman and, if not sanctioned by marriage and convention, the possible son of a Lord. James, however, does not leave his divided self but a symbolic representation of the divided world of man, into social and economic spheres, but represents Hyacinth as a thoroughly motivated and analyzed character of both worlds. Miss Pynsent, the dressmaker who brings him up, loves the possibility that Hyacinth may be indeed a member of the nobility, and secretly hopes that Hyacinth will be taken up by his high-born relatives. That is the bit of romance in her life. The opening scenes of the novel show us how Hyacinth becomes conscious of his own differences, of the possibilities that exist for him and no one else of his class (just as he later finds that his sensitivity is matched by few if any members of the nobility), which set him apart from everyone else. This consciousness of difference is revealed by James through Hyacinth's French background, which in London offered him some distinctiveness, as well as through the fact that Hyacinth becomes, not merely another working man, but a highly skilled, even artistic craftsman. Bookbinding captures his skillfulness, his artistic sensibility—he has even read some books—and his awareness of what exists in that other world from which the average working man is completely banned. Hyacinth's French background is important too in another way than that of setting him apart, for it leads to his friendship with the Poupins; and if the latter are more talkers than doers, they talk as Frenchmen do, passionately and furiously. Hyacinth's French background thus brings him to revolution. His aristocratic background is another thing altogether.

Perhaps the greatest quality of *The Princess Casamassima* is to be found in James' sensitive awareness of human motivations and behavior, his portrayal of the subtle forces surrounding Hyacinth and molding him. Miss Pynsent's aspirations for Hyacinth—her hopes in the midst of her quite real poverty and struggle for existence—cannot but set Hyacinth apart. What in her is but excitement and romantic fascination—a hope too empty of content to have a significant impact on her life—becomes a basic need in Hyacinth. "Miss Pynsent was very timid, but she adored the aristocracy." (PC26)[2] "What endeared him [Hyacinth] to her most was her conviction that he belonged, 'by the left hand,' as she had read in a novel, to a proud and ancient race." (PC27–28) Miss Pynsent is an ordinary woman with love of the great. Raised by her, Hyacinth cannot but chafe at his condition as she never would at hers. Thus others close to us wreak effects that go far beyond a mere reproduction of their own distortions and prejudices.

Here too we find Mr. Vetch, "a lonely, disappointed, embittered, cynical little man," (PC35–36) whom Miss Pynsent knew well and turned to often in doubt, and who "displeased her only by one of the aspects of his character—his blasphemous republican, radical views, and the licentious manner in which he expressed himself about the nobility." (PC36) There was no other man in Hyacinth's childhood, so Mr. Vetch's convictions, particularly after his great interference in Hyacinth's life, could not but penetrate Hyacinth's sensibilities, and perhaps lead him the closer to secret plotting and conspiracy of revolution. In fact, Mr. Vetch's concern for Hyacinth, after Miss Pynsent has died, when he has somehow grasped or intuited Hyacinth's commitment to revolution and willingness to sacrifice himself to a new order of things, marks a miniature version of the fundamental moral problem of the novel.

Mr. Vetch, despite his bitterness and virtual despisal of the aristocracy, dearly loves Hyacinth, far too much to wish him to destroy himself for the overthrow of that aristocracy. It may be that Mr. Vetch's own passivity and inactivity make him disinclined to violent deeds, and that he seeks to save Hyacinth out of nothing but a sense of the futility of sacrifice. Mr. Vetch himself is no revolutionary; he is content to complain cynically and revile the current aristocratic order (he would probably complain whatever the social order). His temperament, like Ivan's in *The Brothers Karamazov*, keeps him from harm, but has great impact on others. His cynicism is only verbal; but to a small child who has deep yearnings and fantastic aspirations, that cynicism is the seed of rebellion and flowers quite readily. James is almost unbelievably perceptive of the subtle ways in which character is formed and dreams are spun.

The general principle—which Mr. Vetch and Hyacinth perhaps both accept, in some vague form or other—that "the people" are exploited and used unjustly, that a better world must be created from the ashes of the old, fails for both of them in a particular case. This is the general moral problem of the novel, revealed in the large by Hyacinth's final suicide, but mirrored in the small by Mr. Vetch's concern for him. Mr. Vetch does not seek revolution; but even if he did, the problem that faces him would be the same. That is, that in the name of mankind, "the people," the downtrodden, the poor—a mass of people, faceless and anonymous—a person dear to him must sacrifice himself. What must be weighed, if any judgment of value is to be reached, is one loved person against the many, the imperfect present against a doubtful future. Perhaps Mr. Vetch has indeed mellowed as he has grown older, as he says. Once "I wanted him to quarrel with society. Now I want him to be reconciled to it." (PC395) But it is also possible that Mr. Vetch in later life does indeed see further than do the younger people in the novel—that great battles tend to use people like grains of wheat, tossing and milling them without consideration or particular regard. And that such disregard of particular human beings cannot have genuine moral worth, which depends on a concern for people in their particular needs and qualities. Put another way, moral judgment depends on love for one's fellow man—while great wars for justice can succeed only by destroying particular men, usually without love or even notice. Someone must be sacrificed for the good of all; but if we seek the good of mankind from love of the many, what of our love for the ones to be sacrificed?

Mr. Vetch, then, whose opinions of society and its ills were as bitter and vengeful as anyone's in Hyacinth's childhood, and who contributed at least as much to Hyacinth's revolutionary character and yearnings for a better world as anyone else, cannot face the possibility that Hyacinth will be the sacrifice for "the people." In response to the Princess's remark that he has "ceased to care for the people," (PC393) Mr. Vetch replies: "why are some human beings the people, the people only, and others not?" (PC394) Taken on one level, this question points out the presuppositions involved in singling one group of human beings out as moral objects: all men are of intrinsic value from a moral point of view. But on the level that concerns him, Mr. Vetch's question points to the impossible moral comparison of any one individual and any mass of mankind. In what moral context is an individual worth sacrificing to a mass— particularly if that individual is loved, or even worse, if he is exceptional and noteworthy? What qualities has this mass of people that makes it a worthy object for sacrifice? It is not at all clear that this last question has an answer.

Hyacinth's own problem has now been reached also. He finds that it is not possible for him, once directly acquainted with the aristocracy and its products, to destroy them in the name of the poor, the miserable. As he puts it after his stay at Medley with the Princess:

What has struck me is the great achievements of which man has been capable in spite of them [want and toil and suffering]—the splendid accumulations of the happier few, to which doubtless the miserable many have also in their degree contributed. . . . The monuments and treasures of art, the great palaces and properties, the conquests of learning and taste, the general fabric of civilization as we know it, based if you will upon all the despotisms, the cruelties, the exclusions, the monopolies and the rapacities of the past, but thanks to which, all the same, the world is less of a "bloody sell" and life more of a lark—our friend Hoffendahl seems to me to hold them too cheap and to wish to substitute for them something in which I can't somehow believe as I do in things with which the yearnings and the tears of generations have been mixed. . . . I don't want everyone to have a little piece of anything and I've a great horror of that kind of invidious jealousy which is at the bottom of the idea of a redistribution." (PC334–335)

What Hyacinth says can be laid, of course, to his torn and ambivalent soul, to his aristocratic yearnings and desires, to his upbringing as having raised his hopes too high for his true station in life. To
a genuine revolutionary, there is nothing so despicable as a man who
lets bourgeois values so corrupt him as to make him incapable of
action to his own benefit. Hegel's conception of alienation applies
only too well to Hyacinth—a man whose yearnings and whose material capacities lie at polar extremes. To Hegel, a genuine union of
consciousness and material must be created (shall I say *will* be created?), and every dichotomy of consciousness and power must be
transcended to create a union of all the elements in human life. The
alienated consciousness is a weak, powerless, and unhappy consciousness. So long as its yearnings are incommensurable with its finite
powers, it will strive for Absolutes that cannot be attained, or struggle
with finite powers that fail to have value in terms of its desires. And
the most natural result of all is that the alienated man will be incapable of action or definite judgment, paralyzed by the split in his
consciousness. In Hermann Hesse's *Steppenwolf*, a man of like
ambivalence—between a sense of the good and beautiful, and the poverty of action in a world filled with stupid and insensible middle-
class people—is similarly paralyzed, and desperately miserable as
well. Alienation of self, when recognized on a conscious level, cannot
but be extremely painful to its subject. What we wish to cry out to
such desperate men is, "cease your anguish; settle yourselves one way
or the other." Or, as Mr. Vetch cries to the Princess: "Try what you
like, madam, but for God's sake get the boy out of his muddle."
(PC396)

To Mr. Vetch, Hyacinth's muddle is that he may die for
something not worth the candle—for Mr. Vetch does not believe in
creating a better world by democratic innovations. It is difficult to
believe that were Hyacinth dedicated to justice for all, Mr. Vetch
would then be happy at his willingness to sacrifice himself for it. For
the latter says, "I don't care a fig for his sense of justice—I don't care
a fig for the wretchedness of London." (PC397) "I only want to get
Hyacinth free." (PC398) On the other hand, surely Hyacinth's renunciation of justice in the name of the beautiful and valuable in
the world of wretchedness and injustice is of crucial importance for
*him*. Mr. Vetch's problem is that he loves Hyacinth too much to see
him sacrificed for anything, especially for what will not be as wonderful and remarkable as Hyacinth. Hyacinth's problem however, is a

deeper one: it is rooted in an inescapable ambivalence, not one love can solve.

Hyacinth has been raised to love the beautiful and hate the ugliness and wretchedness of life. His own dislocation leads him not to a quest after personal advancement, but to a search for beauty and goodness for everyone. His revolutionary attitudes are not so much principles as values: he values and loves the beautiful; he scorns and hates ugliness, sterility, poverty, and suffering. It is not to gain *personal* advantage that he enlists in the service of an organization seeking to promote a new world, but out of a moral (perhaps even aesthetic) hatred of the condition of the common man. His outrage is moral, general, and generous.

It is precisely the same values and qualities that lead him to reject the revolutionary alternative: revolution offers only destruction of older, secure values, without definite cognizance of the new. Most people suffer, and their lives are desperate and ugly. But the world in which they lead such lives contains also beauty, art, grace, and charm. The Princess is willing to throw herself away on a cause; but Hyacinth can see as she cannot (and most of the others cannot) how beautiful she is—and also that her beauty is a matter of her being a member of that nobility which she is willing to destroy. Grace and charm are not gifts available to all men, and it is not at all probable that a new and "better" order will bequeath them to them. How then destroy such beauties in the name of loving the beautiful and good?

Perhaps it is worth standing back from our own time and looking objectively at the achievements of technology and democracy. It is quite true that more people have more gadgets, more food and creature comforts, and entertainment of their very own in television. But many wonderful things have been lost—still enjoyed, it is true, by the very few, but for most people replaced by common enjoyments of far less obvious value—such as leisure, grace, and charm, all that is implied in the breeding of a nobility. Education for the few produced very few, but truly deeply educated men. It is not at all clear that education of the many endows them with anything of lasting value, even in their own lives—at least, not if what television provides is the result of their education at work. An aristocracy breeds excess, sterility, and callousness. But it also breeds ease, taste, and grace. Democracy raises the very poor considerably higher, but

perhaps at the price of all that is beautiful in an aristocratic hierarchy. Some products of aristocracy are indisputably beautiful, and
of enduring value. Are any in a democracy? Has not modern life
brought with it a chaotic and disordered world, wherein secure
values are very few and far between?

All such remarks are in a democratic world beside the point—
we live in democratic societies (at least in some of the Western part
of the world) and can see its benefits. But to a man unable to envisage the benefits of destroying the nobility to help "the people," there
is only the guaranteed destruction of the old, with its beauties and
its excesses, to elevate and help those who do not seem worthy of being helped. Perhaps a parallel lies in the civil rights movement in
the United States, where whites and blacks of great conviction, who
believe in values of justice and individual freedom, fight to help
negroes achieve nothing better than a materialistic and often unsatisfactory middle-class life. Here the price paid to gain that end is
relatively small—though the danger of somewhat lowering the standards and quality of their children's schools has led many middle-
class whites to violently oppose integration, even against their own
moral convictions. If the price to be paid were a whole social order,
what is so wonderful about what is to be gained?

The fundamental issue is not the general one of justice against
injustice, democracy against aristocracy, comfort against suffering.
Between these alternatives the choice is generally quite clear. The
issue is that whenever general moral values are taken from the domain of principle to that of cold and definite action, to particular
cases and concrete circumstances, they become transformed. The particular issue at hand brings with it considerations that are of equal
or even superior value to that of the pure principle. Democracy is
better than aristocracy only in a very general, perhaps gross and
empty sense, where we ignore the people, the beauties and values,
the lives involved in the transition from one to the other. Only a cold
and callous man can ignore the price paid for justice. Hyacinth
recognizes too clearly that something wonderful will be lost in accom-
plishing something rather doubtful and unclear. And it is not weakness of spirit or imprecision of thought that makes this so. It is his
wish to preserve the good, or not to give it up except for a definite
higher good. The latter is what he cannot find clearly; for it is not
clear or definite.

What James does that is so remarkable in *The Princess Casa-massima* is to show that Hyacinth Robinson's ambivalence, though we see it develop and understand its causes and his motivations, is in every way morally superior to the convictions of the other characters in the novel—who find it far easier than he does to make decisions and act on the basis of them. That ambivalence stems from a genuine concern for things, for human misery and at the same time the beauties of human life. By comparison all the other characters who preserve conviction and dedication come off as cold and unconcerned, as selfish and self-interested.

I have already discussed Miss Pynsent and Mr. Vetch. Both are instrumental in Hyacinth's upbringing, and both are motivated by their own passions and desires creating in Hyacinth yearnings and wishes that neither really wanted to. In an unthinking manner, people use each other for their own needs without thought of the consequences upon their friends. Parents treat their children as they wish and desire, even need to. The residuum of that use is the burden the children must bear for the rest of their lives. One might say that this fundamental form of selfishness marks all parent-child relations, and all too many interpersonal relations among men. Yet Hyacinth does not come off as selfish this way, nor does he use people to his devices. This most of all reveals his utterly moral quality.

Though instrumental in creating Hyacinth's character, which becomes fundamental in his moral situation, Miss Pynsent and Mr. Vetch do not define the problem for him. This can only be done by the people who represent the significant alternatives for him—the two most important of which are Paul Muniment and the Princess Casamassima. The former is the model Hyacinth seeks to imitate when an active revolutionary, and the instrument of his dreadful vow. Yet despite his possessing a strong, even charismatic personality, Muniment is finally shown to be not even trusted by the highest circle of the organization, perhaps because of his friendship with Hyacinth, but more likely because of some fundamental defects that are shown to the reader very late in the novel. Basically, Muniment has no moral convictions at all. He scorns Lady Aurora for leaving her rich life to help the poor. As his sister says early in the novel, "when you're up so high as that you've got to stay there; and if the powers above have made you a lady the best thing you can do is to hold up your head." (PC103–104) And as Paul Muniment puts it later, "As regards caring for the people there's surely no obligation at all. I wouldn't if I could help it." (PC379) Muniment is a revolutionary out of sheer self-interest, to better himself, because he hates the way he and his fellow men live. But as for what he wants—he wants the Princess's middle-class, ugly little home. He seeks to gain, but has no sense of beauty, no standards of judgment by which to measure his success. He will use people to achieve his ends, as he uses Hyacinth, and his ends are shallow, ugly, and completely self-centered. To use people for empty and ugly ends is not good or right, so Muniment cannot be held to be the moral hero of the novel. If he is the man of action, he is so from a self-interested and very narrow point of view. He uses Hyacinth, knowing that the latter has changed his attitude toward the issues at hand, and when all is said and done, only to help himself. Moreover, he risks nothing at all personally, under the guise of being so very important. But to the reader, he seems overblown, worth little if anything beside Hyacinth.

The Princess is another matter. She has everything to lose by joining revolutionary organizations: her wealth, position, even her honor and her life—and she says so many times. But her extreme generosity and self-sacrifice also make her use Hyacinth—to her extremely devious purposes. It might be possible to examine how the Princess' rebellion against her husband has led her to such willingness to destroy her aristocratic heritage, even herself along with it; or that she can be expected to change her mind casually at any moment, as Madame Grandoni repeats many times. Hyacinth too cannot take her seriously—for there is throughout her behavior an atmosphere of slumming, of reveling in poverty and disgrace, to no purpose except self-flagellation. For example, Hyacinth "noticed how resolutely the Princess had withheld herself from any attempt to sweeten the dose she had taken it into her head to swallow, to mitigate the ugliness of her vulgar little house. . . . It was plainly her thinking that the right way to acquaint one's self with the sensations of the wretched was to suffer the anguish of exasperated taste." (PC357) A poor person must live poorly—but he would, if sensitive, seek to bring as much beauty into his life as he could, as he could afford. The Princess indulges herself, her desire to demean herself, to destroy herself, even to destroy everything beautiful around her. It is difficult to interpret her behavior as stemming from a moral quest after justice and beauty for all. Her desire is to destroy herself for "the cause" at the end. It is unbelievable that this is genuine conviction, particularly rooted in the misery of others. It is a form of self-gratification, albeit of a strange sort. The main difficulty, however, is that genuine or not, the Princess' passions are extremely destructive. She takes up people who serve her as she needs them, and casually discards them when she is through. In the name of a better world, she uses Hyacinth—much as she uses Captain Sholto—and when she meets Paul Muniment through him, drops him with but a passing thought—or at least, with little sensitivity to his needs or his person. She loves him, but the great cause and her self-sacrifice come first. And again we see the problem of a general moral principle in its conflict with the particular needs of particular human beings. So also many revolutionaries have fought to save the world, and neglected their families and friends in their zeal. When she needs Hyacinth, the Princess takes him, without a thought either to his job or to what exposure to her might do to him. And when she no longer needs him, he is dropped, as she drops everyone else. This is truly an aristocratic mode of behavior, and we can forgive her for it—after all, she is an aristocrat; that is why Hyacinth loves her. But she cannot be trusted to save the world at the same time.

It cannot be seriously maintained, then, at least in the context of the novel, that Hyacinth Robinson is a sick and worthless member of the revolutionary organization, unless we too hold that men can be used to great purposes, which is the violently immoral attitude the aristocracy can be condemned for holding. Hyacinth Robinson is rendered impotent because he genuinely cares about beauty and goodness, about what is to be gained by eliminating suffering. The active members of his organization are more self-interested than he, more self-destructive than he, less passionately moral than he is. Thus the moral problem James reveals to us is the desperate uncertainty of moral choice in a world of pain and suffering, given that one has genuine moral convictions. It would appear that ease of moral decision stems from fundamentally nonmoral sources: self-interest, self-destructiveness, even sexual love as in Lady Aurora. Hyacinth, ambivalent because of the nature of moral values in opposition, is destroyed because of his sensitivity.

There does, of course, appear to remain within the novel the chance that Hyacinth could survive his moral conflict, if he could find around him a basis on which to act, even in his own immediate life. We cannot be sure, but he might break his vows and retire from active life to seek his own interest, to gain some peace. He thinks on this when he goes to find Millicent Henning his last day of life. But there is no escape for him that way—in self-interest and self-seeking, in rejecting his love of beauty and his fellow man. For the other people of his life, Millicent Henning in particular, are both self-seeking and ambitious as well. And it may even be thought that Hyacinth's suicide is not a desperate act motivated by an inability to choose, but is rather a refusal to be used any longer to others' purposes. He has been used by everyone to their desires, often useless and vain desires. Only suicide can free him finally.

# III

*Conclusion*

# 13

## Restatement
## of the Argument

It is quite natural to describe the function of a work of art as that of *displaying, revealing,* or *exhibiting,* rather than *asserting.* It is quite plausible, then, to deny the assertive or judgmental character of art. Furthermore, it is often said, and very persuasively, that not only does art display rather than assert, but it displays nothing but itself, for the beholder to enjoy, to experience, to respond to immediately. Michelangelo's *David* stands before the onlooker, complete in itself as a work of art. It points to nothing outside of itself. Although it is possible to imagine the statue to be a commentary on the King David of the Old Testament, even Michelangelo's sense of the kind of person who is revealed in the story of the youth who slew a giant, it is by no means necessary to do so in order to respond to the work of art as such. What an artist does is to create something new from materials available to him. He brings something into the world which is not to be enjoyed because it is like anything else, nor because it reveals the nature of other things, but just for itself—something that stands before the observer to be witnessed and accepted. Particularly in the twentieth century, when art has become detached from whatever apparent content it always had in the past, works of art represent and reveal nothing but themselves. Nonobjective paintings, contemporary music—as always, but to a greater extreme—are not windows through which one can look out on other scenes: they are the only scenes to be found in the art. Art stands only for itself, exhibits only itself for contemplation.

This view of art is, I believe, quite correct—up to a point. Its limitations, however, render invalid the inference that art cannot assert or judge. A work of art does stand before its audience to be taken in and for itself, in a manner quite different from scientific reports, historical chronicles, or philosophic analyses. But it is precisely because in literature the achievement of such complete self-identity is a complex and difficult task that literature can take on philosophic significance, can even adopt explicit philosophic positions, though in its own particular style and with its own particular techniques.

The limitation of the above conception of art is that it assumes that being complete in itself—revealing nothing but itself—is a simple and straightforward role for a work of art. No doubt painting, music, sculpture, and perhaps architecture are the specific examples held in mind. Music has always held a special fascination for aestheticians who emphasized the content or expressive function of art, for music is, superficially at least, contentless and expresses nothing but itself. It is what it is, and great music is even more self-complete than second-rate music. With the rise of abstract painting —from cubism on—in the twentieth century, painting has shown itself capable of self-revelation also, to the exclusion of other content and functions.

A brief comparison of a nonobjective painting and one with definite and recognizable content reveals, however, that no theory of self-revelation can account for the power and force of paintings with significant themes exhibited within them. Picasso's *Guernica* has the kind of power and emotional effect it has *because* the agonized horse and dead bodies are so recognizable. Abstract painting has demonstrated its viability as a self-revelatory form of art. But it cannot possibly justify the view that all other art should be judged in its terms. It is true that some aestheticians have let the obvious success of self-complete art persuade them to take the view that all art should be rendered self-complete. But such violation of common and ordinary experience is altogether too frequent in philosophy and almost never justifiable.

The key point is that the achievement of self-revelation at the expense of other emotional qualities is much simpler for some arts than others. And if properly understood, it makes clear the fact that this achievement is almost always gained through definite and explicit techniques which *negate* other possibilities of response. Music is not "naturally" without content—there are compositions that imitate various common noises and patterns, as well as compositions that play upon rather trite feelings, like patriotism, sadness, and nostalgia. Music can imitate bubbling brooks, galloping horses, and automobiles. But these are all considered trite and second-rate— so great music refrains explicitly from such imitation, and becomes self-revelatory. Contemporary painting must set aside explicit representation to become complete in itself.

Thus a work of art achieves its unique self-integration only by explicit negation of alternative ways of conceiving it that would lead the observer to confuse it with what it is not. It does not carry a sign on it: "do not treat me as if I testify to the world; I am what I am." Rather, it reveals itself by itself only when it shows that intrinsic to it are dimensions that nullify its being taken in other ways. (It must create Distance, that is, or it will be responded to in inappropriate ways.) Propagandistic literature fails to withhold from the reader the possibility of a didactic and judgmental response; that is its major failing. It tends to become something other than a work of art—a diatribe or theoretical analysis.

Prose literature, unlike painting, music, and even poetry, must wage continual effort to avoid being misconstrued. It is by no means a simple thing to create a novel that is revelatory only of itself. In dealing with people and their circumstances, a novel tends to call for a reader to think of its characters as real—as like people he has known, of circumstances as resembling circumstances he has witnessed, and so on. The temptations are enormous to enter a novel by the wrong door, and to look for moral wisdom, psychological insight, even anecdotal chronicle. All of these tend to nullify the primary function of art—which is to stand by itself as a created and novel work which is valuable in itself.

There are, of course, relatively simple ways of solving this problem. A novel may be set in a remote time, in bizarre circumstances, or contain unusual characters—which lead the reader to accept it for what it is, rather than to try to make something else of it. A novel fantastic enough in some respects compels its readers to take it on its own terms, rather than to seek the wrong kinds of emotional or intellectual satisfactions within it.

Unfortunately, such techniques smack of evasion of the problem. Some wonderful works of literature have been written which are so fanciful and strange as to compel the reader to look no further than to the events and people revealed in them. But a much more difficult and risky path remains—to portray vitally important circumstances in human life, to exhibit people typically human in at least some of their aspects, to reveal desperately important moral dilemmas and human beings dealing with them, and yet not to overpower the peculiarly aesthetic values of the work with extraneous considerations. Such an achievement is truly the sublime in art.

What must be done to reveal situations of great moment in a work of literature and yet prevent misconception of the self-revelatory character of art has already been described—it is a matter of maintaining proper Distance. It can be accomplished through the use of artificial style and language, as in the writings of Henry James and James Joyce; by the portrayal of men so much larger than life as to render identification with them unlikely, as in the tragedies of Aeschylus, Sophocles, even Shakespeare; by emotional exaggeration to the extent that overidentification is prevented—as in Dostoievski. But it can also be accomplished by the presence of sufficient intellectual content as to mitigate the exaggerated tendency to psychoanalyze the characters in a novel or play. Symbolic content provides a negation of the outright humanity of a work of literature, at least on the level of immediate or emotional response.

A work of literature which struggles to achieve sublimity must avoid two deadly evils: it must avoid leading the reader to toogreat emotional identification with its characters, for that would make him treat the novel as a slice of life, which it is not; and it must avoid so overt an argument as to lead the reader to think of it as mainly either a scientific report or philosophic argument. One way of doing this (and there are many others), is to play the two liabilities against each other, when they remarkably become assets instead. A work in which the development of character is so rich as to preclude treating the persons of the book as mere ciphers or symbols, in which the circumstances are so richly described as to prevent thinking of them as mere intellectual devices—but in which as well some intellectual thesis is portrayed through the characters and events, which do represent in addition types of men or aspects of life, to preclude too literal or unthinking a response on the part of the reader—can be truly sublime. It avoids being misconstrued by being so richly endowed as to make too literal or too intellectual a response quite inappropriate. Such a work of literature achieves its own integration of its various elements and on such a high level of accomplishment as to stand complete in itself as such a unity of various elements. It reveals itself as the integrated and sublime unity it is—but it is a sublime unity only when what it unifies does tend to lead the reader at least temporarily into other than artistic and self-complete directions. Various tensions are set up—here, in particular, emotional and intellectual ones—that nevertheless are integrated in the work of art.

Works of literature which present philosophical thesis do not necessarily harangue the reader with philosophical diatribe—as shown by *The Trial*. Nor, if there is present in a novel definite and explicit philosophical argumentation, need this be the philosophic *point* of the novel. The presence of such theoretical aspects, however, does provide both enrichment of the novel and sufficient intellectual material as to balance the emotional intensity of the other aspects of the novel—as in *The Brothers Karamazov* and perhaps *The Princess Casamassima*. Sometimes, where the characters portrayed must be relatively colorless, the emotional intensity of the novel is too weak to provide a balance for its intellectual force, and a certain degree of ambiguity is taken advantage of to weaken the discursive elements of the novel—as in *Magister Ludi* and *The Stranger*. But in all these cases, the philosophic nature of the novel does not imply that it is but a vehicle for the transmission of a thesis. It is partly a vehicle, but only partly—and no vehicles can run in so unbalanced a fashion. The novel reveals itself to be the only created thing that could use such a peculiar mixture of character, place, and idea.

Such works of literature are not alone among the great ones, but they are indubitably to be found there. And yet they do not reach the pinnacle of aesthetic success by revealing anything that belongs more properly in a philosophic or scientific work, except as an aspect of their totality. They succeed in negating misinterpretation by the addition of richness rather than by limitation. That is why they are sublime.

# Notes

## Part I

### Chapter 1.

1 For an example of this, see Gustav E. Mueller: *Philosophy of Literature*, Philosophical Library, New York, 1948.

2 Plato: *Republic*, 605. The quotation is from the Cornford translation, Oxford University, London, 1941.

3 *Ibid.*, 602.

4 *Ibid.*, 606.

5 I. A. Richards: *The Principles of Literary Criticism*, Routledge and K. Paul, London, 1949, pp. 274, 279. And according to Sir Herbert Read, "a work of art exists not by virtue of any meaning, but by virtue of aspects of art that have no meaning," while to Rudolph Carnap, the logical positivist position is that "only verifiable statements of specific empirical sciences can be logically conceived as knowledge of the states of nature or of matters of fact. . . . No object in any mode of art can be of any value in acquiring new knowledge. Whatever therefore we take from a work of art may offer emotional or formal pleasure but cannot offer intellectual meaning."

### Chapter 2.

1 E. Bullough: "Psychical Distance as a Factor in Art and in Aesthetic Principle," British Journal of Psychology, V (1912), pp. 87–98; reprinted in E. Vivas and M. Krieger: *The Problems of Aesthetics*, Rinehart, New York, 1953, pp. 396–405.

### Chapter 3.

1 Cf. Albert W. Levi: *Philosophy and the Imagination*, Indiana University, Bloomington, 1962.

2 Benedetto Croce: *Aesthetic*, tr. Douglas Ainslie, Macmillan, New York, 1909, p. 1; reprinted in Vivas and Krieger: *op. cit.*, p. 69.

3 Levi: *op. cit.*, p. 225.

## Chapter 4.

1 C. L. Stevenson: *Ethics and Language,* Yale University, New Haven, 1944, p. 243.

2 *Ibid.,* p. 139.

3 See Plato's *Republic,* Book II, for a discussion of something "good in itself"—that which is simply good, not because it leads to something else which is.

4 J. P. Sartre: *Being and Nothingness,* tr. Hazel E. Barnes, Philosophical Library, New York, 1956, Part I, Ch. 2.

## Chapter 6.

1 Perhaps some literature is not beautiful at all when sublime, in that its content does not permit harmonious arrangement which would violate it.

## *Part II*

## Chapter 8.

1 All page references to *Magister Ludi* are to the M. Savill translation, Ungar, New York, 1949.

2 *The Philosophy of Schopenhauer,* Modern Library, New York, 1928, pp. 217–219.

3 *Ibid.,* p. 304.

4 Nietzsche: *Beyond Good and Evil,* tr. Helen Zimmern, Modern Library, New York, 1927, par. 265, pp. 590–591.

5 J. Kepler: *Harmonice Mundi,* Book V, Ch. 10, quoted from M. Polanyi: *Personal Knowledge,* Routledge & Kegan Paul, London, 1958, p. 7.

6 A. Camus: *The Stranger,* tr. Stuart Gilbert, Knopf, New York, 1946, p. 152.

7 J. Dewey: *Experience and Nature,* 2nd ed., Dover, New York, 1929, p. 412.

8 Schopenhauer: *op. cit.,* p. 210.

9 *Ibid.,* p. 214.

10 Plato: *Theaetetus,* tr. B. Jowett, Bobbs, Merrill, New York, 1949, 176.

11 Nietzsche: *The Geneology of Morals,* Third Essay, par. 13. The quotation is from the H. B. Samuel translation, Modern Library, New York, 1927, p. 745.

12 Augustine: *The City of God,* Book XXII, Ch. XXX, Random House, New York, 1948, p. 661.

13 Kant: *The Fundamental Principles of the Metaphysic of Morals,* Bobbs, Merrill, New York, 1949, p. 64.

14 Plato: *Republic,* 577.

15 E. Fromm: *Escape from Freedom,* Rinehart, New York, 1941, p. 4.

16 *Ibid.,* p. 36.

17 Nietzsche: *Beyond Good and Evil,* par. 33.

18 *Ibid.,* par. 44.

19 *Ibid.,* par. 272.

20 Plato: *Republic,* 499.

## Chapter 9.

1 All page references to *The Trial* are to the Knopf ed., tr. W. and E. Muir (the Modern Library as well), New York, 1937.

2 Four interpretations are found in the parable, which I am indicating in this manner.

3 Cf. here E. Fromm: *The Forgotten Language,* Holt, Rinehart and Winston, New York, 1951.

## Chapter 10.

1 Cf. also chapter 12.

2 All page references to *The Brothers Karamazov* are to the Modern Library ed., tr. Constance Garnett, New York, 1950.

3 E. Fromm: *Escape from Freedom,* Rinehart, New York, 1941. Fromm argues that a productive, free relationship *can* be found for men; but whether that thesis is correct or not, the key point is that men *have* indeed sought to abdicate freedom when it was bestowed on them.

## Chapter 11.

1 All page references to *The Stranger* are to the Vintage ed., tr. S. Gilbert, Vintage, New York, 1954.

2 D. Hume: *Treatise of Human Nature,* III, I, 1.

## Chapter 12.

1 See also pp. 177–181.

2 All page references to *The Princess Casamassima* are to the Harper ed., New York, 1959.

DATE DUE

OCT 3 0 1990

DATE DUE

RETURNED
FEB 5 79

JUN 1 8 1985 UWI